HEROES

PEOPLE
WHO
MADE A
DIFFERENCE
IN OUR
WORLD

HEROES

PEOPLE
WHO
MADE A
DIFFERENCE
IN OUR
WORLD

HAROLD J. SALA

PROMISE
PRESS
An Imprint of Barbour Publishing

Published by Promise Press, an imprint of Barbour Publishing, Inc., P.O. Box 719, Uhrichsville, Ohio 44683, http://www.barbourbooks.com

 Member of the
Evangelical Christian
Publishers Association

Printed in the United States of America.

Dedicated to

William, Andrew, Taylor, Ryan,
and my yet-to-be-born grandchildren
along with
Amanda, Jefferson, Lincoln,
and my young friends everywhere
who, with God's help,
will make a difference in our world.

CONTENTS

PREFACE

A national magazine recently featured a story decrying the fact that there are no real heroes for today. The article mentioned a survey of young people who were asked who their heroes were. Their answers primarily included rock stars, sports heroes, and movie personalities. A few political activists were named. But no scientists or educators were included in the list. Neither did the name of Billy Graham nor Mother Teresa make the roster. Most of those who responded have never heard of Athanasius or Maximillan Kolbe to say nothing of John Huss or Amy Carmichael.

At least the article made me start thinking about my heroes. Who are they? And from my perspective, what sets them apart? I readily admit that my heroes are in a different class than the heroes of the average youth today, and maybe these people aren't the sort of folk to whom today's young people can relate—though I have to say most of the people whom I have admired were just as high in my book when I enrolled as a college freshman at age seventeen as they are now. This book is an outgrowth of my admiration for men and women who have made a difference in our world—real heroes who are not to be confused with celebrities.

As I started thinking about my heroes, I noted that they are not perfect individuals at all. Each of them was completely human, flawed in certain ways, yet they all seemed to possess three qualities: 1) integrity, 2) commitment to their ideals, and 3) the willingness to stand apart from the crowd. They marched to the beat of a different drummer. The world could not force them into its mold, nor could it label and box them. They were their own person entirely.

For instance, Dr. Timothy Lin, who is a seminary president in Taiwan today, will always be one of my heroes. This quiet, scholarly man left a real impact on my life during my graduate studies. He showed me that spirituality and scholarship complement each other. But most importantly, he was a man after God's heart.

Bob Pierce, the man who founded World Vision, was another hero. What I most admired in Pierce was his compassion and genuine love in a world that knows so little real tenderness today.

Another hero of mine was George Mueller, the great man of faith and prayer who built the orphanages in Bristol, England, a man who walked away from the German rationalism of his day and learned the simple lesson of faith.

In the same vein as Mueller is a Norwegian-American who has been instrumental in calling millions to prayer, Armin Gesswein. Now in his nineties, Gesswein still heads a ministry known as Revival Prayer Fellowship and travels the world speaking on prayer. He, in my opinion, is made of the sterling stuff that you don't often see today.

Hudson Taylor, Adoniram Judson, and David Livingstone are also high on my roster of heroes. These three dared to be different by leaving behind family and aspirations to be God's men, blazing trails of missionary service. I often quote Taylor as saying, "God's work done God's way will never lack God's supply." We have found that to be true in many years of broadcasting here at Guidelines. David Livingstone, whose frail body was finally brought back from Africa to Westminster Abbey to be interred with the world's great, had a simple life motto which was, "I will place no value on anything I have or possess except in its relationship to the kingdom of God."

"Are there any women included in the list of heroes in your book?" a friend asked as I was working on this book. I laughed and said, "Yes, lots of them." Frankly, women often put men to shame when it comes to courage and the fortitude it takes to walk the hard road and face the difficult task. Among the many women whom I regard as heroes are three in particular who did what few men would dare to do. Mary Slessor, the Scottish lass who defied centuries of tribal customs in Africa and became affectionately known as Mary, Queen of the Calabar, is one of them. Another is Mother Teresa, who worked among the poor of the world. The third is Amy Carmichael, who founded Donavuhr Fellowship in India and rescued hundreds of girls from temple prostitution in India.

There is another woman who ranks high on my list of admired women. She translated Scripture into her own life, and her character and integrity helped me to see Christ. She is my own mother.

No, the selections in this book are not definitive. There are others who ought to be included, but I have selected men and women who made a difference, and knowing what made them outstanding can contribute to the character of our lives and give us insights as to how we should live today. I am convinced that we can learn a great deal from the lives of men and women who have accomplished something for God. Although their circumstances may be different from yours, the God who met them at the point of their needs, their humanity, and, at times, their failure is here to meet you as well.

Instead of reading this book through from cover to cover in a few hours, I would like to suggest that you read one selection each day. Then take a few minutes to read the resource reading from Scripture. I've given you several questions that bring your life into focus, helping you think about the qualities of the person's life that make him or her outstanding.

May God use this book to help you focus on your own life and help you be all that God wants you to be.

Harold J. Sala
Mission Viejo, California

A PLAN FOR LIVING

Pat Williams

"Whatever you do, work at it with all your heart, as working for the Lord, not for men, since you know that you will receive an inheritance from the Lord as a reward. . . ."
Colossians 3:23, 24

In his book, *Go for the Magic*, Pat Williams, general manager of the Orlando Magic, one of the best basketball teams in the NBA, tells how he borrowed five principles from Walt Disney in producing champion teams. Pat and his wife, who have raised nearly a dozen foster children as well as four of their own, are convinced that these principles will produce magic whether it is in basketball, parenting, or in business.

"Why limit what He might want to accomplish through you?"

Principle #1: Think tomorrow. When you live only for the moment, you lose the connection to tomorrow. Everything you do should count for tomorrow. Some folks think only of the past—yesterday's achievements or failures. Most people live only for the moment. In so doing, they sacrifice tomorrow on the altar of today. "Eat drink and be merry," they think, forgetting that tomorrow is connected to the end of today.

Principle #2: Free up your imagination. Dream the impossible dream; think in large measures. If God is a big God and doesn't know the word "impossible," why limit what He might want to accomplish through you? After all, doesn't faith see the larger picture? Have you ever considered the possibility that your dream might well be the outline of what God wants you to do?

Principle #3: Build for lasting quality. That's the attitude of giving your very best. Most people give enough to get by, and no more. Paul wrote, "Whatever you do, work at it with all your heart, as working for the Lord, not for men, since you know that you will receive an inheritance from the Lord as a reward . . ." (Colossians 3:23, 24).

Principle #4: You need "sticktuity." Never heard that word before? Walt Disney, who repeatedly failed before he succeeded, coined it. It means sticking to the task, keeping on keeping on, when you feel like quitting. Everybody thinks only of the Disney dream succeeding, but few remember his financial failures before he finally put his Magic Kingdom together. The bottom line is that winners never quit, and quitters never win. If you have a dream, a goal, an ambition, stick to it until you succeed.

Sir Edmund Hillary, the New Zealander who was the first man in history to climb Mt. Everest, had "sticktuity." Writing of his success after the expedition, a reporter from *National Geographic* explained, "When others turned back, Hillary took one more step." And, I could add, another and another until he and Tensing, the Sherpa guide who accompanied him, stood where no other human being had ever stood.

Principle #5: Have fun. Simply put, enjoy what you are doing. Life is too short to be miserable. There is no great reward in drinking vinegar and simply enduring what you do. When he was seventy-five, Billy Graham, who has preached to more people than any person in history, was asked how he wanted to be remembered. He replied, "I want to be remembered for being fun to live with!" Surprised? I was when I heard his response. Robert Ingersol, an agnostic, was once asked why he had never become a Christian. He replied that he would consider it if he met more people who *looked* like they had been redeemed.

Pat Williams has not only used those principles in building a champion team, but a champion life as well. They are the embodiment of biblical principles that work wherever they are applied. By the way, you might want to ask yourself the same question I asked myself, "Just how much fun am I to be around, anyway?" Touché.

RESOURCE READING
Colossians 3:23-4:6

INSIGHT
A game plan for life is just as necessary as a game plan for sports.

APPLICATION
What are your immediate goals?

How important is it to you to have "fun"?

Why are Christians sometimes not characterized as being joyful and pleasant to have around?

A PURPOSE IN LIFE
David Livingstone

"And surely I am with you always, to the very end of the age."
Matthew 28:20

He left his heart in Africa, but his body is interred with the great in Westminster Abbey in London. At his death, natives gently removed his heart and buried it in the Africa he so loved. Then his body was carried to the coast, where it was shipped back to England for burial. His name: David Livingstone, born in Blantyreshire, a mill town in Scotland where he grew up.

"I will place no value on anything I have or possess, except in its relationship to the kingdom of God."

When I was in my early twenties, I had the privilege of visiting the birth site of this great missionary doctor and explorer. The small flat where he grew up is now a museum, and on display there are artifacts and memorabilia from his years in Africa. What I shall never forget is reading the open page of his diary where in a firm hand he wrote of the devastating loneliness and pain he experienced following the death of his wife, Mary. Though the page was beginning to yellow with age, it was not the antiquity of the text that caused my eyes to fill with tears. It was the message. "Oh my Mary," he wrote, "how often we wished for a quiet home since we were cast adrift in Koloburg, and now you have gone to a better home, our home in heaven."

What sustains men and women who leave behind family and comfort to go to another country for the gospel's sake, as did Livingstone? More directly, what kept Livingstone there when, as a medical doctor, he could have lived comfortably in his native Scotland?

Livingstone, himself, answered that question. After sixteen years of service in Africa, he returned to Scotland and was asked to speak at the University of Glasgow. One of his arms had been rendered useless, the result of a lion's attack. His body bore physical evidence of the suffering he had endured with twenty-seven bouts of jungle fever. His face, a leathery brown from exposure to the elements, was creased from the cares of a hard life battling the Turks and the slave traders, both of whom had little use for Livingstone.

A hush crept over the students who listened to this man, realizing this was no ordinary person. "Shall I tell you what sustained me amidst the trials and hardships and loneliness of my exiled life?" he asked, and then he gave them the answer. "It was a promise, the promise of a gentleman of the most sacred honor; it was this promise, 'Lo, I am with you always, even unto the end of the world.'"

At Livingstone's death, they found his body bent in prayer as he knelt by his bed, beside him a small, well-worn New Testament opened to Matthew 28. In the margin beside verse 20 was this notation: "The Word of a Gentleman."

Did Livingstone feel, though, that he had made a great sacrifice? Not in the least. He answered that very issue by saying, "People talk of the sacrifice I have made in spending so much time in Africa. Can that be called a sacrifice which is simply paying back a small part of a great debt owing to our God which we can never repay? Is that a sacrifice which brings its own best reward in healthful activity, the consciousness of doing good, peace of mind, and a bright hope of glorious destiny hereafter? Away with the word in such a view and with such a thought. It is emphatically no sacrifice. Say, rather it is a privilege."

As the body of Livingstone was carried through the streets of London on its way to its final resting place in Westminster Abbey, one man wept openly. A friend gently consoled him, asking if he had known Livingstone personally.

"I weep not for Livingstone but for myself," the first man said, adding, "he lived and died for something, but I have lived for nothing."

Livingstone's life motto was, "I will place no value on anything I have or possess, except in its relationship to the kingdom of God." He lived that motto.

RESOURCE READING
Hebrews 13:1-6

INSIGHT
True greatness is not dependent upon accomplishments alone but in fulfilling God's purpose for your life.

APPLICATION
Take time to read a biography about Livingstone, or read an encyclopedia article about him.

Make a copy of Livingstone's life motto and put it where you will read it every day. Then think about your values and your goals in life in relationship to what God would have you do.

Did Livingstone have any regrets about serving God wholeheartedly?

BEING A DISCIPLE
Dawson Trotman

"For me to live is Christ, and to die is gain."
Philippians 1:21, KJV

If ever a person started out in life as a Roman candle that quickly fizzled, Dawson Trotman was that person. In high school he was student body president, chairman of the student council, and captain of the basketball team. He graduated with honors as the class valedictorian. But then for the next several years, his life was all downhill. He gambled, he drank to excess, and caroused.

"Raising a hand to receive Christ, or joining a church, or saying that you are a Christian is not enough."

Drunk and unable to find his car, which was parked nearby, he was staggering through the streets when a policeman saw him. Stopping him, the policeman took his car keys and asked, "Son, do you like this kind of life?"

"Sir," replied Trotman, "I hate it." The policeman was convinced. Instead of arresting him for drunkenness, the policeman encouraged him like a father to change his life.

For Dawson Trotman, that encounter was a turning point. Days later he attended a church gathering where he was challenged to memorize ten Bible verses stressing salvation. Of those who were there, Trotman was the only one who memorized the verses. Then he memorized another ten verses in the next week. What he had committed to memory began to speak to his heart.

Several weeks later as he pondered the meaning of what he had learned, he quietly prayed, "Oh God, whatever it means to receive Jesus, I want to do it right now."

Dawson Trotman never got away from the power of the Word. As his knowledge of the Word grew, Trotman also realized that a combination of elements produce spiritual growth: prayer, worship, and service, as well as the study of Scripture.

As Trotman began to share what he had learned with others, a pattern of discipleship began to emerge that God eventually used to touch the lives of millions of men and women. Though Trotman never set out to establish an organization, he eventually gave birth to Navigators, which now reaches into almost ninety countries. Based on a nautical theme, with Christ at the helm, Navigators grew into a ministry which has produced strong disciples—not simply converts to Christianity.

At the heart of Trotman's philosophy was the belief that raising a hand to receive Christ, or joining a church, or saying that you are a Christian is not enough. The great work of the church—the often neglected task, believed Trotman—is the making of disciples, which requires not only a knowledge of what Scripture says but application of those truths in such a way that your life is vitally affected.

In 1956, at the height of his ministry, Trotman's life was prematurely cut short. Attempting to rescue a swimmer who was in trouble, Trotman himself drowned. At his funeral, Billy Graham said, "I think Dawson Trotman has personally touched more lives than anybody I have ever known."[1] Graham spoke from experience. Trotman developed the follow-up materials Billy used in his campaigns during the early years of the evangelist's own ministry.

His untimely death was disturbing to many thoughtful people. "Why should someone so dedicated to the Lord and so widely used by the Lord have his life cut short by drowning?" Eventually, though, others stepped into the gap and carried on what Trotman had begun. His life was genuine and authentic, but far more impressive was the truth of what he demonstrated: "For me to live is Christ, and to die is gain" (Philippians 1:21, KJV).

When Jesus called His disciples He said, "For whosoever will save his life shall lose it: but whosoever will lose his life for my sake, the same shall save it" (Luke 9:24, KJV). Dawson Trotman, the disciple of Jesus Christ.

RESOURCE READING
Luke 9:23-27

INSIGHT
The life of Dawson Trotman is a vivid example of the fact that when a person becomes a disciple and follower of Jesus Christ, his or her life can be radically transformed. Trotman's death is a reminder that God's ways are different from ours and that it is far better to live even a short, purposeful life than a long, empty one.

APPLICATION
In your opinion, what is a disciple? (See Luke 9:23-27.)

Would you agree that many who call themselves Christians today have only an intellectual understanding of the gospel and, in fact, have never become disciples and followers of Jesus Christ? What's the difference?

BOLDNESS
Simon Peter

"Peter, an apostle of Jesus Christ . . .
Grace and peace be yours in abundance."
1 Peter 1:1, 2

Meet Mr. Simon Peter. Oh, some folks put a halo over him and call him St. Peter, and some history books use his Aramaic name and call him Cephas, but Jesus gave him the name Peter, meaning "Rock." If Jesus thought of him as being as hard or as tough as a rock, it's pretty obvious to me that Peter didn't wear black, have lace on his handkerchief, or sit around singing hymns all day, drinking vinegar to keep from smiling.

"The God who changed his life is still in the business of changing people."

Peter was a pretty tough character in his younger days. Born to Jonah, a fisherman who lived in northern Galilee on the shores of the sea, Peter joined with a couple of buddies, James and John, and ran a fishing business that gave them a pretty fair living. I have yet to meet a commercial fisherman who put perfume behind his ear or frosted his hair. I'm sure Peter was no different. The wind and weather bronzed and etched his face, and the long hours of labor battling the seas and the nets hardened his muscles and strengthened his back.

As I think of Mr. Peter, I think of four qualities or attributes. First, he was a man of action. He never vacillated. He didn't play the grandstand. He may not have always been right, but you knew where he stood. He did what he thought was right. It was this quality that made him a leader. Second, Peter was a man of commitment and loyalty. Once Jesus entered his life, Peter quickly walked away from his nets and vowed allegiance to the Carpenter-Messiah from Galilee. "Lord, no matter what others may do, I'll die for You. I'll go to the wall with You!" That was Peter's temperament! And third, Peter was a man of courage. When the temple guards seized Jesus as He prayed alone in the garden, it was Peter who quickly drew his sword in defense. Yes, I remember that Peter denied Christ as he warmed his hands outside the house of Caiaphas, but I am also reminded that he was the only one who even tried to stay close by Jesus in His hour of trial.

The closer he was, physically, to Jesus, the more secure he was psychologically; and inversely, the farther away he was physically, the greater his insecurity and difficulty.

As I think of Simon Peter, I also think of him as a man of conviction. "I say You are the Son of God!" shouts Peter as he waves his fist in the air to drive home his point. It was that same conviction that, fired by the outpouring of the Holy Spirit, caused Peter to become the leader of the early church and eventually give his life for the cause of Jesus Christ. According to tradition, Peter was crucified upside down, because he did not deem himself worthy to die as his Lord had died. After Pentecost, Peter was a changed individual.

Why bother to talk about the life of a man who lived and died 1900 years ago? I see myself in Peter. I also see my neighbors and friends in him. Perhaps you see yourself in Peter as well. There's something of this man in us all, and the way God used him with his faults and failures gives me hope, for the God who changed his life is still in the business of changing people.

RESOURCE READING
1 Peter 1:1-14

INSIGHT
Peter's genuineness made him a valued friend of Jesus, one who stood with Him when others fled.

APPLICATION
Note the qualities and character traits of this man that made him a valued friend and colleague in ministry.

Do you think that we are too tough on Peter for denying Christ? Note that after the Resurrection, Jesus told the women: "Go tell my disciples and Peter." Why "and Peter"?

CARING FOR OTHERS
Doug Nichols

"Inasmuch as you did it to one of the least of these
My brethren, you did it to Me."
Matthew 25:40, NKJV

Doug Nichols describes it as "what seminary can't teach." It's one of the lessons learned in the school of experience that is otherwise described as "the school of hard knocks." In 1967, Doug, who today heads a Christian mission known as Action International Ministries, was serving as a missionary in India. When he contracted tuberculosis, he was eventually sent to a sanitarium to recuperate.

"The world doesn't care how much you have or what you know; they want to know how much you care."

Though he was living on a support scale not much higher than the nationals who also were hospitalized in the government sanitarium, people thought that because he was an American, he had to be rich. Doug said, "They didn't know that I was just as broke as they were!"

While he was hospitalized, Doug tried unsuccessfully to reach some of the patients, but his efforts were generally met with rebuffs. When he offered tracts or Gospels of John, he was politely refused. It was obvious that the patients wanted nothing to do with him or his God. Discouragement set in and Doug began to wonder why God had allowed him to be there anyway.

Doug would often be awakened in the night by the rasping sound of coughing, both his and others. But then, what would you expect in the TB ward of a sanitarium? Unable to sleep because of his raspy cough, early one morning Doug noticed an old man trying to sit on the edge of the bed, but because of weakness, he would fall back. Exhausted, the old man finally lay still and sobbed. Early the next morning the scene was repeated. Then later in the morning, the stench that began to permeate the ward certified the obvious: the old man had been unsuccessfully trying to get up and go to a rest room.

Says Doug, "The nurses were extremely agitated and angry because they had to clean up the mess. One of the nurses in her anger even slapped him. The man, terribly embarrassed, just curled up into a ball and wept."

The next morning– about 2:00 A.M.–Doug noticed the old man was again trying to generate enough strength to get himself out of bed. This time, though, without thinking, Doug got out of bed, went over to where the old man was, put one arm under his head and neck, the other under his legs, and gently carried him to the rest room. When he had finished, Doug carried him back to his bed.

But what happened after that is what makes the story. The old man, speaking in a language Doug didn't understand, thanked him profusely, and then. . .gently kissed him on the cheek.

The story doesn't end there, either. Eventually Doug drifted off to an uneasy sleep. In the morning he awakened to a steaming cup of tea served to him by another patient who spoke no English. After the patient served the tea, he made motions indicating that he wanted one of Doug's tracts.

"Throughout the day," says Doug, "people came to me, asking for the Gospel booklets. This included the nurses, the hospital interns, the doctors, until everyone in the hospital had a tract, booklet, or Gospel of John. Over the next few days," he adds, "several indicated they trusted Christ as Savior as a result of reading the Good News!"

A final thought. The world doesn't care how much you have or what you know; they want to know how much you care. "I simply took an old man to the bathroom," says Doug, adding, "Anyone could have done that!"

RESOURCE READING
Matthew 25:31-46

INSIGHT
Until people know that you care about them personally, they will never be very interested in your faith.

APPLICATION
Doug Nichols is one of the most respected mission leaders today because he models the message he proclaims, just as this selection records. Though this question is tough to face, would you say that your life measures up to what you believe and say?

What are some practical applications for putting your faith into practice?

CHARACTER
Mrs. Noah

"The world was not worthy of them. . . ."
Hebrews 11:38

She is the mother of everyone you will ever meet, yet we don't know her name. For someone who was so very important, it is amazing how little we know about her. We know neither where she was born nor where she lived—not even where she died. We do know, however, that she lived during a period of world calamity and distress—unlike anything the world had ever known before or since. We also know that she supported her husband and became a woman who rightfully takes her place in the annals of world history.

"The world was not worthy of them. . . ."
Hebrews 11:38

Do you know the answer to this riddle? No—not Eve! This woman was at least ten generations removed from Mother Eve. In the Bible, she is identified only as "the wife of Noah." For lack of better identification, let's call her Mrs. Noah! Does it ever strike you as strange that for someone who was so very important, so little has been written about her?

Her husband is mentioned over fifty times in the Bible. Ezekiel, living hundreds of years after the flood, describes Noah as being a man of righteousness (Ezekiel 14:14). In the New Testament, Peter mentions Noah in both of his books (1 Peter 3:20 and 2 Peter 2:5). He describes him as "a preacher of righteousness" (2 Peter 2:5).

Today, all the people of the world, whether they be Chinese, Spanish, Filipino, Arab, or Jewish, can trace their lineage to this woman. And when you look at the record carefully, you have to immediately recognize what a great woman she was and how much she contributed to the history of humanity. Mrs. Noah is a woman whose true worth has never been recognized. In this selection, I'd like to give you three snapshots of Mrs. Noah that may help you better understand her true value and worth.

First, there is Mrs. Noah, the wife of an unpopular preacher. Behind almost every successful man there is a woman, and few ever consider what it must have been to live with a man who was the mockery of his day. Think how discouraged old Noah must have been facing the crowd of hostile men and women who laughed at him when he pronounced the coming judgment of God. Then, too, Mrs. Noah knew the heartache that comes to preachers' wives today when there is failure. After the flood, Mrs. Noah suffered the heartache of seeing her husband struggle with alcohol, yet she stood by her husband and worked through their problems.

The second snapshot of Mrs. Noah is that of the mother of three sons who grew up playing with the children of those whose values were so much different from what she and her husband believed. Mrs. Noah did a good job with her boys. Surely Mother Noah had to wipe tears from her boys' eyes when their friends mocked them because of their father's strange ideas. She was there when they needed her, and subsequently, not a one of her three sons was lost, something that cannot always be said of mothers of three boys today.

The third snapshot of Mrs. Noah is that of Grandmother Noah. All children want grandmothers to tell them bedtime stories, but none who has ever lived could rival the stories Mrs. Noah told when innocent grandchildren asked, "Grandma, tell us a story!" What vivid, eyewitness accounts of the flood those grandchildren must have heard!

Mrs. Noah was all of the above, plus a great deal more.

Surely she must have been included in those of whom the writer of Hebrews wrote, "The world was not worthy of them . . ." (Hebrews 11:38). Hats off to Mrs. Noah, at one time the most influential woman in the world.

RESOURCE READING
Genesis 6:1-8

INSIGHT
A person can have a profound influence in our world and never receive much publicity or notoriety. Such was Mrs. Noah, yet she influenced not only her children but generations to come.

APPLICATION
How would you evaluate your mother's influence in your life? Who influenced her?

To what degree does a mother shape the direction of a child?

In situations where a mother's influence is absent, what can replace this? Anything? Explain.

COMMITMENT
Mother Teresa

"The King will reply, 'I tell you the truth, whatever you did for one of the least of these brothers of mine, you did for me.' "
Matthew 25:40

She was born in what is now known as Macedonia, just north of Greece. Her parents were constantly hounded by poverty. Her father died when she was seven years old, and her mother was forced to start a business selling embroidered cloth. Her brother, determined to make something of his life, became an army officer, and when his sister, at the age of eighteen, decided to give her life in missionary service, he chided her, "Why don't you make something of your life!"

"We are called on not to be successful, but to be faithful."

Defiantly she hurled back the words, "You think you are so important as an officer, serving a king of two million subjects. Well, I am serving the King of the whole world."[3]

In 1976, the brother stood in the company of admirers in Stockholm, as his sister—the one whom he first thought was wasting her life—received the Nobel Prize for her work with the poor.[4]

The brother was known as Lt. Bojaxhui. Never heard of him, right? But the sister will be remembered affectionately as Mother Teresa. When the frail figure who won the hearts of the world died of cardiac arrest at the age of 87, the world mourned.

Dynamite comes in small packages, and this woman less than five feet in stature, so light and fragile that people threatened to put rocks in her pockets so the wind wouldn't blow her away, created a tremendous explosion of care and compassion for the outcasts and suffering of the world.

At her death accolades came pouring in from both the rich and famous and the poor and insignificant. "The saint of the gutters," "a living saint," "the hero of the poor," "angel of mercy," and a host of other titles were bestowed on this little woman who hobnobbed with the great and mighty but never varied from her absolute commitment to the poor and destitute of the world. While some may differ with her theology, none can fault what she did.

A few paragraphs are totally insufficient to describe the qualities of this great woman who is a hero's hero. She was her own person who never hesitated to rebuke those who disagreed with her, yet she wept with the suffering and dying. When the situation demanded it, she was as tough as nails. At a prayer breakfast in Washington, D.C., she singled out President Bill Clinton and strongly rebuked him for his position on abortion.

Among the many qualities I admire in Mother Teresa–her humility, her compassion, her loyalty, her love for the suffering and outcasts, even her keen sense of humor–perhaps more than any other, I admire her unswerving commitment to God's calling, no matter how difficult, no matter how great the personal cost, or how lowly the task to which she felt God had directed her. When she ministered to the poor, she thought of it as ministry to Jesus Christ. A colleague who knew her well said, "She didn't look at masses of people. She looked at. . .one face, one smile, one heart, one person at a time."

She told her biographer Chawla, "We are called upon not to be successful, but to be faithful."[5] And faithful she was, even unto death. Her last words were, "Jesus, I love You. Jesus, I love You." It was this that drove her and kept her pressing on.

Jesus said, "Whenever you did one of these things to someone overlooked or ignored, that was me—you did it to me" (Matthew 25:40, *The Message*). At Mother Teresa's death, India's president K. R. Naryanan, said, "Such a one as she rarely walks upon this Earth."

When she died, her light was not extinguished. By the time of her death, more than four thousand sisters had joined her, ministering in orphanages, homes for the poor, AIDS hospices, and centers for the poor and destitute. They will carry on the work she began. What a woman who touched the lives of so many for God!

RESOURCE READING
John 13:1-17

INSIGHT
Faithfulness to the calling of God—whether the task is great or very lowly—is the greatest act of worship we can render to the Lord.

APPLICATION
How can you serve others with the same humility that Mother Teresa showed? Is there anyone in your family who needs your help?

Do you ever ignore those who are unpleasant or destitute, thinking, "I'm not responsible?" How does God view this?

What might have happened if, like her brother, Mother Teresa set out to make a name for herself?

COMMITMENT
Samuel Zwemer

"You did not choose me, but I chose you to go and bear fruit. . . ."
John 15:16

The term "Christian" was first used as a term of derision to describe those who had followed Jesus Christ. When Adoniram Judson was in Burma, he faced the same kind of derision when he was often called "Jesus Christ's man in Burma." And when Samuel Zwemer walked down the streets of Bahrain, where he had gone to work among Muslims, he was often identified as "The Do You Pray? Man" because he had authored a little tract by that title, which had been widely circulated.

"The sheer joy of it all comes back. Gladly would I do it all over again. . . ."

Zwemer not only wrote tracts about praying, he prayed; and the God who answers prayer used this energetic, scholarly man to help change the world.

Samuel Zwemer was not an ordinary person in any sense of the word. The thirteenth of fifteen children born to a Reformed Church pastor, it seemed natural that Samuel would follow his father in Christian work as did four of his five surviving brothers. From the beginning, Zwemer never asked for an easy lot in life.

Zwemer worked among the Muslims of Arabia and in so doing became the "Apostle to Islam," as missionary history has dubbed him. His was not an easy lot. Turned down by the Reformed Board of Missions because the board considered a mission to the Muslim world "impractical," Zwemer teamed up with James Cantine, a fellow classmate; and they established their own mission, each raising support for the other until enough had been raised for them both to sail.

"Lethargy of the pastors," wrote Zwemer, "is the great drawback." But it wasn't only lethargy that annoyed him; it was legalism as well. In some churches he could speak on Sunday, but he wasn't allowed to hang on the wall his chart showing the concentration of Muslims in the world.

In the year 1890, Zwemer sailed for Arabia, settling in on the little island of Bahrain in the now oil-rich Persian Gulf. For five long years, he labored there alone. Then in 1885 Samuel met and married Amy Wilkes, a beautiful missionary nurse who became his companion and co-laborer.

The rest of Zwemer's life was far less romantic, however. It was not only the difficult language that he wrestled with but loneliness and suffering as well. In July 1904, the Zwemers' two little daughters, ages four and seven, died within two days of each other. For a period of time he was not allowed by local authorities even to bury the girls lest the soil be contaminated by the bodies of these non-Muslim pagans. Finally, he dug the tiny graves himself and laid the bodies of the two children in the ground.

Eventually, the Zwemers located in Cairo, where this brilliant intellectual influenced thousands of young men and women in the universities. It could hardly be said, though, that Zwemer was a great evangelist who swept multitudes of Muslims into the kingdom of God. The fact is that he was able to bring no more than a dozen people to a saving knowledge of Jesus Christ, yet Zwemer did what no one else had yet done. He confronted the claims of Islam and began to awaken the church to the impact of Islam on the world. In his lifetime Zwemer traveled all over the world, speaking in conferences, raising large sums of money, challenging the narrow view of the Christian world, asking them to consider the vast number of people in the Muslim world whose knowledge of Jesus Christ is unclear and fragmented.

Toward the end of his life, Zwemer looked back over fifty years of missionary ministry and said, "The sheer joy of it all comes back. Gladly would I do it all over again. . . ."[6] Samuel Zwemer, Apostle to the Muslims.

RESOURCE READING
2 Timothy 2

INSIGHT

Individuals who have accomplished something for God have always been willing to go the second mile, to sustain personal discomfort. Taking the easy path never results in achievement in education, business, or touching the world for God.

APPLICATION

Do you think that Zwemer would be surprised at the growth of Islam in our generation?

Zwemer considered lethargy to be one of the greatest foes of reaching Muslims with the Gospel. Have things really changed any?

Do you know any Muslims? Do you know what they believe as opposed to what you believe?

COMMITMENT
William Borden

"For to me, to live is Christ and to die is gain."
Philippians 1:21

Two wills were probated within a few days of each other in the spring of the year 1913. Both were handwritten. One was signed by the financier J. Pierpont Morgan, the other by a twenty-five-year-old Princeton Seminary graduate, William Borden.

Only weeks before, Borden had taken pen in hand—just in case anything should happen—and as a slow-moving ship sailed to Egypt, where he hoped to share the love of God with Muslims, Borden wrote his last will and testament.

"No reservation,
no retreat,
no regret."

Both men were wealthy; both were believers in Jesus Christ. Borden was heir to a family fortune, and Morgan had built one of the world's largest financial empires. But when their wills were probated, it was discovered that when Morgan died at age seventy-five, he left to Christian work less than half of what Borden did, who died at one-third of his age.

William Borden, however, left far more than a legacy of money when his life was cut short by cerebral meningitis. Borden's money wasn't what impressed people; it was his life, his integrity, his thoughtfulness, and his commitment to Jesus Christ. Born into a wealthy family, Borden could have had a life of leisure. Instead, he chose to become a missionary serving in one of the world's most difficult places.

Converted as a teenager, Borden never let his money get in his way. In fact, people were often shocked to learn that this caring young man was actually quite wealthy. Borden never considered that his money belonged to him. He refused to buy a car, saying it was "an unjustified luxury." Even in Cairo, he rode oxcarts and lived with a local family.

During his seminary days, he established a mission on skid row to reach alcoholics. At age twenty-three, he wrote what became the doctrinal charter for the Moody Bible Institute in Chicago. And when he died, newspapers around the world carried the story of this young man's untimely death. "What a waste of human potential," cried many. "Just think what he could have done with his life!"

Friends cried, "Lord, why did You take him when missionaries are so needed and so few are willing to pay the price?" From a human perspective, his death was hard to understand.

From our limited viewpoint, many things in life are difficult to understand. Our hearts cry out, "Why, Lord? Why did this have to happen?"

Writing of those whose lives were tragically cut short in death, Jim Reapsome asks, "Whose side is God on?" He wrote, "From my rationalistic perspective, the tragic death of Paul Little in an automobile accident was not the right way to run the universe. He was one of the nation's most effective campus evangelists, teacher and author, and was sold on world missions. What about Chet Bitterman, executed by Colombian terrorists? Or John Speers, gunned down in the Philippines?"

Then Jim says, "It will always look that way, unless we undergird our minds with God's supremacy, His right to do as He pleases (even to remove missionaries), and His right to bring glory to Himself any way He chooses."

William Borden would have agreed with Jim—and he would have agreed even more with the Apostle Paul when he wrote to the Philippians that "Christ will be exalted in my body, whether by life or by death." Paul went on to write, "For to me, to live is Christ and to die is gain" (Philippians 1:20, 21).

Borden's life motto was: "No reservation, no retreat, no regret." If, as the Westminster confession of faith suggests, our chief end in life is to glorify God, William Borden did just that. He also demonstrated that it is not how long you live that counts but how you live. Think about it.[7]

RESOURCE READING
Philippians 1:12-26

INSIGHT
While God does not expect each of us to give away our money as did Borden, He does expect to have first place in our lives (Matthew 6:33).

APPLICATION
What is first or most important in your life? What was it, do you think, in Borden's life?

Look up Matthew 6:33 in your Bible (if you have not already done so) and answer the question, "How important are these 'other things' in my life?"

COMMITMENT

Byrd Brunemeier

"I am not ashamed, because I know whom I have believed,
and am convinced that he is able to guard what I have
entrusted to him for that day."
2 Timothy 1:12

On the wall of our Guidelines' studio is a rusty 30-caliber rifle shell mounted on a wooden base. It is a rather strange artifact to adorn the wall of a Christian recording center, but a story lies behind it.

"For the child of God there are no 'accidents' —only 'incidents.' "

It was one of the thousands of shells and implements of warfare gleaned when engineers on the island of Saipan cleared a site for the installation of the Far East Broadcasting Company's powerful radio station. The rifle shell was found at the base of "suicide hill," where thousands of Japanese soldiers had flung themselves to their deaths when it seemed that capture by the Allied Forces was imminent. On that death site has risen a tremendous antennae field that will broadcast the message of life to men and women throughout Southeast Asia.

No one individual has done more to convert the scene of tragedy to a field of victory than Byrd Brunemeier, a quiet, unassuming engineer who spent most of his life as a missionary—much of it in missionary radio. I first met Byrd in 1974 when we were living in Manila, Philippines, the center for our Asian radio ministry. Byrd was never one to waste words, but when he said something, people listened. When my son, then nine years of age, embarked on a science project building a miniature radio station, Byrd was the one who had to take me aside and explain that Steve was hopelessly in over his head. He spent hours with Steve, helping him design a project he could handle. Byrd was the one who had the patience to sit down with kids and explain the difference between transistors and vacuum tubes—but he also had the knowledge to put together super-power stations that reached around the world.

Byrd was my kind of a man—tough, resilient, and committed. He was totally dedicated to the cause of Jesus Christ, whom he served with reckless abandon. When equipment had to be procured, instead of spending mission funds, Byrd would scour the alleys and electronic junk-yards of Manila for parts and then put something together far superior to anything that could be bought.

On July 22, 1983, Byrd made radio contact with his wife, Angie, who had been sent to the United States for surgery. He had just finished cleaning up the field under the shortwave antenna and was preparing to fine-tune the powerful KSAI transmitter. Finishing the contact, Byrd said, "Good-bye until next Friday."

By Friday, however, Byrd's body lay in a simple grave in the Protestant cemetery on Saipan. Here is what happened: while adjusting the equipment, a fire broke out in the transmitter. Racing to hit the power cut-off, Byrd stumbled and fell into a high voltage power line. As Angie put it, "He fell into the arms of His Savior."

"For the child of God there are no 'accidents'—only 'incidents'" wrote someone long ago. That had to be true of Byrd.

Telling of his "homegoing," his wife, Angie, wrote, "In our years together I was often alone with the children, never knowing in what condition he would return. . .or if he would return at all. I learned that when one is in God's perfect will, there are no such conditions as 'danger' or 'safety.' Time after time Byrd was near death, or just barely missed being killed. It is because of this that I have the assurance that his death at this time was no accident. It was our Father's perfect plan." The Apostle Paul made it clear: "For to be absent from the body," he wrote to the Corinthians, "is to be present with the Lord" (2 Corinthians 5:8).

RESOURCE READING
2 Timothy 1

INSIGHT

Byrd Brunemeir was gifted and talented, somewhat of a "loner" individual, who accomplished great things for the Lord because he had determined that everything he had already belonged to the Lord.

APPLICATION

As a student at John Brown University, Byrd took a metal coiled innerspring (from a mattress) and made a transmitter, broadcasting low power to fellow students. If he didn't have something, he made it. Question: How can we develop the "improvise and make it work" mentality today, when we have so much readily available merchandise?

What is your primary interest in life? How can this be used for the Lord?

COMMITMENT

Lim Cheong

"And my God will meet all your needs
according to his glorious riches in Christ Jesus."
Philippians 4:19

When Lim Cheong bought a three-bedroom house with two bathrooms and moved into it, it represented far more to him than the mere pleasure of owning his own home. For him, it represented a kind of spiritual victory as well.

You see, Lim Cheong's father, a silversmith, earned his living by making silver gods and selling them to the people who came to the local temple in Cambodia. As he grew up, undoubtedly, Lim Cheong thought a great deal about the gods that his father made, but he also began thinking about what they could do, or could not do. He knew that people prayed to them, but what this young man wanted to know was, "Were those prayers answered?"

"Let your God take care of you!"

At the age of twelve, Lim Cheong went to his uncle, a Buddhist priest, and asked him if he knew of a prayer that had ever been answered. The uncle had to admit that he was uncertain of any definite answers. Not satisfied, Lim Cheong went to a missionary and asked him the same question. Without hesitation, the missionary related numerous incidents in which God very definitely answered prayer; the missionary went on to tell Lim Cheong about God's love in Christ Jesus. Lim Cheong decided that he would serve the God who is alive and answers prayer.

When he came home that evening, he told his father what he had done. In anger the father shouted to his twelve-year-old son, "Get out of my house. Go sleep with your Jesus!" It was then that Lim Cheong had to put his newly found God to the test. Would God take care of him? What does a twelve-year-old boy do who has been thrown out of his own home?

God did take care of him. After graduating from Prince Sihanouk High School, Lim Cheong received a full university scholarship but turned it down, feeling that God was calling him into Christian service. After he completed his education at a Bible college, Lim Cheong married and became a pastor to his people in Cambodia.

Then in 1964, foreign missionaries were asked to leave the country. Fearlessly, Lim Cheong still carried on God's work. He was imprisoned in a test case that eventually resulted in his release.

And what happened to his family? First, his little mother became a follower of Jesus Christ, and then one by one his brothers and sisters followed. Undoubtedly, his father thought much about God and the silver images that he designed and made, but finally his father came to realize that God is bigger than the images he had spent his life making. Then his aged father also embraced Jesus Christ as his personal Lord and Savior.

When Lim Cheong moved into his own home, he couldn't help but remember the words of his father who once said, "Let your God take care of you!" God certainly had done just that.

Today Lim Cheong is a pastor and broadcasts God's love to his fellow citizens. He can no longer shepherd them directly, for the religious freedom that Cambodia once enjoyed has been lost. But the God who took care of a twelve-year-old boy and proved His care for him is just the same as ever.

How about your life? Does the God you serve really answer prayer? Or would you have to admit, as did Lim Cheong's uncle, that in spite of your religious activities, you cannot be sure that you have ever heard directly from heaven? "My God," promises the Bible, "shall supply all your needs according to His riches in glory in Christ Jesus" (Philippians 4:19). Going through the motions of religious experience is not enough, but there is a God in heaven who will hear and answer prayer if you become His child, and He can change your life. Lim Cheong discovered that those who come to God in faith will be amply rewarded, for God will take care of them. And you can make that same discovery.

REFERENCE READING
Jonah 1, 2

INSIGHT
God answers prayer for us—not because of our goodness—but because of our position in Jesus Christ.

APPLICATION
If you were locked up in prison, what prayer promises have you memorized that you could stand on? Take inventory and determine to memorize at least one this week, beginning with Mark 11:24.

If someone asked you to tell about the answer to one of your prayers, what would you say?

COMPASSION
Ed Rosenbaum

"In everything, do to others what you would have them do to you,
for this sums up the Law and the Prophets."
Matthew 7:12

The movie, *The Doctor*, is based on the real life experiences of Dr. Ed Rosenbaum. He relates these experiences in his book, *A Taste of My Own Medicine*. In the movie, the life of a young surgeon, Dr. Jack McKee, is drastically changed by a raspiness in his voice and a cough that won't go away. The cause: cancer of the larynx.

"We are all very much the same when it comes to matters of life and death."

Dr. McKee has surrounded himself with the trappings of luxury —a powerful sports car, a picture-perfect home, expensive suits, and a beautiful wife. He has no use for compassion. In fact, he views it as weakness. He tells the doctors he is training that a surgeon's responsibility is to be good, get in and get out, and save the patient's life. Being emotionally involved with your patient, he says, is a hindrance.

McKee does his surgery with music filling the operating theater, making borderline remarks to the nurses and wise-cracking with fellow doctors. Then one day in a fit of laughter, Dr. McKee begins to cough up blood, and a subsequent exam by a brisk, pretty female doctor bursts his bubble of superficiality. "Doctor," she says, "you have a growth on your larynx." Bang, just like that! His future is "on hold." His expensive toys become meaningless.

Soon the doctor becomes a patient, and his status as a staff surgeon is reduced to being that of the bearer of a blue hospital medical card. Now he's a number, a statistic, who has to wait his turn like everybody else, and he chaffs at the system. Yelling, "Do you know who I am?" doesn't really matter to the core of nurses and hospital attendants. Minus his white coat and stethoscope, he's just another patient.

The movie, based on Dr. Rosenbaum's real-life experiences, is a graphic picture of how easily we lose touch with the reality of what is happening to those whose lives we touch every day. Following unsuccessful attempts to treat the growth with radiation, the doctor is forced to confess his dislike and abuse of a fellow surgeon and asks him to remove the growth. The surgery is successful, and following a frustrating recovery, Dr. McKee again begins to brief his surgeons in training.

This time it's different. McKee begins by lecturing his interns on the fact that the people they are working with are human beings and that someday they will be on the other end of the knife, so they had better learn what compassion is all about. He orders them to remove their white coats, put on hospital gowns, and be patients for seventy-two hours to learn how a person feels who has to depend on the professional.

If Dr. Rosenbaum understood the spiritual ramifications of the change in his life, the movie doesn't indicate it. But the doctor was really acting out what Jesus said long ago: "In everything, do to others what you would have them do to you, for this sums up the Law and the Prophets" (Matthew 7:12).

There is one thing for sure. A surgeon who is reduced to being a patient never again presumes to be a skillful manipulator of organs and sick bodies. He's learned compassionate care by being on the other side of the scalpel. I have to say in defense of the medical profession, most of the people I have worked with in medicine are not there because of the money they make, but because they care for people. But all of us need to be reminded once in a while of the same lesson Dr. Rosenbaum had to learn: no matter how much we think we care about people, are we truly treating them the way we'd want to be treated in their place?

Whether you are a minister, a doctor, a nurse, a bus driver, or a social service worker, it is people with flesh and blood to whom you minister—not clients, patients, or customers. People are individuals with fears, hopes, expectations, and disappointments, and beneath the professional veneer or the image we project, we are all very much the same when it comes to matters of life and death.

Putting yourself in the position of the one with whom you work will help bring compassion and healing to humanity. Think about it.

RESOURCE READING
Matthew 7

INSIGHT
Putting ourselves in the position of the other person means that we will treat individuals with compassion and care.

APPLICATION
Have you ever been a victim of "the system"? Have you felt that someone didn't listen to your complaint or treated you as though you were just a number? How did it make you feel?

Answer honestly: Do you strive to treat others as you would have them treat you? Most of the time? Sometimes? Never think about it?

COMPASSION
Bob Pierce

"When he saw the crowds, he had compassion on them, because they were harassed and helpless, like sheep without a shepherd."
Matthew 9:36

World War II was winding down when Bob Pierce visited a mission school and orphanage run by a group of German sisters near the Tibetan border. While he was there, Pierce noticed a little girl hunched at the bottom of the cold, stone steps. The little girl was obviously undernourished and lacked proper clothing for the cold climate.

The child could not have been more than nine or ten, yet her gaunt little face and coal-black eyes reflected as much suffering as some endure in a lifetime.

"What am I going to do about it?"

Deeply concerned, Pierce asked one of the sisters about her. "Oh," she replied, "she comes and sits there everyday. She wants to come to school. But we have no room."

The reply did not satisfy him, so he said, "Surely one child won't make that much difference. If she wants to come so badly, could you not make room for just one more?"

The sister turned to Pierce and said, "We have made room for 'just one more,' time and time again. We have already four times the number of children we were originally prepared to care for. We have stretched our food as far as it will go. I myself am feeding three others out of my rice bowl, as are all the other sisters. If we do not draw the line somewhere, there will not be enough rice to keep the children we already have alive. We simply cannot take one more child!"

The brutal reality of the situation hit home, but Pierce did not want to accept it. "That is crazy, ridiculous!" he said. "A child cannot come asking for help and be turned away at the door. Why isn't something being done?"

Without saying anything, the sister walked over and swooped the little girl up in her arms. Walking over to Pierce, she deposited the girl in his strong arms and said, "What are *you* going to do about it?"

That incident led to the founding of World Vision—an organization that has helped feed and clothe thousands of boys and girls. Pierce did what I think you would have done. He dug into his own pocket and gave the sister enough money to buy rice for the little girl.

Bob Pierce was a warm-hearted man whose compassion deeply touched my life as well as thousands and thousands of other people. I will never forget sitting with Bob late one Sunday night in a coffee shop after the evening service. Nobody was there but myself, another friend, and Bob Pierce. Nobody to impress, but what spoke to my heart was the way Bob sat there and told us of the suffering of the Korean people. His eyes filled with tears that coursed down his cheeks, mingling with the coffee grounds in the bottom of the cup.

Men of lesser stature would have turned the other way. I have lived in Asia and seen the wretchedness of poverty and disease and the disgust of ignorance. I have also noticed that when you look the other way, passing by becomes so much easier, until eventually you do not see at all. The pain of suffering has been totally masked by the little world you live in. Hunger—be it physical or spiritual—lies at our doorstep. We did not ask for it; we do not like it; but nevertheless it is there.

A sister's question founded a great organization. "What

are *you* going to do about it?" It is the question that every person must face. When you think of the needs of all the world, you are overwhelmed, but if you can think of the one person outside your gate and face the question, "What am I going to do about it?" you will find that the darkness is driven back at least one step. The needs of people come one at a time; eventually every person must answer the question: "What am I going to do about it?"

RESOURCE READING
Matthew 9:9-38

INSIGHT
Just because you cannot do everything, you should not neglect doing what you can. Remember, little is much when God is in it.

APPLICATION
Does the emphasis on ourselves keep us from asking, "What can I do?"

Jesus gave us an example of being a servant (John 13) and then said, "Now that you know these things, you will be blessed if you do them" (John 13:17). Are we missing something today with our emphasis on "fun" as opposed to service? How does this principle speak to your life?

COMPASSION
Joseph Damien

*"I tell you the truth, unless a kernel of wheat falls
to the ground and dies, it remains only a single seed.
But if it dies, it produces many seeds."*
John 12:24

Anyone who has ever known the darkness of discouragement should be able to relate to Joseph Damien, who left
his home in Belgium to work among the lepers on the
island of Molokai in Hawaii.

"Take a lingering look at the cross. . . proof positive He cares."

In 1873, when someone em-
barked on a mission such as
Damien undertook, he didn't
come home for vacations or ask
for a transfer when he got home-
sick or discouraged, and before
long, Father Damien, who was a
Catholic missionary, experienced
both. Though he tried to make friends with the native
islanders, he was rejected and his little chapel was almost
empty week after week. "Is this what I have come for? Is
this what I have spent years in preparation for?" he asked
himself.

For twelve long years, he tried to penetrate the culture
and minister effectively to the men and women whose limbs
became horribly deformed with leprosy. When they were
desperate enough, the lepers let him dress their sores and
provide help. When they died, he stood over the disfigured
remains and prayed for their souls. But the living would not

allow him to pray with them, nor would they listen to what he had to say. Gradually his hopes turned to despair.

He finally reached the end of his patience, and that's when he decided to quit. After all, there is a limit to what anyone can endure. He was finished. He was sure that he had given it his best, but his best wasn't good enough. He made the decision to quit and go home.

Dennis Cone writes, "While standing on the pier about to board the ship that would take him back to Belgium, he looked down at his hands. The white spots he saw could mean only one thing. He had contracted leprosy. So instead of going home, he returned to his work in the leper colony."

As he turned and slowly walked up the hill, the word spread. Hearts were melted. Now he was one of them. He understood their pain, their loneliness, their rejection by society. They started coming–some crawling, some hobbling along helping each other–until literally hundreds of them gathered outside the little hut that was his home.

The next Sunday Father Damien went to his little chapel as he had done Sunday after Sunday, but this time it was full to overflowing. They listened to him as one of them. For a period of four more years, he gave himself completely to his flock until he was too sick himself to rise from his bed. On April 15, 1889, he died and was buried among his parishioners.

Since 1965, a likeness of Father Damien has stood in the Statuary Hall of the U.S. Capitol building, a tribute to the man who gave his life for others. When Damien stood on the pier with a small group of loyal friends, ready to quit, and saw the unmistakable signs of leprosy, he turned and walked up the hill, forever closing the door on the luxuries of life in his homeland. There was no going back. He was committed.

Those who lived before Jesus came to our world could at times wonder how much God really cared for those who faced life on earth. After all, He seemed to pass a great deal of judgment on those who sinned. But then Christ came; and when He came, God became flesh and lived among us, experiencing our pain, our loneliness, and our discourage-ment. One of the names of Jesus is the name Immanuel, which means "God with us!"

Understanding what Father Damien did should help you, friend, to see something of God's care for you. When Jesus came to our planet, He took a step He could not reverse; He was committed, a human being like ourselves. Still, He could have called on legions of angels to deliver Him from the painful death He experienced on the cross. But He chose to give His life so that we might have life.

When you become discouraged, wondering whether or not God really cares for you, take a lingering look at the cross and remind yourself that this is proof positive He cares about you.

No matter how far you have wandered from the pres-ence of the Father, no matter what you have done, He will still receive you with open arms and wipe away your tears and love you. "Come to me, all you who are weary and burdened," said Jesus, "and I will give you rest" (Matthew 11:28).

RESOURCE READING
Luke 15:11-31

INSIGHT
Our greatest accomplishments in life are the result of great sacrifice.

APPLICATION
In dying to self, we live to others. In your life, what per-sonal sacrifices can you make that would result in touching the life of another person?

If Father Damien had gone back to his native Belgium and lived out the rest of his life in health, would he have enjoyed the same sense of accomplishment and satisfaction?

Is the length of life as important as the fullness of life?

CONVERSION
Basilio Clark

"Therefore, if anyone is in Christ, he is a new creation."
2 Corinthians 5:17

Any of the old-timers living in Olongapo, Philippines, near Subic Bay (once the home of the American Seventh Fleet), will tell you that Basilio Clark, the warm Baptist pastor who plays his guitar and sings so beautifully, is a different person from the one who terrorized the same city in his youth.

A clue to his background is found in his name—Basilio Clark. Basilio is a Filipino name; Clark, an American name. Basilio's father was an American serviceman; his mother, a Filipino who met and fell in love with the handsome American. After several children were born, Basilio's father was killed in an automobile accident. Without enough food at home, the boy began to run the streets, stealing from the sidewalk vendors and shop keepers in the open markets of Olongapo.

"How amazing, how marvelous is God's grace!"

As a teenager, Basilio was the head of a gang who robbed, plundered, murdered, and pillaged at will. Holing up one night with his gang, Basilio slept as police surrounded the hideout. They took him and his companions captive.

The judge, glad to be able to rid the area of such terrors, showed no mercy. Basilio and his eight companions were sentenced to die in the electric chair. They were quickly moved to Bilibid prison in Muntinglupa, just outside of Manila. The massive steel doors of the fortresslike prison closed, ominously signaling the end.

I've spoken in Muntinglupa prison and have seen the electric chair, with levers outside the door that send thousands of volts of electricity into a frail body, short-circuiting the heart and stopping life. Basilio and his gang feared death this way and chose rather to die at their own hands.

Mixing insecticide, which had been smuggled into the prison, with paint thinner they were able to steal, the nine of them formed a circle and drank the deadly potion. Of the nine, only one survived: Basilio, and he was blind.

He had failed in life and he had failed in death. While he awaited his appointment with the electric chair, Basilio began to listen to a little radio that Olga Robertson, a faithful prison worker, had given to the prisoners. This little radio, known as a PM (Portable Missionary), played but one station, DZAS, the voice of the Far East Broadcasting Company. Day after day as Basilio listened, God began to speak to his heart. Kneeling on the concrete floor beside his steel bunk, Basilio was converted.

Gaining his confidence, Mommie Olga, as the prisoners affectionately called her, began to disciple and teach Basilio the Word of God. Then going from cell block to cell block, Basilio began to tell other prisoners that God had forgiven him and that he had repented of his sins.

It quickly became obvious that this was no longer the tough youth who had terrorized Olongapo, but a changed man whose eyes no longer saw—but they did shed tears over his fellow prisoners. Something had happened! Something big.

Eventually, the president of the Philippines issued a pardon to Basilio Clark, and he was released. Going back to his home a changed man, Basilio continued to share his faith.

I'm tempted to say, "Hats off to the unknown programmer on FEBC's Christian radio voice and to a brave little woman, Olga Robertson, who goes where most men fear to walk and takes a radio." Both of these thoughts are valid, but I know that our friends at FEBC and Olga Robertson, whom I know very well personally, would want me to say that God was the one who worked the miracle—and what He did for a thug and gangster He can do for you. Changed lives are what the Gospel of Jesus Christ is all about. Paul was right, "If anyone is in Christ, he is a new creation. . ." (2 Corinthians 5:17).

RESOURCE READING
2 Corinthians 5

INSIGHT
All the government social programs in the world have not brought the change that the Holy Spirit brings when a person is converted to Jesus Christ.

APPLICATION
Do you know of someone whose life was turned around by the Gospel of Jesus Christ?

Can a person be a Christian and have nothing change in his or her life?

CONVERSION
John Newton

"In my distress I called to the LORD, and he answered me. From the depths of the grave I called for help, and you listened to my cry."
Jonah 2:2

Talk about a man with a past! Few can rival the story that John Newton must have told to his grandchildren.

Though he was born into a Christian home, he was orphaned at the age of six. But before his mother died, she talked to her little boy about the depravity of mankind and the grace of God that leads to repentance.

"Amazing grace how sweet the sound That saved a wretch like me!"

After six-year-old John became an orphan, he was passed from relative to relative. Finally a distant relative took him in, a man who scoffed at his mother's faith and abused him severely for the slightest infraction of the rules he laid down. John quickly stopped talking of both his mother and God.

As a teenager, John went to sea to escape the home he had grown to despise. After an apprenticeship, he joined the Royal Navy; but finding the life too hard, he deserted and went to Africa. Eventually he joined himself to a Portuguese slave trader in whose home he was treated like a slave. On occasions the wife of the trader would vent her hatred for John by throwing his food on the floor, and if he ate, he had to eat it on his hands and knees as an animal.

Fleeing again, Newton made his way to the coast and

attracted the attention of a passing ship by building a large fire. Thinking that Newton either had ivory or slaves to sell, the captain of the ship sent a dory to trade with him. Disappointed that Newton had neither, the captain reluctantly allowed him to come on board as a navigator.

On one occasion, Newton opened a cask of rum to entertain the crew, who promptly got drunk. This so enraged the captain that he threw Newton overboard and then hurled a harpoon at the youth floundering in the waters, tearing a gaping hole in his body and leaving a wound large enough that Newton could put his fist into it.

Eventually Newton became the captain of a slave ship that made its way between the coasts of Africa and the New World. Now, some two hundred years later, biographers are uncertain as to when the crisis came that changed the direction of his life. Some say it was on the same journey as when he experienced the harpoon in the back. They say that the ship was caught in a storm and that as the ship floundered, Newton was forced to man the pumps along with slaves being transported to England. Fearful for his life, Newton cried out to God for forgiveness and deliverance.

Others say the crisis came when Newton's own ship was caught in an Atlantic gale that threatened its destruction. He then knelt beside the wheel of the vessel he feared he would lose and cried out, "O thou God of my dead mother, have mercy on me!"

At any length, Newton was genuinely converted and walked away from the ship to spend the rest of his life as an Anglican clergyman.

In his lifetime he authored more than 280 hymns, and when he died, these words, at his own request, were graven on his tombstone:

John Newton, clerk
Once an Infidel and Libertine
A servant of slaves in Africa
was, by the rich mercy of our Lord

and Savior, Jesus Christ, preserved,
Restored and pardoned and appointed to
preach the faith he had long labored to destroy.

Of all his hymns, perhaps one of the dearest of all is the
one that goes,

"Amazing grace how sweet the sound,
That saved a wretch like me!
I once was lost, but now am found,
Was blind but now I see."

John Newton understood how amazing, how marvelous
is God's grace! May we, too, learn that truth today.

RESOURCE READING
Jonah 2

INSIGHT
No matter what you need, the grace of God is sufficient for
you.

APPLICATION
Do you see the biography of Newton's life in his hymn,
"Amazing Grace"?

Conversion is an about-face. Take time to look up
2 Corinthians 5:17 and ask how the "old has gone" and "the
new has come" in your personal life.

CONVERSION
William J. Murray III

"Therefore, if anyone is in Christ, he is a new creation;
the old has gone, the new has come! All this is from God,
who reconciled us to himself through Christ. . . ."
2 Corinthians 5:17, 18

That God has a sense of humor is without question. Take, for instance, what happened to Madalyn Murray O'Hair, who won the 1963 Supreme Court case against prayer in public schools.

Perhaps you recall something of the furor of the mid-sixties when she and her colleagues decided to take God out of public life in America, and certainly out of the classroom. She made some headway, too, as the Supreme Court interpreted the First Amendment in such a way that decreed there should be no prayer in public schools—a ruling that, I suppose, could be set aside in the event of nuclear attack.

"There is a God-shaped vacuum in the heart of every man that can be filled only by Jesus Christ."

William J. Murray, III, Madalyn's son, was a seventeen-year-old high school junior at Baltimore's Poly Western High School in 1963, when the Supreme Court rendered its decision. Perhaps Mrs. Murray was more engrossed in the battle than in indoctrinating her son, because—believe it or not—her son William is now an outspoken, committed Christian, who wants to see his own mother find the same faith that has been born in his heart.

In a letter that appeared in the *Baltimore Sun,* William Murray III said that he wanted to "apologize to the city of Baltimore" for his part in removing "Bible reading and prayer from the tax-supported schools of the city." In a similar letter of apology published by the Austin, Texas, *American-Statesman,* he said that he was no longer an atheist and probably never had been. He also said, "It is only with a return to our traditional values and our faith in God that we will be able to survive as a people. . . ."

The turning point in his life came in September 1979. Let me quote his words verbatim, as printed in the *Orange County Register:* "After living with atheism for thirty years. . . I threw myself on my knees and asked for God's help in my life. Mine was not a lightning-fast conversion; but in September of 1979, once and for all, I gave myself to the Lord. I pledged that I would do His will each day and, you know, things always managed to work out."

When Murray shares the testimony of the change in his life, he tells how he became a successful business executive and had a good life but was not happy. His search finally led to a personal commitment to God, the God who his mother says does not exist. In the same city where his mother built an Atheist Center, Murray now attends a non-denominational church.

When a reporter asked his mother to comment on what had happened to her son, she replied, "Pretty strange . . .I think what this is," she said, "is that he is after his mother again." Yes, it is pretty strange how God works!

It was Augustine, who wrote, "There is a God-shaped vacuum in the heart of every man that can be filled only by Jesus Christ." I am wondering where you stand in relationship to our Heavenly Father. Are you asking, "Could He fill the empty void in my heart?" Every person was born to have communion with our Maker, and denying His existence does not satisfy that spiritual hunger that cries out for the Father's presence.

What God has done for the son of Madalyn Murray

O'Hair, He can do for you, for there is no favoritism with God. Jesus said, "Whoever comes to me, I will in no wise cast out" (John 6:37). It is God's invitation to you.

RESOURCE READING
2 Corinthians 5:11-21

INSIGHT

Though the influence of parents is profound in our lives, it is not absolute. The conversion of William Murray is another illustration that God not only wants each of us to think for ourselves but also holds us accountable for our actions.

APPLICATION

Do you know anyone who is a Christian today who grew up in a home where parents rejected Christian values and the gospel?

If you had a friend whose parents were unbelievers, what advice would you give your friend in striving to win them to the Lord?

CONVERSION
Augustine

*"I am not ashamed of the gospel, because it is the power of God
for the salvation of everyone who believes:
first for the Jew, then for the Gentile."*
Romans 1:16

Amidst the crumbling ruins of the Roman Empire in the
year A.D. 354, one of the greatest champions of Christian
faith was born in a small North African province. His name
was Augustine. In capsule form, here is his biography.

*"Thou has made us
for Thyself, O God,
and our heart is restless
until it finds its
rest in Thee."*

As a youth, Augustine was
reared in the church of his day,
though at first the church seemed
to make no great impression on
him. His mother was a Christian;
his father was a noble Roman. In
his late teen years, Augustine, like
many young men and women
today, turned to philosophy, and under its influence he
turned from the church. His heart was seeking for an
answer to the questions of life. At first he thought he found
peace in a pagan religion called Manicheanism, but soon
Augustine was seized with doubt and agnosticism. For a
period of time, he drifted and doubted, still seeking anchors
for his restless heart.

In his autobiography that bears the title *Confessions*,
Augustine tells about this period of great turmoil and
unrest. He indicates that he shared in the vices and corrup-
tions of his day. For a number of years he lived a double life

of immorality. Then quite suddenly in the year 387, Augustine found faith in God through Jesus Christ His Son. Augustine's seeking heart found an answer that has satisfied the restlessness of people in all ages.

Many today lead lives that parallel the life of Augustine–born in the shadow of a church, reared in a Christian atmosphere, but in college years confronted with periods of doubt and unbelief. But the restless seekings of the human heart in this twentieth century can still find peace through faith in Jesus Christ.

Why is Augustine important? In spite of the life that he lived before he found Christian faith, he made one of the greatest contributions to Christianity that has been made since the time of the Apostle Paul. He is one of the few men in history who is equally loved and respected by Catholics and Protestants alike.

Augustine experienced the depths of sin, yet he found that the grace of God is greater than the greatest sin. Augustine's approach to Christian faith began with his assertion that the human heart is entirely corrupted by sin, which he defined as "choosing our own way rather than God's way." He believed that humans were created perfect, but in the garden of Eden humanity rejected God and fell to the depths of degradation. He believed everyone has sinned and come short of God's standard. He said there is nothing in the heart of human beings that is worthy of God and that all we could ever do would never bring us to a place where we could be worthy of the Savior.

Augustine held that only by the grace of God could anyone find eternal life. And he was right, for the Apostle Paul said, "By grace are you saved through faith, and that not of yourselves, it is the gift of God; not of works lest any man should boast." Augustine's life was really no different than the lives of countless thousands today–seeking, restless, drifting. In his *Confessions,* Augustine wrote, "Thou has made us for Thyself, O God, and our heart is restless until it finds its rest in Thee."

In relation to Augustine's life, where are you? Have you found reality in Jesus Christ, or are you still seeking? You, like Augustine, can discover that the answer is not in sin, loose living, or in philosophy, but in a personal relationship to Jesus Christ.

RESOURCE READING
Colossians 3:12-17

INSIGHT
As long as people live with one foot in the world and one on Christ's side, they will never have peace of heart or know where they stand in relationship to salvation.

APPLICATION
When you have questions about life and its meaning, where do you turn for answers? Where *should* you turn?

After his conversion, Augustine was confronted by a former acquaintance with whom he had been immoral. She called his name and Augustine didn't answer. Finally, he said, "That was the old Augustine; I am the new one." Should the difference in a person's life be evident following conversion to Jesus Christ?

Conversion

Malcolm Muggeridge

"In reply Jesus declared, 'I tell you the truth, no one can see the kingdom of God unless he is born again.' "
John 3:3

I never met the old gentleman, but when newspapers reported his death at the age of 87, I felt a profound sadness and loss. In his youth, Malcolm Muggeridge had a tongue that was as sharp as a sword, and he never spared anyone of position or influence when it came to using it. He referred to Britain's monarchy as "a royal soap opera." He wrote of the American president, Dwight D. Eisenhower, as "a meandering old President." When he edited *Punch* magazine, he wrote a lot of things that caused a wisp of smoke to rise as people read them.

"In the Gospels he discovered a new world."

As a young Marxist, he went to Russia for two years, then returned to write a scathing bestseller condemning the entire system. Muggeridge could be described as a brilliant man of letters, a cynic and a skeptic, a liberal, one who was able to penetrate the hypocrisy and veneer of society and describe it as it was. In his more skeptical hours, he dismantled the entire household of Western life and dethroned God, venerating science and power.

Later in life he admitted that he had moments of doubt when he secretly read the Bible. Actually he said that he read it at all stages of his life—in Egypt, India, the USSR, and, of course, at home in his native Britain. In the Gospels he "discovered a new world" that was entirely different from twentieth-century life. In his *Confessions,* which he wrote at the age of 84, he admitted that the most marked-up passages of his Bible concerned the Passion and bore "stains that might be from tears."

A variety of experiences slowly caused his doubt and skepticism to erode, such as the time he was serving with British intelligence in Mozambique during World War II. Depressed, he decided to terminate his life by drowning. He started swimming but saw a great light that caused him to turn back toward shore. He didn't drown, but neither did he convert to Christianity at that point.

Mother Teresa left her mark on his life as well, as he saw in her the selfless spirit of Christ-likeness. Russian Christians with whom he worshipped also left their mark on him. Of his experience with them he wrote, "I should have found myself nearest to You, Jesus, in the land where for half a century past the practice of the Christian religion has been most ruthlessly suppressed."

On November 27, 1982, Muggeridge was received into the Roman Catholic Church, but this does not really date his time of conversion. It was his way of making a statement condemning the carnality and depravity of life today and a reaffirmation of his commitment to life, including his opposition to abortion.

When a news magazine reported his death, it ended by saying his life "ended last week at 87." No, for Muggeridge, life had just begun.

In his book, *Christ and Media,* he wrote, "As the old do, I often wake up in the night, half out of my body, so that I see between the sheets the old battered carcass I shall soon be leaving for good, and in the distance a glow in the sky, the lights of Augustine's City of God." For the old British journalist, the distant light that was a glow in the sky has become a reality.

As Paul put it, "Now we see through a glass darkly, but

then we shall see face to face. Now we know in part, but then we shall know even as we are known" (1 Corinthians 13:12, KJV). Malcolm Muggeridge, promoted to heaven at age 87. For him, life has just begun.

RESOURCE READING
Acts 9

INSIGHT
At times those who attack Christianity are themselves convicted by it.

APPLICATION
Is there something in the Bible you don't understand? Do you use that as an excuse to keep from doing what you *do* understand?

Never believe all your doubts or doubt all your beliefs. Hold on to what you know is true, and ask God to let that base of truth expand.

CONVERSION
Paul

"Christ will be exalted in my body, whether by life or by death.
For to me, to live is Christ and to die is gain."
Philippians 1:20, 21

Some are born great; some have greatness thrust upon them; and some could be dumped out of an airplane in a brown paper bag over a country where they had never set foot, and they would still achieve greatness. These are the ones who are truly great. Such was the individual born long ago of Jewish parents in the university town of Tarsus, located in the Zagros mountains of Turkey. During the first part of his life, he was identified as Saul of Tarsus, but following a dramatic encounter with the risen Christ, he became known as Paul, the Apostle.

"We are hard pressed on every side, but not crushed; perplexed, but not in despair; persecuted, but not abandoned; struck down, but not destroyed"

No other individual so shaped and molded the future of Christianity as did this scholarly and dedicated individual. As an author he contributed thirteen books to the New Testament, writing more books than any other person and second only to Luke in volume. As the theologian of the first century, he settled doctrinal issues, set in order rules for church government, and became the missionary who spread the Good News through the known world, from Jerusalem to Rome and perhaps as far west as Spain.

Following his conversion, which you can read about in the ninth chapter of the Book of Acts, Saul, as he was then known, went on to Damascus, where he recovered his sight following the blindness that had occurred as he traveled to Damascus. His conversion was immediate and complete. Whereas he had been the greatest enemy of Christianity, he now became its great proponent and evangelist, traversing seas and continents in the relentless pursuit of converts.

When Paul appeared before a hostile mob in Jerusalem, he tried to explain what had happened. Here are his words: "I am a Jew, born in Tarsus of Cilicia, but brought up in this city [meaning Jerusalem]. Under Gamaliel [one of the chief theologians of Jewish law], I was thoroughly trained in the law of our fathers and was just as zealous for God as any of you are today. I persecuted the followers of this Way to their death, arresting both men and women and throwing them into prison, as also the high priest and all the council can testify. I even obtained letters from them to their brothers in Damascus and went there to bring these people as prisoners to Jerusalem to be punished" (Acts 22:2-5).

Following his conversion, Paul met with much skepticism from the Christian community, something that was to be expected. After three years in exile in Arabia, he returned to Damascus and then to Jerusalem to meet with Peter and James, the Lord's brother, who had become a leader in the church. He then went back to his hometown in Tarsus and made tents until, about seven years later, Barnabas sought him out and said, "Brother Saul, the Lord has need of you!"

Paul and his traveling companions made three extensive missionary journeys and, in the process, planted the flag of Christianity in many a town and city. He discovered how it was to be on the receiving end of a jail sentence and was often abused and imprisoned for his faith. Writing to the Corinthians, he opened his heart, saying, "We are hard pressed on every side, but not crushed; perplexed, but not in despair; persecuted, but not abandoned; struck down, but not destroyed" (2 Corinthians 4:8-9). He also told how he had received the traditional thirty-nine lashes from his enemies on five occasions. Three times he was beaten with rods, once stoned.

Tradition says that Paul sustained two long periods of prison, once for almost two years under house arrest in Rome, where he wrote letters to the churches, and then a final imprisonment about A.D. 67, when he was martyred. Paul's goal: "Christ will be exalted in my body, whether by life or by death. For to me, to live is Christ and to die is gain" (Philippians 1:20, 21).

What a man! He's one to whom we are all indebted.

RESOURCE READING
Philippians 2:1-11

INSIGHT
What has happened in the past isn't important, for when a person becomes a Christian, everything changes (see 2 Corinthians 5:17).

APPLICATION
How many years had Paul spent in preparation before he really began his ministry as a believer?

How many years had probably elapsed between his conversion and his ministry? What does that tell you?

CONVICTIONS
Martin Luther

"For it is by grace you have been saved, through faith—
and this not from yourselves, it is the gift of God—
not by works, so that no one can boast."
Ephesians 2:8, 9

While October 31 is Halloween to many people, to others it marks the anniversary of the day a German priest, outraged by abuses he saw in the Roman Catholic Church, nailed a document to the door of the cathedral in Wittenburg, Germany. Known as the *Ninety-five Theses*, Martin Luther's document created an uproar unlike anything that had troubled the church for centuries—perhaps ever. Before his death in 1546, this man was responsible for dividing the church, establishing the Protestant Church, *"A mighty fortress is our God, a bulwark never failing."* inaugurating the Reformation, translating the Bible into German, and introducing the Christmas tree into the nativity observance. Who was this village priest, an apparent troublemaker who couldn't just live and let live as everyone else did?

The son of a Saxon miner, Luther was born at Eisleben on November 10, 1483. At the age of eighteen, he entered the University of Erfurt, where he studied pre-law. Then in the summer of 1505, Luther was caught in a thunderstorm that threatened his life. So thankful was he that he escaped unharmed, he vowed to become a monk. True to his promise, he entered the Augustinian monastery at Erfurt and was ordained in 1507. Eventually Luther received a doctorate in theology and was appointed as a professor of Scripture—a position he held for the rest of his life.

On a visit to Rome in 1510, on business for his Order, Luther was shocked at the practice of buying and selling indulgences. Today we think of an indulgence as when we have a second or third piece of dessert. However, in Luther's day, as a kind of prepayment for sins the buyer had not yet committed, indulgences (thought to bring God's forgiveness) were sold in the streets to pay for the construction of massive St. Peter's Cathedral in Rome.

This angered Luther, and an angry Luther troubled the conscience of the Middle Age church that had compromised the Scriptures. Luther never intended to split the church of his day; he simply sought to bring them back to the historic position held by the apostles and the early church fathers.

Visitors to Rome today can still view the Church of the Scala Sancta, or the Church of the Sacred Steps—thought to have been the ones Jesus walked up as He approached Pilate's judgment hall and later moved to Rome. As Luther was crawling up these steps, kissing each one, the impact of what he had been studying came crashing down upon him: "The just shall live by faith" (Romans 1:17, KJV). Luther's keen mind struggled with the issue of how sinful man finds forgiveness: By what he does as good deeds? Or by what Jesus did when He died on the cross? The impact of what Paul wrote—"the just shall live by faith"—finally caused Luther to cry out, "Fide sola!" (Faith alone!). And the Reformation was born.

Scripture led Luther to evaluate the practices of his day, and the Word of God alone became the foundation of Luther's teaching and preaching. Paul's letters played a prominent part in Luther's theology. He stood against anything he felt was in defiance of God's Word. As one historian put it, "His studies had led him to the conclusion that

Christ was the sole mediator between God and Man and that forgiveness of sin and salvation are effected by God's grace alone and are received by faith alone." As Luther wrote, "A mighty fortress is our God, a bulwark never failing."

Martin Luther–the man who changed the church, which changed the world!

RESOURCE READING
Romans 1:1-17

INSIGHT
Martin Luther's strong convictions resulted in changing the course of history. His convictions, however, were based on the authority of Scripture, which helped bring Christianity back into conformity with biblical principles.

APPLICATION
What is the difference between a conviction and a prejudice?

What does Scripture mean when it says that the "just shall live by faith"?

CONVICTIONS
Hannah Whitall Smith

*"For I have chosen him, so that he will direct his children and
keep his household after him to keep the way of the LORD
by doing what is right and just, so that the LORD will bring
about for Abraham what he has promised him."*
Genesis 18:19

One of the greatest tragedies that can confront a Christian
mother is to feel very strongly about certain values—such as
faith in God, fidelity in marriage, honesty, and commitment—and to see her children grow up and turn their backs
on almost every value she believes
is important. When that happens, a
mother cries out, "God, where did
I go wrong?"

*"The real heroes of our
time are those who in a
faithless age hold, live
and share their faith in
God."*

Undoubtedly that is how
Hannah Whitall Smith felt when
her three surviving children all
married unbelievers and gave up
the faith that their famous mother
wrote and spoke of. If the name Hannah Whitall Smith
doesn't ring a bell, let me give you a brief biographical
sketch of the life of this godly and influential woman who
was born to Quaker parents on February 7, 1832.

At the age of nineteen, Hannah married Robert
Pearsall Smith, seemingly a good man who eventually
developed mood swings we would identify today as manic-
depressive. Soon after they were married, leadership of the
family fell on Hannah's shoulders. Eventually, suspicion
turned to sadness as her husband, who at one time

preached to thousands in both Europe and the United States, became openly unfaithful to her. They never divorced, something that was unthinkable in their culture and day, yet they were far from happy.

Though not perfect, Hannah was yet saintly and encouraged her children to trust God. Her life was constantly challenged by heartache, sorrow, disappointment, and loss. Of her seven children, four were eventually taken from her in death, not an uncommon occurrence in the nineteenth century before the day of antibiotics and miracle medicines.

Of the three who grew to maturity, one married the son of a British Lord, Bertrand Russell, who eventually hated his mother-in-law with a passion and wrote to defame Christianity as much as his mother-in-law defended it. Another daughter shocked her mother by marrying an Irish Catholic and then walked out on him and their two children to live with an Italian lover who promised her an exciting life in Italy.

Eventually Hannah's husband, demented and debauched, abandoned his faith and openly flaunted his infidelity. Of the surviving son, Hannah's biographer, Marie Henry, says, "Logan claimed to have lost his faith as a boy of eleven, sitting in a cherry tree."

Question: How could it have been that a woman so godly should not have even one child to grow up in the faith of their mother? The answer is complex. Striving to have the best education possible, something denied her since she was a woman, Hannah insisted that her daughters be in the finest schools, where their faith was constantly assaulted.

At the same time, the Smith home became a center for radical discussions involving men such as Walt Whitman, the American poet, and others who were philosophers, agnostics, and free-thinkers. Is this to suggest that in the forum of free discussion, Hannah's faith was indefensible? Not really. Each of her children grew up with a knowledge of right and wrong in spite of the fact that Hannah had no help with parenting from her husband, whose very example became a negative influence and force. Then there was the will of each child, who ultimately had to decide which way to go.

Any single parent who has faced the challenge of raising children without the help of a spouse knows how easy it would have been for Hannah Whitall Smith to have withdrawn into a shell of discouragement and failure. But she did not, and for this I admire her.

Among the books that came from the pen of this godly woman was *The Christian's Secret of a Happy Life,* which continues to be sold in bookstores today. Individuals of lesser personal strength would have given up in despair. No, she not only experienced the sufficiency of the Almighty in her personal life but shared her spiritual strength with others the world over. Carl Henry was right when he observed, "The real heroes of our time are those who in a faithless age hold, live and share their faith in God."[8]

RESOURCE READING
1 Samuel 15

INSIGHT
Though you may grow up in a Christian home, there comes a time when you must decide for yourself that you will live for God because it is the right thing to do and because living for Him is your choice.

APPLICATION
How could it have been that a woman so godly should not have even one child grow up in the faith of their mother?

Do you think that when parents are overly strict (which obviously the Smiths were not), a child rebels? Is this equally as wrong as being too lax and lenient?

CONVICTIONS
Paul Tournier

*"If we claim to be without sin, we deceive ourselves and
the truth is not in us. If we confess our sins,
he is faithful and just and will forgive us
our sins and purify us from all unrighteousness."*
1 John 1:8, 9

Dr. Paul Tournier, the late physician-physicist of Geneva,
Switzerland, never quite fit the stereotyped mold. Tournier
had a unique freshness in his professional practice and in
his personal life as well. The
French-speaking Swiss physician
pioneered a new approach to
medicine when he insisted that
man is a composite of body, soul,
and spirit, and the whole person
must be treated.

*"God has a purpose for
every person's life."*

Tournier believed that life can
not be separated into three compartments that we label
body, soul, and spirit. He recognized that these three are
but different aspects of one being. When one part of life is
affected by stress, the other two areas are affected as well.
He said that, like the levels of a tri-part honeycomb, a person's state of being is a composite of these three factors.

Tournier's approach to healing is that if you are physically depressed, then mentally and spiritually you are
affected as well. By the same token, he contended that
physical or moral disobedience to God's purpose has its
consequences—physically, mentally, and spiritually.

What led Tournier to pioneer this approach to psychotherapy and medicine? The bushy-browed physician was the son of a noted doctor-author who died while Paul was quite young. World War I also affected Paul as he worked on the repatriation of prisoners and their children. After he became a physician, he became quite active in his church and in the Oxford group. It was there that he made a personal commitment to Jesus Christ, a step that vitally influenced his life and practice.

Leslie Stobbe describes what happened after that: "During his years as a physician, in the 20's and 30's, Tournier became more and more convinced that the usual approach of diagnosing an illness and prescribing medicine was not enough." Boldly, he changed the direction of his service toward a study of the role played by the spiritual and moral life in health, diseases, and healing. Despite the discouragement of friends, he embarked on an adventure that became an absorbing passion. Three years later, greatly encouraged by his wife, he began writing down some of his experiences.

Leslie continues: "He submitted his first draft to six friends, who discouraged him from publishing it. Disheartened, he let the manuscript lie. One day, Tournier's wife went to a friend's house to ask for prayer that her husband would gain the courage to submit the manuscript to a publisher. Hearing of this, Tournier took the manuscript to a publisher. It was rejected. Tournier was turned down twice before a third publisher agreed to publish the book. Success came almost overnight.

"Tournier believed that a doctor cannot approach his patient as just another case. He must think of him as a person, a total person in his relationship to God and man. Naturally, Dr. Tournier had developed deep personal friendships with his patients. He said, 'I must always try to see my patient, not as a case to be labeled, but as a unique being, an opportunity for an unique experience.'"

Underlying his practice was his commitment to the belief that God has a purpose for every person's life. He believed that the conflict between humanity and God is sin and that this alone separates us from a loving God. Confession of that sin, he taught, restores the fellowship between God and humans.

The Apostle John penned these words to fellow believers: "If we claim to be without sin, we deceive ourselves and the truth is not in us. If we confess our sins, he is faithful and just and will forgive us our sins and purify us from all unrighteousness" (1 John 1:8, 9).

And how does Paul Tournier qualify to be included in my roster of heroes? In spite of professional criticism and even hostile reviews, he stood by his convictions and became a pioneer in a biblical approach to mental healing. He refused to use the "psychobabble" other psychiatrists used to lessen the impact of biblical concepts of sin and wrongdoing and led the way in a biblical approach to personal and spiritual restoration and healing. Not only did he personally help thousands of patients, his influence was widely felt in the field of psychiatry. He made a difference.

RESOURCE READING
Mark 5:1-20

INSIGHT
Truth that is based on Scripture can stand unashamedly in the world, regardless of how hostile some may be to it, and eventually God honors the person who is committed to a biblical position regardless of how unpopular it may be.

APPLICATION
What might have happened if Dr. Tournier had not been encouraged by his wife to resubmit the manuscript?

Have you personally faced discouragement or rebuff and were tempted to give up or quit? Do you know anyone like that? What can you do to make a difference?

CONVICTIONS
Anne Frank

*" 'I will gather you from all the nations and places where I have
banished you,' declares the LORD, 'and will bring you back to
the place from which I carried you into exile.' "*
Jeremiah 29:14

Four years after Anne Frank was born in the city of
Frankfurt, Germany, Adolph Hitler came to power. Shortly
thereafter Otto Frank began to have concern for his family.
You see, the Franks were Jewish, and it soon became apparent that Jews did not fit into Hitler's grand scheme for a
master race. Thinking that they
were escaping the increasing
hatred against the Jews, the family
fled to Amsterdam.

*"May God help us to
remember there is
but one race: the
human race."*

Then in May 1940, the Nazis
marched on Holland, and the feeble resistance of the underground
quickly collapsed. The Nazis were
in control. Within days, new regu-
lations were issued that sought to identify Jews and restrict
their movement. Eventually, it became illegal to befriend a
Jew or to provide sanctuary for one.

In June 1942, as a birthday gift, Anne Frank was given
a diary, a little book containing blank pages that were eventually used to chronicle the sad days of confinement as she
and her family strove to escape the fate of thousands of
other Jews who were loaded into cattle cars and sent to
their deaths in the concentration camps of Europe.

Otto, fearing that the time would come when his family would be forced to either board one of those ill-fated death trains or go into hiding, prepared an annex at the back of a row house on the Prinsengracht canal—a tiny attic that could be reached by a narrow, steep stairway concealed by a bookcase.

On a warm morning in July 1942, a letter was delivered to the Frank house that forever changed their lives. Margot, Anne's sixteen-year-old sister, was ordered to report to the police. On July 8, Anne made an entry in her diary: "Margot is sixteen; would they really take girls of that age away alone? But thank goodness she won't go, Mummy said so herself; that must be what Daddy meant when he talked about us going into hiding."

For the next two years, the family existed in a tiny attic with inadequate food and sanitation. Day by day in the pages of this little book, Anne penned her thoughts, her dreams, and her despair.

On July 11, 1942, she wrote, "I can't tell you how oppressive it is never to be able to go outdoors. I am afraid we shall be discovered and be shot. That is not exactly a pleasant prospect."

Eventually what they had feared happened. On August 4, 1944, a truck stopped outside 263 Prinsengracht. Soldiers ran up the three flights of stairs and headed for the bookcase concealing the entrance to the attic. The family was taken to the police station, then on to Westerbork, a transit camp in Holland where Jews were held before being sent to forced labor or an extermination camp.

Sadly, the family was placed on the very last train for Auschwitz, where Anne, then sixteen, died of typhus. Anne's father, Otto, was the only one of the family who lived through the horrible ordeal. Of the 140,000 Jews living in Holland at the beginning of the war, only 30,000 survived.

Anne's diary was left lying on the floor of the attic hiding place, and eventually it was found and has been translated into more than fifty languages. Because Anne recorded her thoughts and dreams, the world can see life through the eyes of a child who would never live to see the tulips of Holland bloom again in the spring.

One entry in her diary reads, "What, oh what is the use of war? Why can't people live peacefully together? Why all this destruction?" May God help us to remember there is but one race: the human race. If we fail to remember we are all made in the image of God, it could happen again. Anne's little diary is a reminder to us, and though her life was short, her words have made a difference.

RESOURCE READING
2 Chronicles 32

INSIGHT
Anne Frank's courage has touched the lives of millions.

APPLICATION
Her home at 263 Prinsengracht Street in Amsterdam is now a museum. Should you ever get to visit Amsterdam, be sure to go there.

Do you suppose that Anne—in her wildest imagination—ever thought that her diary would be read by so many people?

Look up James 4:1 in your New Testament and ponder Anne's question: "What, oh what is the use of war? Why can't people live peacefully together?"

COURAGE
Athanasius

" 'Are you then the Son of God?' He replied, '. . . I am.' "
John 22:70

It can fairly be said that in the history of Christendom, never has so much been owed to one man as is owed to a pugnacious, argumentative preacher by the name of Athanasius. You probably know several individuals who would fit that description. Frankly, if Athanasius were alive today, or if we had lived in the early third century, it is quite probable that we wouldn't much care for him.

Folks didn't then, either.

Athanasius was born in Alexandria, Egypt about A.D. 297. When he was five years old, Diocletian, the Roman emperor, proclaimed himself to be a god and demanded to be worshipped.

"If Jesus Christ is God, then He demands our allegiance and our worship."

When he was eighteen, Constantine became the emperor, and things began to change fast.

Historians don't know much about Athanasius's mother, but I suspect that she helped her son to realize something that kids still need to know today: You don't have to go along with the crowd. It's okay to stand alone when you know you are right. But doing that made him pretty unpopular.

For one thing, Athanasius didn't win friends and influence people. He was tough, everybody agreed. He used words like a street fighter uses left jabs. "Why can't he just love people and mind his own business?" folks said of

Athanasius. Surely he must have been told, "Why create such a furor over something when everyone disagrees with you?" Exiled five times in forty-five years, he should have gotten the message, "To get along, you've got to go along." Not Athanasius. He stood by his convictions when friends and supporters abandoned him.

To appreciate this man to whom we owe so very much today, you must understand the issues. Athanasius believed the Bible taught that Jesus Christ was very God of the very God. In other words, He did not become God when He was born. He always was God. He believed that Jesus Christ laid aside His exercise of authority as God, or His attributes of deity, as theologians describe it, and became man. But he was no ordinary man, believed Athanasius. He was the unique fusion of man and God.

Others, though, disagreed. Led by Arius, who was Athanasius's archenemy, others taught that Jesus became God, the highest of all created beings. In the last 150 years, some groups have adopted Arius's teaching, which makes Jesus merely a good man who rose to the same spiritual heights as we can today.

With the overview of history, church historian Bruce Shelley says that if Athanasius had gone along with the crowd, "It would have meant that Christianity had degenerated to a form of paganism. The Christian faith would have had two gods and a Jesus who was neither God nor man. It would have meant that God himself was unapproachable and totally removed from man. The result would have been a Christianity like a host of pagan religions."[9]

The one teaching that separates Christianity from Judaism, and more recently from the teaching of cult groups, is the truth that God exists as one in three persons: Father, Son, and Holy Spirit. Yet, contended the pugnacious Athanasius, there is one God, not three.

If Arius had won, Christianity would have been just another religion, and Jesus Christ would have been a great teacher but nothing more. If Jesus Christ was God, as

Athanasius contended, then He demands our allegiance and our worship. One man against the world was eventually vindicated by the truth, and for that we owe Athanasius a great debt of gratitude.

RESOURCE READING
2 Timothy 2

INSIGHT
The true measure of a person is the ability to abide by his or her convictions, no matter how lonely he or she may be. In the case of Athanasius, one man stood against the religious world, yet he was right and, in time, God exonerated him.

APPLICATION
Do you see God's providential hand in helping to strengthen Athanasius, giving him the courage to do right?

When you feel pressure "to go along," what do you do? Can you disagree, agreeably?

COURAGE
John Huss

"The grass withers and the flowers fall,
but the word of our God stands forever."
Isaiah 40:8

It Doesn't Take a Hero is the title of General H. Norman Schwarzkopf's autobiography that modestly downplays his part in the 1991 Gulf Conflict. I am not sure whether John Huss, the Bohemian reformer who died in 1415, had much in common with Schwarzkopf–but I do know he would have agreed with his premise. I doubt that he thought of himself as a hero but merely as an ordinary man who had the courage to stick to his convictions.

"May God give us more men and women who have the courage to stand for what they believe is right."

And who was John Huss?

Visit Bethlehem Chapel in Prague today and you will see busloads of children who visit what remains of Huss's home and the chapel where he proclaimed a message that was not well received. Today, Huss is a Czech national hero–a champion of the common man–but in his day, he was a controversial Roman Catholic priest who took on the establishment.

John Huss was born of peasant parentage in Bohemia, now part of the Czech Republic. At the University of Prague, he took his bachelor's and master's degrees and became a lecturer in theology. In 1402 he was ordained to the priesthood and became rector of the university.

As a progressive thinker, Huss felt that the church needed to reform. When an Englishman by the name of John Wycliffe translated the Bible into English with the goal of making it so simple that a plowboy could understand it, John Huss decided that the same thing would be good for the people he served in Prague. Huss translated some of Wycliffe's writings and certainly used some of his ideas in his fiery sermons, which inflamed the minds of those who heard him.

Recently, I was in Prague and stood over the desk where Huss wrote his messages. I couldn't help wondering how Huss might respond to some of the issues confronting us, were he alive today. Described by his biographers as "a loyal member of the Roman Catholic church," Huss became disturbed when, following the papal election of 1378, two men claimed to be the legitimate pope. Then, in 1409, a third claimed the papal throne, with all three, like politicians in a close race, denouncing each other. Huss strongly voiced his dissent.

In matters of faith and practice, Huss held unswervingly to the Bible as the Word of God, and it was this that he expounded to the masses who embraced his teaching. No man of his leadership and stature could say and do the things he did without making enemies. And soon he had plenty of them. Their power threatened, the clergy branded him as a heretic and denounced his teaching, but the nation of Czechoslovakia rallied around their favorite son.

It was the church versus the state, and the state lost. Promised safe conduct by King Wenceslaus of Bohemia, the emperor, and even the pope, he was summoned to the Council of Constance to explain his teaching and defend himself against the charges made against him. Forget the promise of "safe conduct." The council condemned him to death. Shortly thereafter, in 1415, he was taken outside the cathedral and burned at the stake.

Several years ago, I was in Switzerland and visited the cathedral. A guide took us throughout the massive gothic structure, but said nothing of John Huss or the Council of Constance. At the conclusion of the tour, I asked, "Could you show me where John Huss stood when he was condemned to death?" Reluctantly, the guide took me to the spot. I stood there, pondering the great debt of gratitude and obligation we owe to those such as Huss who were willing to pay the supreme price of abiding by their convictions.

May God give us more men and women who have the courage to stand for what they believe is right. Maybe, as Schwarzkopf says, it doesn't take a hero—but it takes courage. John Huss, absent from the body, at home with the Lord.

RESOURCE READING
Revelation 21

INSIGHT
Convictions always come with a price tag attached, yet when those convictions are based upon the Word of God, they become more meaningful than a life of compromise and appeasement.

APPLICATION
What do you most admire in the life of John Huss?

If he were alive today, what question would you want to ask him? What do you think would be his answer?

COURAGE
"Pongo"

"In the same way, any of you who does not give up everything
he has cannot be my disciple."
Luke 14:33

Ernest Hemingway once said that "courage is fear that has prayed!" If he's right, then a Zamboanga man has that kind of stuff. (In the event that the city of Zamboanga doesn't register with you, allow me to explain that this is one of the principal cities in Mindanao, southern Philippines, an area that has been torn by strife in recent years.)

The nickname of this man from Zamboanga is "Pongo" and he's a radio engineer with the Far East Broadcasting Company. He was there the day that Muslim gunmen drove a motorcycle into the FEBC compound, ran into the studio, and with guns spewing deadly bullets, shot and killed Greg Bacabis, the FEBC engineer who kept the station running, as well as Greg Hapalla, a pastor whose gospel program was aired over the stations.

"Fear that has prayed can motivate a person to tremendous acts of courage."

That was enough for Pongo. He had had it. He knew that he might very well be the next person to be gunned down. He had a wife and children, and he didn't want to take the risk.

Pongo had a motorized pedicab–a motorcycle with a side-car attached, which is used for inexpensive transportation.

Pongo reasoned that with a degree of luck, he might even be able to turn the sideline into a real money-making business, at least enough to support his family. The risk of being killed in traffic was less than being shot by a terrorist. Quit while he was ahead–that's what he thought he was doing.

In the days that followed, however, as Pongo drove his pedicab, he thought of the two men who had died for the cause of Jesus Christ, and he began to understand how the disciples felt when they all fled as Jesus was arrested in the garden.

"Enough!" Pongo finally thought. He went back to the radio studio and told the staff that he would be ashamed to die in a traffic accident. If he had to be killed, he wanted to die for the cause of Christ.

He went about his work quietly, apprehensively. He prayed and waited. Then it happened. In the words of a colleague, "A few days after Pongo returned to work, a motorcycle raced into the studio compound. Remembering that the gunmen had come in on a motorcycle before, the staff feared they had returned to finish the job of killing all the broadcasters. People dove under tables and desks . . . hid behind cabinets . . . scrambled to get into closets.

"But not Pongo. He deliberately walked to the console in the studio and sat down. 'If I'm to be shot,' he said, 'I'd rather be broadcasting the gospel–not hiding under a table!' "

It was a false alarm and nobody was hurt, but Pongo didn't know that when he walked into the studio and took his place at the controls.

What a display of courage! Hemingway was right: Fear that has prayed can motivate a person to tremendous acts of courage. Over the years I have heard of numerous acts of bravery and courage, and Pongo joins the ranks of those whom I consider to be real heroes.

The real heroes of the faith are not the media celebrities whose faces are often seen on TV or applauded by the crowds. They are the unknown, unnamed men and women who are willing to lay down their lives for what they believe. The Book of Acts describes Paul and Barnabas as "men who have risked their lives for the name of our Lord Jesus Christ" (Acts 15:26).

Question: What would you be willing to risk for your faith? Your name? Your reputation? Even your life? Pongo has made the decision. He's decided to follow Jesus.

RESOURCE READING
Luke 14:25-34

INSIGHT
Courage has nothing to do with your education, your money, or your strength. It depends on personal character and the strength that comes by trusting the Lord.

APPLICATION
Have you faced a situation that demanded courage? Describe it.

What would you be willing to risk for your faith? If you had been Pongo, would you have stayed with your pedicab business or gone back to serve the Lord?

COURAGE
William Carey

"By faith he [Abraham] made his home in the promised land like a stranger in a foreign country. . . . For he was looking forward to the city with foundations, whose architect and builder is God."
Hebrews 11:9, 10

When Chuck Wickman polled some 1500 youthful Christians and asked them, "Who was William Carey?" he was in for the shock of his life. How many of those 1500 could identify Carey? Not a single one, yet William Carey has appropriately been called the "Father of Modern Missions," and his book on missions, written in 1792, so stirred the Christian world that it ranks alongside Martin Luther's Ninety-five Theses in its influence and consequences.

"Expect great things from God; attempt great things for God."

Who was William Carey? Born to a poverty-stricken family in 1761, near Northampton, England, Carey suffered from allergies that kept him from pursuing his goal of becoming a gardener. At the age of sixteen, he was apprenticed to a shoemaker; but then shortly thereafter he was converted to faith in Jesus Christ.

A lack of formal education didn't stop this determined young man who set out to change the world. Of Carey, Warren Wiersbe wrote, ". . . by the time he was in his teens, he could read the Bible in six languages. He later became Professor of Oriental Languages at Fort William College in Calcutta, and his press at Serampore provided

Scriptures in over 40 languages and dialects for more than 300 million people."

Never was there a more unlikely candidate for success than this young man, who at the age of nineteen married the sister-in-law of the man to whom he was apprenticed. Following his now famous sermon to a group of ministers where he uttered his famous quote, "Expect great things from God; attempt great things for God," he volunteered to go to India as a missionary.

At first Carey's wife, Dorothy, adamantly refused to go. His father considered his going to India an act of absolute madness. Meanwhile, the shoemaker to whom he was apprenticed died, and Carey assumed the financial responsibility for his widow. Boarding a ship for India with his eight-year-old son, Carey was turned back before the ship left England. When he finally boarded another ship, his wife reluctantly relented and joined him on the journey to India. She knew she would never be happy, and she wasn't. Neither did she adjust to her new surroundings. Her health and disposition both deteriorated. She constantly belittled Carey, urging him to quit and take the family back to their native England.

Carey, rebuffed by the East India Company, sought work in an Indian factory and spent evenings each week translating Scripture or preaching. The tragic death of their son, little eight-year-old Peter, caused Dorothy's mind to snap, and she never regained her mental equilibrium. Until her death in 1807, Dorothy never shared her husband's desire to make Christ known. Yet Carey struggled and endured in the face of failure. For seven long years among the Bengali people Carey had grown to love, he could not claim a single convert.

If ever a man had cause to relent and give up, it was William Carey. In 1812 a warehouse fire destroyed his two grammar books, his massive polyglot dictionary, and whole versions of the Bible that he had translated, yet Carey knelt, thanked God that he had strength, and started the task all over again.

Carey died in 1834 but not before he left an indelible mark on his beloved India and, more than that, on the mentality of missions around the world.

RESOURCE READING
Hebrews 11:1-12

INSIGHT
Dedication and hard work will take you further than talent without commitment.

APPLICATION
If you had sustained the disappointment that Carey faced, would you have quit?

Are you faced with apparent failure in your life today? Remember, God can use even your failures, just as He used William Carey's.

COURAGE
William Carey's Secret

"Forgetting what is behind and straining toward what is ahead,
I press on toward the goal to win the prize for which
God has called me heavenward in Christ Jesus."
Philippians 3:13

When William Carey entered the pulpit of the chapel of Lall Bazaar in Calcutta and found a pair of old shoes tied to the desk, he was reminded of his humble origin as a cobbler. He was also reminded that leather workers in India are among the lowest castes. Seeing the shoes, Carey said, "The God who can do for and through a poor shoemaker as much as He has done for and through me, can bless and use any. The very humblest may trust Him."

> *"I can plod.*
> *That is my only genius.*
> *I can persevere in any*
> *definite pursuit.*
> *To this I owe*
> *everything."*

If ever a person had every cause to give up in failure and yet overcame and succeeded, it was William Carey, the man who eventually became known as "The Father of Modern Missions."

Carey was basically self-educated in an era when Oxford and Cambridge validated the credentials of men of learning, and individuals who studied on their own were still cast in the mold of the uneducated, uncultured. By the age of twelve, Carey had mastered Latin, and at the cobbler's bench, he studied Hebrew and Greek, becoming proficient in at least six languages.

When Carey began to formulate his idea of world

evangelism, he was discouraged because the heathen were considered by the formal church unworthy of the sacrifice necessary to convert them. One minister told Carey, "Young man, sit down. When God pleases to convert the heathen, He will do it without your aid or mine." Carey neither sat down nor was silenced. He believed that each individual is important to our heavenly Father and that Christ died for the sins of the world, a world that needed to hear that people are saved by grace through faith in the Lord Jesus Christ.

To his nephew Eustice, Carey once said, ". . .if after my removal anyone should think it worth his while to write my life, I will give you a criterion by which you may judge its correctness. If he gives me credit for being a plodder, he will describe me justly. Anything beyond this will be too much. I can plod. That is my only genius. I can persevere in any definite pursuit. To this I owe everything."

Commenting on Carey's ability to plod, Warren Wiersbe writes, "The etymologists tell us that our word plod comes from an old Middle English word that means 'a puddle.' The Danish have a similar word that means 'mud.' A 'plodder' is someone who is willing to get his feet wet and wade through water to get to his destination. He keeps going."

As I read those words I couldn't help but think of Sir Edmund Hillary, the man who conquered Mt. Everest, who was once asked about the secret of his success. Hillary responded that when others had turned back, he took one more step. Ask the athlete who presses on in spite of pain, his body screaming with thirst, what his secret is. He'll tell you he paces himself in the marathon and keeps on running.

Considering throwing in the towel and quitting? Ready to resign, pack up, and try it again somewhere else where people appreciate you and pay you what you are really worth? The test of your character is what it takes to stop you.

To the Philippians Paul wrote, ". . .one thing I do:

Forgetting what is behind and straining toward what is ahead, I press on toward the goal to win the prize for which God has called me heavenward in Christ Jesus" (Philippians 3:13, 14).

Be encouraged and plod on, as did the man who eventually left his mark on the world. The daily routine of doing what you know you should be doing—whether it is raising your children, taking the mail to the post office, or preaching to a small handful of critical, ungrateful people—is your means of pleasing God. And it may take just that to succeed.

RESOURCE READING
Philippians 3:12-4:1

INSIGHT
Most of life is not terribly glamorous—getting up and doing the same thing every day, yet learning to be faithful in the small task is the key to accomplishing great things. Remember, when others turned back, Hillary took one more step.

APPLICATION
What is the most unpleasant task you have to perform regularly? Does it help to do this first? Can you take it as a personal challenge to see how well you can do it?

Does it help to know that God knows your faithfulness when others don't recognize your effort? He does.

COURAGE
Alexander Solzhenitsyn

"And they took offense at him. But Jesus said to them, 'Only in his hometown and in his own house is a prophet without honor.' "
Matthew 13:57

In 1974, *Time* magazine called Alexander Solzhenitsyn "the world's most celebrated writer."[10] Only four years before, he had received the Nobel Prize. Then in 1976, the Solzhenitsyns were allowed to emigrate to the United States via Switzerland, and the U.S. press had its hero—one who anathematized the Soviet Union for wreaking its vengeance on this fiery spirit.

"The line separating good and evil passes not through states, nor between classes, nor between parties either— but right through the human heart."

Alexander Solzhenitsyn was born in the North Caucasus, six months after his father had died as the result of a hunting accident. In 1951, he completed a university degree in science and joined the military, where he rose to the rank of captain. Then he made a political blunder. In a letter that fell into the hands of the secret police, he described Stalin as "the mustachioed one." That was it! And this brought exile in the Soviet prison system for eight years.[11]

During that period of time, however, Solzhenitsyn underwent a transformation that resulted in his regeneration— spiritually and intellectually. In prison he saw both the absolute baseness of humanity and "great courage and comradeship among fellow prisoners" along with the "fearlessness of those who have lost everything."[12]

Speaking of his losing battle with the system, Solzhenitsyn once told of the progression that came as he first lost his friends, then his position, his books and papers, then his wife and family, and finally his personal freedom. But he said that he was never stronger than when all his treasures were within, where they could never be taken from him.

This he described as "the heavenly kingdom of the liberated spirit," and he warned that even a food package "transforms you from a free though hungry person into one who is anxious and cowardly."

After he had come to the United States in 1978, Solzhenitsyn was invited to speak at Harvard University in a both acclaimed and denounced message that partly ended the love affair that the free world had with this bearded modern Jeremiah. He scathingly denounced the shallow values, the materialism, and the withering spirit of the West.

He blasted "destructive and irresponsible freedom" that has "little defense against the abyss of human decadence, such as, for example, misuse of liberty for moral violence against young people, motion pictures full of pornography, crime and horror" and so forth.[13]

Telling the unvarnished truth has never been popular no matter where it is proclaimed. In 1991, Communism collapsed, and the Solzhenitsyns eventually felt they could return to their native Russia, but after a brief honeymoon with the new government, they received the same "we don't know what to do with you" treatment they encountered at the hands of the Western press.

Alexander Solzhenitsyn is not an angry man who only hurls angry words at the world. He's his own man. His analytical and penetrating analyses go to the very heart of society and life. "The line separating good and evil," he said, "passes not through states, nor between classes, nor between parties either—but right through the human heart." Human nature, he believed, "changes not much faster than the geological face of the earth."[14]

It is questionable that Solzhenitsyn's fiery rhetoric changed the course of either the East or the West, but it has had the same effect as the preaching of John the Baptist, whose generation may have not repented but knew fully well they had turned their back on God. Thank God for a man who made a difference, who spoke and wrote with the conviction of conscience, whether it was in the gulag of a Soviet prison or the hallowed halls of Harvard. Jesus said, "Only in his hometown and in his own house is a prophet without honor" (Matthew 13:57). But if a measure of disdain is a measure of true greatness, Solzhenitsyn must be close to the top—a prophet with honor in God's sight.

RESOURCE READING
Hebrews 11:32-40

INSIGHT
While courage and honesty are not always applauded by everyone, they are deeply treasured and honored by God and those who love Him.

APPLICATION
As a "guest," did Solzhenitsyn have the right to speak out against the decadence and sinfulness of the West?

Is it surprising that those who "tell it like it is" often are denounced? Can you think of another instance when the same thing happened?

Have you discovered the "blessing" Jesus pronounced on those who are so treated? (See Matthew 5:11, 12.)

COURAGE
Peter ten Boom

*"Let us not become weary in doing good, for at the proper time
we will reap a harvest if we do not give up."*
Galatians 6:9

The name of his famous aunt, Corrie ten Boom, is still
widely known in Christian circles, while few have heard of
the nephew. Yet Peter ten Boom felt just as strongly about
saving the Jews as did Aunt Corrie (*Tante Corrie* as Peter
called her, using the Dutch word for "aunt"). The ten Boom
house, located off the main plaza
in Haarlem, a short train ride from
Amsterdam, became a safe house
to which Jewish people could
escape; and like the ancient cities
of refuge mentioned in the Old
Testament to which people fled,
the ten Boom house provided a
haven and an escape from the Nazis, who were determined
to destroy every Jew in Europe.

*" Forgiveness is the
only answer to hatred
that never dies."*

When Dutch patriots learned that the S.S. troops were
systematically raiding the orphanages and taking the children who were Jewish, sending them to their deaths in the
concentration camps of Europe, brave Dutch men would
impersonate S.S. officers at the risk of their lives, raid the
orphanages, and take the Jewish babies to the ten Boom
house, where they were out of danger until they could be
sent to safe houses and farms where people adopted them
as their own.

107

How many children were thus saved? Only God knows for sure, but it is certain that their numbers were in the hundreds before the Germans finally raided the family home and sent the ten Booms to prison.

After the war, Corrie ten Boom went all over the world and told people, "Forgiveness is the only answer to horrible and indescribable crimes of the holocaust." And where does Corrie's nephew Peter fit into this scenario?

Peter was a committed Christian first and a Dutch patriot second. During the German occupation, Peter served as an organist in a country church, playing the pipe organ for services. Though it was forbidden by decree of the Germans, on one occasion Peter pulled out the stops of the organ and at full crescendo played the Dutch national anthem, while shocked but proud churchgoers stood to their feet and sang the words. For this act of defiance, Peter, then age sixteen, went to prison.

After the war, Peter also went throughout the world with the same message as his famous aunt: that forgiveness is the only answer to hatred that never dies.

Peter was in Israel on one of his speaking tours and was felled by a heart attack. Going home was out of the question. Surgery–and as soon as possible–would be the only thing that could save his life. As the cardiologist chatted with his patient before the operation, he said, "I see your name is ten Boom. Hmmm. Are you by any chance related to the ten Booms of Holland?"

"Yes," replied Peter. "That is my family. I am a ten Boom."

The doctor replied, "And I am one of the babies your family saved!"

And the doctor whose life had been saved as a tiny Jewish baby in Holland forty years or so before then saved the life of Peter ten Boom and paid back a debt in full.

Some three thousand years ago, the writer of Ecclesiastes said, "Cast your bread upon the waters, for after many days you will find it again" (Ecclesiastes 11:1).

Whether it is acts of kindness or deeds of wickedness, they eventually come back to bless you or haunt you. Some universal truths in life never change. What you sow, you will eventually reap. It happened with Peter ten Boom and it can happen to you as well.

RESOURCE READING
Galatians 6:1-10

INSIGHT
God always honors the efforts of those who serve their fellow humans, no matter how long it may take.

APPLICATION
Would you say it was by chance or God's design that the cardiologist who saved Peter's life was one of the babies his family had saved a generation before?

Have you ever experienced a situation in which you were rewarded for something you did much earlier?

COURAGE
Wang Ming Dao

"I have fought the good fight, I have finished the race, I have kept the faith. Now there is in store for me the crown of righteousness, which the Lord, the righteous Judge will award to me on that day—and not only to me, but also to all who have longed for his appearing."
2 Timothy 4:7, 8

On July 30, 1991, life in Shanghai, China was pretty normal. Ships and water ferries moved up and down the Huangpu River; streets were crowded and it was business as usual. On that morning, a small group of men and women quietly slipped into a tiny, one-bedroom apartment in Shanghai to blend their voices and prayers in a memorial service for 91-year-old Wang Ming Dao. Actually, the service had been scheduled for the following day, but fearing that far too many people would come, having learned that this godly old saint had slipped into the presence of the Lord, family and friends decided to go ahead with a private memorial service on Tuesday instead of the scheduled Wednesday.

"Walk the hard road!"

Wang Ming Dao was one of the most influential Chinese Christians to have lived in this century, and while some might think it strange that only a small private memorial service was observed in the small, one-bedroom apartment where Wang and his saintly wife lived, things aren't done in Shanghai the same way they are done elsewhere.

110

In China there is a lot more to think about than flowers and special music. You see, Wang Ming Dao was also an ex-convict, having once been sentenced to death row under China's penal code. When visitors from outside would visit the little apartment where the Wangs lived, they would discreetly close the blinds to hide their presence from prying eyes.

What was the crime that sent Wang to prison for twenty-two years and nine months? The Communist government charged and convicted him of being a "counter revolutionary" and sent him to forced labor in the northern part of China, where he worked in a coal mine. His real crime was that Wang was committed to Jesus Christ. You see, when the Communists closed the churches in the early 1950s, Wang, who was a leader, defiantly said, "They can close our churches but they cannot stop us from worshipping God in the confines of our homes!"

Frankly, if ever a man was a saint, Wang Ming Dao was one. Perfect? No! Committed? Definitely. I met Wang and his wife for the first time when he was eighty-nine. He was hard of hearing and almost blind, yet he was alert; and in spite of everything he had been through, he had retained his sense of humor. In 1981, following his release from prison, Wang wrote of the events in his life in an autobiography called, *A Stone Made Smooth.* When I told the aged gentleman that I had read his book, with a twinkle in his eye, he replied, "Stone still not yet smooth!"

Today the stone has turned into a crown! Wang Ming Dao is part of the reason that the church inside China is among the fastest growing in the world in spite of the repression of a government that is committed to atheism.

One of the reasons I admire this great man is that he was so human. Convicted and thrown in prison, Wang began to question the mercy of a God who would allow such punishment on His children, and acknowledging his misgiving, he was released. Then, out of prison, he felt that he had betrayed Christ like Peter and again stood resolutely for Christ. This time, he was sent back to prison for the long haul.

Authentic saints are not made out of plaster of Paris or painted with gloss enamel; they are real men and women who have tasted the fire of bitter persecution but have found in the flame the presence of Jesus Christ to sustain and strengthen them.

Shortly before his death, when asked what lesson he could share with the church elsewhere, he firmly and resolutely replied, "Tell them to walk the hard road!" Wang Ming Dao was one of the greatest of all time. And at the end of the hard road, he met his Master, Jesus Christ.

RESOURCE READING
2 Timothy 4

INSIGHT
The less traveled path—often the hard path—is usually the right one. Quick fixes and shortcuts never satisfy the demands of God.

APPLICATION
What is the "hard path" in your life?

What does the thought of "a stone made smooth" mean? How are stones polished in a riverbed?

DETERMINATION
Ray Buker

"I have fought the good fight, I have finished the race,
I have kept the faith."
2 Timothy 4:7

In the Olympics of 1924–the same one in which the Scotsman, Eric Lidell, took two gold medals–another, little-known athlete medaled as well. His name: Raymond Bates Buker. While Eric Lidell eventually went to China as a missionary, Ray Buker served in Burma, on the China border. Though Buker couldn't recall meeting the Flying Scot who distinguished himself because he refused to run on Sunday, the two would have liked each other.

"The world needs the undiluted Gospel of Jesus Christ."

Both were champions; both chose to champion a cause greater than winning in the Olympics, the cause of proclaiming the Gospel of Jesus Christ.

Meeting Dr. Ray Buker for the first time left quite an impression on me. I was a young seminarian, not especially interested in world missions. Unlike most seminary professors who come to class dressed in something like a brown tweed sport coat with baggy trousers or a slightly worn suit that wasn't quite good enough to wear on Sundays, Ray Buker walked into the classroom dressed in the garb of a Burmese male. As students watched, somewhat mystified, Buker climbed onto the top of his desk and sat cross-legged for the rest of the hour, teaching his class without moving.

113

Don't think, for a moment, that didn't impress us. No matter how you met him, Ray Buker left an indelible impression on you.

In his biography, *Against the Clock*, Eric Fife says that by the time Ray and Dorothy Buker arrived in Burma in 1926, there were already two hundred American Baptist missionaries there, whose lifestyle was anything but hard. The missionaries had "their own banking system. . . , British-trained butlers, finger bowls, and afternoon tea at 4:00 P.M." All of this didn't fit the image of taking the gospel to the regions beyond, which was what Buker had in mind.

Before he went to the mission field, he had asked to be sent to a difficult place. He explained that he was an athlete and was disciplined, accustomed to hardship, and he was willing to go to places other people couldn't handle. It was that spirit that brought him north into China, where he established a missions station and planted the cross.

When he was in his mid-eighties, Dr. Buker did an interview with me for our radio program, and as we sat in the studio chatting together, he told me about some of the highlights of his missionary service. Then I asked, "Could you tell me about some of the dark hours of your service in Burma?" He thought for a few moments and then softly told how his wife had suffered a nervous breakdown and the closest help was a journey of six days by horseback. Buker prayed and courageously nursed his wife back to health by reading to her and by quieting her unrest.

In 1942, the Bukers, continuing to serve though World War II had begun, narrowly escaped death, fleeing before the advancing Japanese army. Joining the ranks of the newly-formed Conservative Baptist Foreign Mission Society, Buker was asked to head the work, which, for the next ten years, became the fastest growing mission society in the world.

The last time I saw Ray Buker, we lunched together near the retirement village where he lived. Instead of finding a rocking chair, Buker had measured out the distance in the halls that would allow him to jog a mile or two each day. And that was when he was in his late eighties.

When Ray Buker died at the age of 92, he left behind a rich legacy scattered throughout the world, for through his life hundreds of men and women, myself included, gained a vision of a world that needs the undiluted Gospel of Jesus Christ. Ray Buker, Olympic athlete and missionary statesman without equal, yet another who is "absent from the body, at home with the Lord."

RESOURCE READING
1 Corinthians 9:19-27

INSIGHT
The will of God will never lead you where His grace cannot keep you.

APPLICATION
Ray Buker asked for the toughest assignment. Would you?

God leads us one day at a time, one step at a time. Try to trust Him for today, and leave tomorrow in His hands.

DETERMINATION
Bruce Olson

"But God demonstrates his own love for us in this:
While we were still sinners, Christ died for us."
Romans 5:8

One of the most unusual stories of personal dedication that has come to light in recent years involves a slender, scholarly man by the name of Bruce Olson. In 1961 at the age of nineteen, Olson shouldered a pack and headed into the dense jungles of Venezuela. His objective was to reach the fierce Motilone Indians and tell them that Jesus Christ died for them.

"Faith that is worth living by is worth dying for."

Today Bruce Olson is a personal friend of presidents and other high officials. He has appeared before committees of the Organization of American States and UNESCO. His articles have appeared in learned journals in Germany and Sweden, and his work with the Motilone Indians has been widely recognized by the Venezuelan and Colombian governments.

The following facts make Olson's missionary enterprise one of the most daring and outstanding of the century: First, in making contact with the Motilones, Olson did what no other white man had ever done. In the previous fifteen years, the Motilones had killed more than five hundred oil-field workers. Sixty-eight had been killed in the previous eight years alone. The governments of Venezuela and

Colombia had considered a joint expedition to wipe out the Motilones because of these murderous raids on oil-field workers.

The second fact that distinguishes Olson is that this slender young man walked into the jungles and spent five years of his life with absolutely no backing, something I would not suggest to anyone. He was a one-man committee armed with tremendous willpower and the knowledge that God had sent Him with the message that Christ loves the Motilones. From the beginning all circumstances pointed to abject failure. Olson's parents strongly objected to his going to Venezuela. He had no missionary training, no seminary work, and only a small amount of training in practical medicine and linguistics.

Feeling that he was doing what the Apostle Paul would have done, Olson bought a one-way ticket to Venezuela. Hurdle after hurdle was crossed before young Olson eventually shouldered his pack and hit the jungle trail. Time after time, brushes with death made him realize that God had His hand on his life. Olson finally made contact with the savage Motilone Indians.

When he approached Motilone country, he heard a rustle in the bushes. In a moment Olson was on the ground with an arrow in his leg. He was surrounded by the savage Indians who slowly circled him, puncturing his skin with their spears. He did not know whether they were going to kill him immediately or torture him to death slowly. Olson was carried to the village, where he was kept a prisoner. Three days later he was hit with amoebic dysentery. Olson knew that he was certain to die unless he could escape.

Under cover of a moonless night, young Olson escaped and miraculously made his way to civilization and medical help. Again Olson returned and was captured. He began his second imprisonment. When the Indians were deciding his fate for the second time, he came down with hepatitis. Olson wondered if he had served God's purpose, but a helicopter saw his distress signal and rescued him. Then the Indians thought that God sent a great bird to take him to eternity to keep them from killing him.

When Olson returned for the third time, the Indians shook their heads in disbelief. Slowly Bruce Olson was accepted by the Indians. In time, he told them that God (Dibodibo to the Indians) sent His Son, who was killed because of the evil and sin of all the world, but then the third day this Son arose from the grave and eventually went back to heaven. Slowly the fantastic hurdles gave way. In his own way Olson demonstrated the love of God that brought Christ to earth two thousand years ago.

Olson's dedication is a rebuke to those of us who put such a price on material things. He has proved that faith that is worth living by is worth dying for.

RESOURCE READING
Romans 10:14-21

INSIGHT
While Bruce Olson's methods were unique and not to be considered a pattern for most people, God used his ability, his desire, and his determination to touch the hearts of people. Understanding that you are a unique individual with gifts and talents and giving them completely to the Lord puts you in a position whereby you can accomplish what He calls you to do.

APPLICATION
When daily obedience is a short step in a long direction, you put into practice what God requires: faithfulness. What does God want you to do today?

Have you considered the possibility that God may want you to do something out of the ordinary that can impact the lives of many people?

Why not think about even a summer of service or a short-term stint of missions?

DEVOTION
Brother Lawrence

"Whatever your hand finds to do, do it with all your might,
for in the grave, where you are going, there is neither working
nor planning nor knowledge nor wisdom."
Ecclesiastes 9:10

There are few people in the world who can honestly say that God disappointed them, yet Nicholas Herman was one of them. He was converted to Christianity at the age of eighteen. Seeing a dry, lifeless tree in the dead of winter and realizing that soon it would burst forth into life as the sap rose in the spring, Herman knew that he was spiritually dead and asked God to give him a re-birth. It happened, too; and after that, for a period of time, Nicholas Herman served as a footman and a soldier.

"We ought not to be weary of doing little things for the love of God."

In 1666 Nicholas Herman was admitted to a lay brotherhood at the Carmelite monastery in Paris. Herman entered the order expecting to suffer at the hand of God as the result of his prior sinful life, but God disappointed him. Instead of a life of regret and suffering, Herman, who was given the name of Brother Lawrence, found forgiveness, joy, and peace beyond expectation.

Brother Lawrence's faith, however, was soon put to the test, for he was assigned to the kitchen. By nature, he was awkward and clumsy. Kitchen duty was a challenge, but the way that he tackled it provides guidelines for victorious living three centuries later.

Lawrence believed that even the most mundane and worldly task can be done in love for God, and doing it for the great King gives the most humble task a spiritual purpose. In his little book *The Practice of the Presence of God,* Brother Lawrence shares what God taught him. He wrote, "The time of business does not with me differ from the time of prayer, and in the noise and clatter of my kitchen while several persons are at the same time calling for different things, I possess God in as great tranquillity as if I were upon my knees. . . ."

How did Lawrence approach his duty as cook for the brotherhood? He wrote that he began each task with fervent prayer and then did it with love for God. At the end of the meal, he prayed again with thanksgiving. Lawrence wrote, "We ought not to be weary of doing little things for the love of God, who regards not the greatness of the work, but the love with which it is performed."

To Brother Lawrence the practical aspects of Christianity could be summed up in three words from the pen of the Apostle Paul: faith, hope, love. He said, "That all things are possible to him who believes, that they are less difficult to him who hopes; that they are more easy to him who loves, and still more easy to him who perseveres in the practice of these three virtues." What a legacy! Putting faith, hope, and love into operation was to Brother Lawrence practicing the presence of God.

Most family arguments occur not in the bedroom but in the kitchen, thirty minutes before the evening meal, when the members of the family converge, hot, tired, and tense. You, like Brother Lawrence, may hate kitchen duty. It may be a wearisome drudgery to you. Then learn his secret and do it with love for the Lord. Lawrence's practical approach to the presence of Christ is biblical. "And whatsoever you do," wrote Paul to the Colossians, "do it heartily as unto the Lord and not as unto men" (Colossians 3:23).

What is the thing that you most dread doing? Whatever your answer, this is your challenge, and applying a generous dose of the presence of Christ in the form of faith, hope, and love can transform it into a work of grace. To the believer there should be no task so lowly that it cannot be redeemed by grace. There is no difference between the secular and the sacred, for all things can become sacred. Yes, as Brother Lawrence, who lived to be over eighty, wrote, "Practicing the presence of God is the best rule of a holy life."

RESOURCE READING
Colossians 3

INSIGHT
For the Christian there should be no difference between the secular and sacred because God has made all things sacred.

APPLICATION
On a scale of 1-10, how often do you give tasks your best effort?

Brother Lawrence expected to suffer a great deal because of his faith. Instead God gave him joy and peace. Look up Isaiah 43:25 and see if this might have had something to do with his "disappointment."

DISAPPOINTMENT
Vincent Van Gogh

"Peace I leave with you; my peace I give you. I do not give to you as the world gives. Do not let your hearts be troubled and do not be afraid."
John 14:27

Vincent Van Gogh, one of Netherland's greatest painters, was a strange enigma, and his paintings were often a reflection of the turmoil within his life—the dark colors of the soul. Today one of his paintings sells for tens of millions of dollars, yet in his lifetime he sold only one painting, for the equivalent of about a hundred dollars. For most of his life he had to depend on the charity of his brother for survival. If ever a man's great talents were unrecognized in his day, Van Gogh was that person.

"The pain passes; the beauty remains."

Van Gogh's paintings have a strange and fascinating attraction about them. Even an individual with little artistic expertise such as myself can see in Van Gogh's painting something captivating, something that lets you see into the very life of the man who painted them.

And what of the man who became an unrecognized great painter? Van Gogh was the son of a preacher who was born in Groot-Zundert. For whatever reasons, he never got along with people very well, yet he had a deep love for others and decided to follow in his father's footsteps as a minister.

He went to Brussels and enrolled in a theological seminary. In 1878, he went to a Belgian mining town and sought to convert the miners. His preaching didn't do it, so he donned the garb of a coal miner and went down into the mines, working among the men he sought to convert. But then something happened. No one today knows exactly what it was, but the Belgian missionary society with whom he was working fired him for being "overly zealous," according to one biographer.

Friendless and an outcast even to his own family, Van Gogh decided to become a painter. He studied the impressionists but he didn't strive to be one of them. He wanted to be himself, and he painted his own way. He painted the countryside, the small towns of France, the rented room where he stayed.

Some say it was because he painted in the sun. Some attribute it to his poor diet; some to his own feelings of insecurity and inner turmoil; but whatever the cause, eventually his sanity gave way. In a fit of anger, he threatened to stab a fellow painter and then in remorse and guilt, he punished himself by slashing off part of his own ear with a razor.

All his life he considered himself to be a failure, and eventually he took his life in a mental hospital on July 29, 1890. Was he really a failure? Your answer depends on how you look at life. In 1987, his painting "Irises" sold for fifty million dollars. Today a massive museum in Amsterdam houses his nearly priceless works of art. He is recognized the world over as a great artist.

Could Vincent Van Gogh have been the same painter had he not gone through the dark valley of depression? Probably not, but who knows? I, for one, will always wonder what happened that caused the Belgian missionary society to ask him to leave. Could the matter have been handled without further scarring the man who was misunderstood and so introverted?

Here's something else to think about. Van Gogh could have been a mediocre preacher (whoever heard of his father?), but instead heartache helped produce some great masterpieces. As another painter, Pierre Renoir, put it, "The pain passes; the beauty remains."

My heart goes out to people like Van Gogh who wander through the darkness of loneliness and failure–people whose lives have genius if only someone could recognize it. These people are failures from the world's perspective– but from God's perspective, who knows? And who knows how many more Vincent Van Goghs are alive today. Yes, who knows?

RESOURCE READING
John 14:15-27

INSIGHT
Whether or not you consider Vincent Van Gogh to be a failure depends much on your definition of success. People succeed or fail only in respect to what they feel is their calling in life.

APPLICATION
How do you think Van Gogh's life might have been different had he not become disappointed with his attempt to convert the miners?

Have you had a disappointment that has threatened your future? Is it possible that God may use difficulty to direct you into a path of more productive service?

Excellence
W. Page Pitt

"I can do everything God asks me to with the help of Christ
who gives me the strength and power."
Philippians 4:13, TLB

W. Page Pitt is a man who should have failed, but he succeeded. For years, Professor Pitt headed the Department of
Journalism at Marshall University. Although he was offered
salaries of two to three times what he made as a college professor, Pitt's first love was teaching journalism.

Pitt's success is enviable because of the record he has made,
but what is most remarkable about
Professor Pitt is that he accomplished all of this practically blind.
When he was only five years old,
he lost ninety-seven percent of his
eyesight. Though almost blind,
Pitt refused to attend a school for the blind and was accepted
in public school. He played baseball, first base, catching a
low ball by the sound of it whistling through the grass. He
played football as a second-string tackle. He worked his
way through college and graduate school, inveigling his fellow students to read his lessons to him. When he became a
professor, Page Pitt earned the reputation of being a "slave
driver." But he also earned the reputation of being a top-
notch professor. They did not come any better than Pitt.

One day, a somewhat thoughtless student asked the
professor which he would consider the worst handicap:

"Lethargy,
irresponsibility,
lack of ambition
or desire: they are
the real handicaps."

blindness or deafness, or no arms and legs, or what? "There was a smoldering, ominous quiet," says his wife. Then Page exploded. "None of those things! Lethargy, irresponsibility, lack of ambition or desire: they are the real handicaps. If I do not teach you anything but to want to do something with your lives, this course will be a magnificent success!"

No one could challenge Pitt. Constantly he would growl at his students, "You're not here to learn mediocrities, you're here to learn to excel." Pitt would often tell his students, "If I send you out on a story and you cannot get it because you have broken a leg, call me before the ambulance comes and I'll forgive you. But do not give me excuses! They wound me, and explanations pour salt in the wound."

Pitt is right. The real enemies we face, the ones that deal us the most severe blows are not the handicaps of blindness or deafness. There are enemies far worse: lethargy, irresponsibility, lack of ambition, and lack of desire. These are the real enemies. You may be like Pitt, who was blind early in his life. You face a handicap, anything, and you are prone to pity yourself. You are so quick to rationalize and make excuses. You can blame it on a physical handicap. Or you can say you were a victim of circumstances. You can always find an excuse. Until you come to realize that your biggest enemy is you, your life will continue to be one big failure.

There is something more important, however, than just results. It is learning how to live, how to overcome your difficulties, how to really make your life count. Nearly nineteen hundred years ago, the Apostle Paul wrote, " I can do everything through him who gives me strength" (Philippians 4:13). There is one thing you can be sure of. You can do anything God wants you to do and you can find His strength and help in accomplishing it. Most of us excuse ourselves with reasons that God could not justify for a moment. We blame Him for our mistakes, for our poor eyesight, our background that makes accomplishment difficult.

When I was a boy I used to hear my mother say, "God helps those who help themselves." Paul never said it, but I think it is something that he would have said. There is usually one of two courses of action open to us: that of self-pity and complacency, or that of accomplishment, rising above the handicaps that ordinarily spell failure. Excuses or results? You hold the answer. The next time you are tempted to think up an excuse, please visualize Pitt Page as a youth, ninety-seven percent blind, striving to catch a baseball as it came whistling through the grass. Then listen for the echo of his words, ". . .do not give me excuses! They wound me, and explanations pour salt in the wound." Yes, indeed.

RESOURCE READING
Philippians 4

INSIGHT
You can accomplish far more than you would otherwise with a "Don't tell me why it can't be done; tell me how we'll do it" attitude. Negative thinking precipitates failure but positive attitudes prepare the soil for accomplishment.

APPLICATION
If God never asks you to do the impossible, why would you need to trust Him for the resources or help you need to accomplish your task?

On a scale of 1-10, how positive are you most of the time?

Is it true that those who have time for excuses seldom have time for anything else?

EXCELLENCE
Bertel Thorvaldsen

"Like clay in the hand of the potter, so are you in my hand. . . ."
Jeremiah 18:6

Bertel Thorvaldsen was Denmark's greatest sculptor and probably one of the greatest people ever to lift a hammer and chisel. After studying in Copenhagen, he went to Rome to complete his training. Someone has quipped that some are born great while others have greatness thrust upon them. Surely Thorvaldsen was among the former. Even as a student his works were outstanding. So good were they that it seemed one could but strike one of his figures and command it to speak.

"God molds us with his hands; at times He takes the chisel to His workmanship."

Today any visitor to Copenhagen would be shortchanged without a visit to the great museum that houses a collection of his works of art. Two of Thorvaldsen's collection seem to rise above all others: the Lion of Lucerne, carved out of solid rock to honor the ten Swiss guards killed defending the French king in 1792, and Christ and the twelve apostles, found in two places in Copenhagen.

How is it that something can be in two places in the same city? Visit the Thorvaldsen museum and you will see the figurines of Christ and the twelve apostles, alright, with Paul taking the place of Judas. But you will also find them in the cathedral, only a short distance from the museum.

The figurines in the museum are beautiful, but nothing compared with the ones you will find in the cathedral. The ones in the museum are gray and discolored; the ones in the cathedral, pure white.

Why have two sets on display? Visitors are told that the figurines found in the museum are made of clay, which eventually absorbs dust and dirt and the oil and residue of a city, gradually turning the composition a putty gray; while the ones in the cathedral are made of pure marble, which will probably stay beautiful for centuries.

I don't usually bother to look for a hidden moral truth whenever I visit a museum, but when I compared the brilliant marble figures of Christ and the apostles with the ones made of clay, I couldn't help but ponder how the Book of Hebrews speaks of the church on earth and the one in the heavens. One is made of clay and the other, having had the dross and clay removed, is made with the purity of marble.

I don't know if it speaks to your heart as it does to mine, but I'm convinced that a lot of folks never quite get their eyes off the clay to see the reality of the marble. Paul talked about vessels of clay when he wrote to the Corinthians and the great treasure we have in them. Clay soils and discolors, yet for Thorvaldsen it served as the pattern for the great masterpiece made of marble, a masterpiece that has left its mark on the world, qualifying its maker as a hero.

One more thing, though, needs to be said about clay, something so profound that a child could tell you: Clay is malleable in the hands of the sculptor, while marble is hard to work with. The master artist molds and deftly shapes the clay, working it with his hands; but when it comes to the marble, it requires the hammer and chisel to make the stone do his bidding.

Long ago Jeremiah, the Old Testament prophet, used the analogy of clay to describe what God was doing with His people, Israel. Still today, God molds us with His hands; at times He takes the chisel to His workmanship, bringing us into conformity with His plan and purpose.

We can hardly expect saints to be made of marble. They are made of clay, which includes their hands and feet. Eventually, however, having stood the test of time, they find their marble counterpart in heaven.

To be honest, I was rather disappointed on my first visit to Thorvaldsen's museum, seeing the disciples made of clay when I didn't know the marble figures existed. It was good news to learn that Thorvaldsen had also made those of marble. Think about it the next time a clay disciple disappoints you.

RESOURCE READING
Jeremiah 18

INSIGHT
God uses imperfect, earthly material to create His eternal perfect kingdom.

APPLICATION
We say someone has "feet of clay" when they fall, but in reality everyone has feet of clay and apart from the grace of the Lord, none of us would come to faith in Christ. Have you known someone who disappointed you? What was your response?

Do we expect too much of Christian leaders today? How do we account for the fact that so many have disappointed us in recent years?

EXPLOITS FOR GOD
Billy Graham

*"Yet when I preach the gospel, I cannot boast, for I am compelled
to preach. Woe to me if I do not preach the gospel!"*
1 Corinthians 9:16

Billy Graham has preached the gospel to more people than
any person in all history. In the flyleaf of his autobiography,
Just As I Am, the publisher notes the following: "Billy Graham
Crusades have reached more than 200 million people in person, and millions more have heard him on radio, television,
and film. He has been welcomed
behind the Iron Curtain, into China
and North Korea and on every
continent."

*"The greatest
ability in the
sight of God is
availability."*

Billy has often said, "The
first thing I am going to do when I
get to Heaven is to ask, 'Why me,
Lord? Why did You choose a farm
boy from North Carolina to preach to so many people. . . ?' "

If the greatest ability in the sight of God is availability, that may be part of the answer. Sherwood Eliot Wirt,
the founding editor of Billy's *Decision* magazine, a man
who worked closely with Billy Graham for nearly forty
years, came to know him very well. He says, "All attempts
to explain Billy Graham fail unless they begin at the
cross."[15] In his biography, *Billy,* which abounds with personal incidents, Wirt shows how Billy's spiritual life not
only began at the cross, but the preaching of the cross has
been central in his life and ministry. He always keeps on

bringing people–whether they are the nine U.S. Presidents whom he knew, or the masses who sat under his ministry on every continent– back to the foot of the cross. Jesus said, "But I, when I am lifted up from the earth, will draw all men to myself" (John 12:32). This, Billy has done consistently. His message has remained unaffected.

William Franklin Graham II grew up just outside of Charlotte, North Carolina and was raised by hard-working, no-nonsense parents who attended the local Presbyterian church. When "Billy Frank," as his family knew him, was a teenager, a group of Christian businessmen held an all-day prayer meeting in the Graham family pasture. "Who are all those men over there in the woods making all that noise?" one of the hired hands asked Billy, who had just come home from school. Billy answered, "I guess they're some fanatics that have talked Daddy into using the place."[16]

At that very prayer meeting, businessman Vernon Patterson prayed that "out of Charlotte the Lord would raise up someone to preach the Gospel to the ends of the earth."[17] Little did Billy realize that he would be the answer to this man's prayer.

By high school, Billy went to church with his family "grudgingly, or of necessity," according to his own confession; but then in 1934, a controversial Southern Baptist evangelist came to Charlotte: Dr. Mordecai Fowler Ham. At first Billy vowed he would not go hear him preach, but when Ham publicly denounced the morality of some of the students in Billy's high school and the students decided to go break up the meeting, Billy decided to go just to see what would happen.

What happened is that the Holy Spirit began to convict Billy, who was converted after attending several times. He soon felt that God had called him to preach.

Frankly, over the years, my admiration for this man has grown enormously. He was courted by the liberals who liked him as a man but would have preferred that he tone down his message and avoid the "conversion" emphasis. He was enticed by politicians who promised undeliverable rewards if he would throw his weight behind them. He resisted using his popularity to gain personal wealth (he continues to live on a relatively small salary set by the Billy Graham Association and has donated vast sums of book royalties to Christian work). He has been viciously attacked by his detractors, yet (and this is one of the things I most admire about the man), he answered them with kindness, even thanking them for pointing out his flaws, which he freely admitted and sought to correct. His moral life has been flawless, and his organization has been free of financial scandal.

Recently, I talked about Billy with Armin Gesswein, now in his nineties, who has known almost every great Christian leader since World War II. Armin led the Billy Graham prayer crusades for years. "Will there ever be another Billy Graham?" I asked. "Never!" Armin quickly responded, adding, "Someone—probably his son Franklin—will be his successor, but no one will ever replace him."

Gesswein is undoubtedly correct.

RESOURCE READING
1 Corinthians 1

INSIGHT
Billy's question as to why God should use a "farm boy" (who never went to a theological seminary) to preach to more people than any other person in all history serves as a reminder that God will use anyone who relies completely on the Lord for strength and wisdom.

APPLICATION
In your personal life, have you tended to rely upon your natural attributes or resources (good family, education,

money) instead of God? If so, confess it to the Lord and strive to remedy that attitude.

Are there "shortcuts" you are tempted to take? What would have happened to Billy's ministry had he taken them?

FAITH

C. S. Lewis

"If anyone chooses to do God's will, he will find out whether my teaching comes from God or whether I speak on my own."
John 7:17

When C. S. Lewis died on November 22, 1963, most newspapers never mentioned that fact. Some papers carried a brief news note on an inside page stating that the Cambridge Professor of Medieval Literature had died of heart and kidney failure. On page one of newspapers, on the day Lewis died, was the vivid picture of an American president, John F. Kennedy, who had been cut down by an assassin's bullets. No wonder Lewis's passing drew only scant mention.

"It is more rational to accept the gospel and its implications than to disbelieve it."

His full name was Clive Staples Lewis, which may account for his using only the initials "C. S.," or simply "Jack" to his personal friends. Lewis was a brilliant man and a keen thinker. He wrote on a vast number of themes, including English literature, theology, and children's stories such as the Narnia Chronicles, filled with mythical beings and fairy tale characters.

Some refer to Lewis as an apologist, or one who defends Christianity, yet Lewis never really intended to defend anything. Nevertheless, his book, *Mere Christianity*, which came from a series of radio lectures during World War II, was the tool that brought Chuck Colson to an

135

understanding of Jesus Christ, and the book has spoken to the hearts of millions of other people. Lewis's logical, intuitive mind simply concluded that it is more rational to accept the gospel and its implications than to disbelieve it.

As a youth, Lewis was a believer. Then, partly because of his own struggles with his sexuality, he abandoned his faith and claimed to be an atheist. Eventually, however, the gospel again became meaningful and he fully embraced Christianity, this time with commitment.

Lewis never based his salvation on feelings or emotional experiences. To the contrary, he later wrote that before he was converted, there were times when Christianity seemed very logical; and after his conversion, there were times when atheism also seemed logical. He believed that you have to tell your emotions where to get off, otherwise you dither back and forth, uncertain of who you are or what you believe.

His personal life was complex and his path to faith was marked by intense struggles and personal conflicts. He never learned to drive a car, and he was a failure when it came to practical things like fixing something around the house. Though book royalties eventually amounted to large sums, he generously gave most of it away and never could handle money. But he was a master at handling words. When it came to making complex things simple, he was good—very, very good.

Having met an American writer who admired him, Lewis eventually married and became a father to her two children. At first, Lewis had admired Joy Gresham but didn't really love her. Forced, however, with either the choice of marrying her or losing her because the British government was going to deport her, he married. But eventually he fell in love with Joy, and she became an inseparable part of his life.

When she died of cancer, Lewis was shattered. He felt as though God had let him down. "I turned to God now that I really need him," said Lewis, "and what do I find?

A door slammed in my face, the sound of bolting and double-bolting, and after that. . .silence."

Yet Lewis held on to his faith, based not on his feelings of pain and loss. If I had to pick one thing about the life of C. S. Lewis that speaks to my heart more than anything else, it is the fact that his faith was never based on emotions or feelings, but the truth of the gospel, which rises above sensations or feelings.

C. S. Lewis, the apostle to the skeptics, a man whose life speaks as loudly as his powerful words.

RESOURCE READING
2 Corinthians 2

INSIGHT
When a person is sincere in asking the truth about the Gospel, God will answer, says Jesus in John 7:17. This was true in Lewis's life, and it can be true in yours as well.

APPLICATION
Is there an issue that baffles you and you would like God to reveal His truth regarding this? What is it? Have you gone to the Scriptures to find an answer? Talk to a mature believer about your doubts, someone who has been down the same path—not to another without experience or maturity.

Ask God in faith to show you the solution and await His answer. Study the Book of Habakkuk for additional insights.

FAITH

David

"For when David had served God's purpose in his
own generation, he fell asleep."
Acts 13:36

When I interview people, I often close the interview by asking, "At the end of your life, how would you like to be
remembered?" Answers to that question tell a lot about the
person who is responding.

A thousand years after King David lived, Luke, one of
the writers of the New Testament,
included a few thoughts about how
David was remembered. He wrote,
"For when David had served God's
purpose in his own generation, he
fell asleep. . ." (Acts 13:36). Another
translation adds a single phrase that
injects even more meaning. It
reads, "For when David had served God's purpose in his
own generation *according to the will of God,* he fell asleep"
(Nestle's Greek text, italics added for emphasis by the
author). The overview of history is often so much different
than how we appear in the smoke and dust of the battle.

"Every person,
no matter how humble
or insignificant,
influences somebody."

For a few moments, measure your life against the bench-
mark of what Luke wrote about David. First, he served
God's purpose. Now translate this in our generation to your
family, your workplace, your neighborhood. Would you
say that you are accomplishing God's purpose for your
life? Or would you have to say that you fall far short of

accomplishing God's purposes?

One of the greatest tragedies in life is to get very close to reaching your goal, arriving at your full potential, accomplishing what you set out to do, only to fall short of what you wanted to accomplish. It's always sad to have to quit a few hundred meters short of the top or to get so very close to winning, only to have victory snatched from your grasp.

Unrealized goals! Unfulfilled potential—what a tragedy! With a sigh we speak of "the man he might have been" or "the woman she could have been."

You tell me what your heart yearns to do, what you think about when you lie awake unable to sleep in the night hours, and I'll tell you what kind of a person you really are. If money consumes your thinking, you are materialistic. If you think only of revenge, you're angry and bitter. If your thoughts are of God and how you can serve Him, you are a person of spiritual sensitivity and dedication.

You may be asking, "What is God's purpose for my life?" Good question! There's a whole book that answers that one. It's called the Bible, and it explains very clearly what God's purpose is for your life in simple, easy-to-understand language.

David was responsible only for his own generation. You can't do anything about what took place a hundred years ago or even a generation ago. That's history. But you can do something about your generation—today, the world in which you live.

Some mistakenly think that the sum total of their influence in life is zero. Not true! Every person, no matter how humble or insignificant, influences somebody. You, like David, can serve God's purpose in your generation.

A final thought: David served God's purpose according to the will of God. That's a powerful thought. "Does God have a will for my life?" you may be wondering. The Bible says He does. The writers of Scripture contend that what happens to your life is of great importance to our heavenly Father. Paul wrote, "Be very careful, then, how you live–not as unwise but as wise, making the most of every opportunity, because the days are evil. Therefore do not be foolish, but understand what the Lord's will is" (Ephesians 5:15-17). There you have it–a life of purpose, touching our generation according to the will of God!

RESOURCE READING
Ephesians 5:1-20

INSIGHT
God has a purpose for each of His children and is far more desirous of revealing that to us than we often are in finding it.

APPLICATION
Probably you have never thought much about the question, "What is God's purpose for my life?" Give it some thought. Then finish the statement, "I believe God's purpose for my life is _____."

Make a list of your strengths and aptitudes. Then for a few moments ponder how these fit into accomplishing God's plan and purpose for your life.

FAITH
Chang Shen

"The King will reply, 'I tell you the truth, whatever you did for one of the least of these brothers of mine, you did for me.'"
Matthew 25:40

The truly great saints of the world are the army of unknown, unclaimed, undecorated little people, the ones who live their lives in obscurity, unrecognized, and undiscovered. Such was a Chinese brother martyred in the backlash against foreigners known as the Boxer Rebellion in the year 1900.

If Rosalind Goforth, a Presbyterian missionary living in Manchuria, had not written about this man, we would never have known what a saint he really was. Chang Shen was poorly educated, and he had a violent temper. Until his conversion in 1886, his death would have been little noticed. At the time today's story begins, Chang was blind, thirty-six years of age, a despised, hard-drinking, violent man who cared for little but himself.

"A changed life was his message."

When Blind Chang, as he was called, heard that foreign doctors, who reportedly could cure blindness, were living 120 miles to the south of his home in Manchuria, he set out on the long journey by himself. On the way, the helpless blind man was beaten and robbed, and by the time he finally got to the hospital, he was forlorn, dirty, and wretched. He arrived, only to be told that there were no beds at the hospital and he would have to go away.

He had no place to "go away" to so he curled up in the entrance and fell asleep. The night watchman had seen it all—poverty and hunger, beggars and the destitute; but when he saw this man, his heart was deeply touched. Surely, God's finger touched his heart and with compassion he went to Dr. Christie, who was the chief of the hospital, and volunteered to let Blind Chang sleep in his own bed.

For a month Chang stayed at the hospital and recovered some sight, only to lose it after his release, when a local Chinese practitioner pierced the pupil of his eye with a needle, thinking that this would heal the man. Now Chang was completely blind. At the hospital, however, Chang had heard the Gospel and realized he was a sinner. He was soundly converted.

When he asked to be baptized, James Webster, the missionary in charge, felt that he just wasn't ready and promised to come visit him at his home in due time. Disappointed, Chang took some tracts and a few papers about Christianity and made his way back to his hometown, where he began evangelizing. But Chang had a past, a black one as locals described it. Who would believe him?

When Webster finally got there, however, he found a small but thriving group of believers, all of whom wanted to be baptized. A church had been born, one that had come to an understanding of Jesus through the changed life of this blind man.

In the year 1900, the hatred of outsiders turned the tide of public opinion, and the persecution of Christians grew, especially foreigners: the Boxer Rebellion. When Christians were imprisoned, Chang agreed to give himself up to free them. Thinking if they killed the Christians' leader, they would put an end to the growth of Christianity, on July 22, 1900, Chang was driven through the streets in a cart used to transport animals. As he went to his place of execution, he sang a song we usually think of as a children's song: "Jesus loves me, this I know for the Bible tells me so."

As he cried out, "Heavenly Father, receive my spirit," the executioner's sword severed his neck. And Blind Chang received his sight as God's child in heaven.

A changed life was his message. The truly great saints, the ones who surely must occupy a special place in heaven, are often the unknown, unrecognized, undecorated men and women whose lives reflect the love of Jesus far more than even their words. These are the real saints.

RESOURCE READING
Matthew 25:31-46

INSIGHT
Some of the most powerful witnesses for the Lord come from those whose lives become the message, uncluttered by personal ambition or pride.

APPLICATION
God uses individuals who have no real agenda of their own, which means that one of the greatest assets you have is your desire to let Christ use you.

Chang wasn't stopped by either his physical handicap or the lack of education, which could have easily been "lame" excuses for doing nothing.

SUGGESTION
Pray, "Lord, please take my life and use me for Your service. Shine through my life and let others see Yourself in me."

FAITH
Tom Landry

"Whatever you do, work at it with all your heart, as working for the Lord, not for men, since you know that you will receive an inheritance from the Lord as a reward. It is the Lord Christ you are serving."
Colossians 3:23, 24

Tom Landry, the former head coach of the Dallas Cowboys, was one of the most successful coaches in the history of American football. In World War II, Landry served as a B-17 pilot in Europe, narrowly escaping with his life on several occasions. Though he didn't understand it then, Landry is now convinced that God was sparing his life for a reason. When the war ended, Landry went back to the University of Texas, where his career in football carried him to the Sugar Bowl and Orange Bowl, then to a career as a professional.

"A person who knows where he is in relationship to God is in a better position to succeed."

Landry says that he thought if he reached the top of his profession, he would be happy, but there was still something missing. The year before he took over as head coach for the Dallas Cowboys, Landry found the missing ingredient.

A friend invited him to a Bible study, and Landry thought the guy was absolutely nuts to be interested in the Bible. For reasons that Landry wasn't quite sure of himself, he went, though. . .and eventually discovered what was lacking—a personal relationship with God. Though Landry had gone to church most of his life, when he received Jesus

Christ as his Savior and Lord, life took on an exciting dimension.

Landry believes that the secret of a winning team and the secret of the Christian life is found in what he describes as his favorite passage in the Bible, 1 Corinthians, chapter nine, where Paul describes the athlete who participated in the Ismian games of Paul's day and then likened the Christian life to an athletic contest. In this formula, Landry sees four ingredients: 1) faith, 2) training, which includes a generous dose of discipline, 3) goals, and 4) the will to win, or determination.

Emphasizing his first point–faith–Landry tells how his first season with the Cowboys was disastrous. After a few games, the owner confronted him and said, "We aren't going to win a single game." Landry knew that, but he had hoped the owner of the team didn't. The owner explained: "They always know who's going to get the ball. Four guys go into the huddle and three come out laughing their heads off, and the fourth is white as a sheet." His team needed more faith.

Tom Landry believes that a person who knows where he is in relationship to God is in a better position to succeed as an athlete. Faith is the confident assurance that something you want is going to happen, the certainty that what you hope for is waiting for you even though you cannot see it. And that definition of faith, which you find in Hebrews, chapter eleven, in the New Testament, applies to the reality of God as well as the reality of winning a game.

Landry is very open about his Christian commitment, having served as chairman of the Billy Graham Crusade and as chairman of the board of the Fellowship of Christian Athletes, as well as in many other Christian causes. One thing I have appreciated about Landry is not simply that he is a great athlete and coach, but that he's a man of integrity who produces winners. And we sometimes think that nice guys always finish last!

"An athlete goes to all this trouble just to win a blue ribbon or a silver cup," writes Paul in Landry's favorite passage, which he often quotes, "but we do it for a heavenly reward that never disappears." Tom Landry has left a lasting impact on American football–something which is easily measured. What can't be measured is the tremendous influence he has had on the lives of men and women who have worked with him, who have played with, for, and–at times–against him, and who continue to look up to him.

I still miss seeing Coach Landry on the sidelines when I watch the Dallas Cowboys play. Perhaps I'm nostalgic, but it seems as though he ought to be there. And who knows? When he has paced back and forth the last fifty yard line in his life, he may still be wearing that hat–a kind of Landry trademark–when he knocks on heaven's door.

RESOURCE READING
1 Corinthians 9:24-27

INSIGHT

Coach Landry's life illustrates the fact that excellence is the result of dedication, training, and commitment–not luck or chance.

APPLICATION

How many outstanding professional athletes can you name who, like Landry, are believers?

Do you believe anything less than our best effort satisfied the One who has called us to serve Him?

FAITH
Abraham

"Trust in the Lord with all your heart and lean not unto your own understanding; in all your ways acknowledge Him, and He will direct your path."
Proverbs 3:5,6

Risk your money on dice and they call that gambling; risk your money on the stock market and they call that business. But risk your future on God, and they call you a fool. Such was the way it was with a man by the name of Abraham who lived long ago.

In the event you don't remember Abraham, he holds the unique distinction of being loved and esteemed by devotees of three faiths–Jews, Moslems, and Christians. Long ago, Abraham lived in Ur, a land known today as Ancient Mesopotamia. When God began to speak to Abraham about leaving his hometown, people thought of him as a fool. Hebrews 11:8 speaks of his step of faith saying, "By faith Abraham, when called to go to a place he would later receive as his inheritance, obeyed, and went, even though he did not know where he was going" (Hebrews 11:8).

"The life of faith has always been contrary to the logic of the world."

Ur, where Abraham lived, was a nice place. Good schools and hospitals; good stores; comfortable homes. Ur was a good address to have on your letterhead. When people saw the address on your card, they commented, "You're from Ur. . .moving up in the world"—but Abraham left this all behind as he set his sights on an invisible goal.

Can you imagine some of the conversations that must have taken place as neighbors said, "We see you are packing up your family, Abraham. Where are you headed?" And Abraham says, "Well, you see, I'm not sure; I just know that God is leading me." "Uh-huh," comments a friend. "How are you going to take care of your family?" Abraham shuffles his feet and says, "Well, I really don't completely know, but I am sure God will take care of us!"

Oswald Chambers, a man who died an early death in Egypt, once wrote, "I am not many kinds of fools in one; I am only one kind of fool; the kind of fool that believes and obeys God." That is the kind of man Abraham was.

Men and women today who live and walk by faith, like Abraham of old, will always be considered to be out of step with their peers, a kind of fanatic who takes the truth of God's Word literally. Such have always been in a minority. The writer of Proverbs put it like this, "Trust in the Lord with all your heart and lean not unto your own understanding; in all your ways acknowledge Him, and He will direct your path" (Proverbs 3:5,6).

Those who have heard the call of God on their lives should not expect contemporaries to understand what they are doing; the voice of God is a still, quiet one, often drowned out by ambition and greed and the desire to be in control. The life of faith has always been contrary to the logic of the world, yet obedience to the plan and purpose of God does not require that you have a full knowledge of the game plan; it only demands that you have confidence in Him who does know the plan.

Mrs. Albert Einstein was once asked if she understood the theory of relativity for which her husband was famous, and she replied, "No, but I know my husband, and I know he can be trusted." Mrs. Abraham probably could have said the same when she followed her husband away from Ur.

Every person's life makes a statement. Mine does, and yours does, just as Abraham's did long ago. And

Abraham's life statement is this: "God will meet the person who responds to His promises in faith, trusting Him to do what He alone can do." Some live for gold, some for fame, some for power and influence, but Abraham lived for God. Thinking over the statement of your life, how would you define its message?

REFERENCE READING
Hebrews 11

INSIGHT
The will of God is like a flashlight in a dungeon: It doesn't shine around corners or into the next room but it gives you enough light for the next step.

APPLICATION
Make a list of issues that require you to make decisions. Put the list in your Bible and pray about them. Then as God answers prayer, make a notation on your list. This will be an encouragement to you.

In your Bible, mark the phrase in Proverbs 3:5, "lean not to your own understanding." Is there any need to worry, provided God knows where He is taking you?

What is the message of your life statement?

FAITH

J. Hudson Taylor

"My food," said Jesus, "is to do the will of him who sent me and to finish his work."
John 4:34

Among the British, Yorkshiremen are known to be tough. They are a "no-nonsense" breed of individuals known for common sense, thrift, and hard work. Understanding J. Hudson Taylor's Yorkshire background may explain why this man quietly impacted China in the last century as no other foreigner ever has done. Yet of all the men whose lives have impressed me—spiritual mentors who have been benchmarks for my personal growth and goals—none is harder to figure out than Hudson Taylor, which may be precisely why he is so important.

"I will place no value on anything I have or possess, except in its relationship to the kingdom of God."

Striving to answer the question, "What made him tick?" is difficult. In many respects, he was very ordinary—a quiet, soft-spoken, compassionate, yet tough individual without dynamic leadership skills or outstanding physical charisma. Yet he was a man great in faith and prayer, great in commitment, and indefatigable when it came to impacting the country he adopted and loved.

Before he was born in 1832, his parents had prayed, "Dear God, if You should give us a son, grant that he may work for You in China."[18] Some twelve years later, a discussion ensued in the Taylor home involving his father, a chemist by trade and lay preacher by avocation, who complained about the fact that there were only a half dozen Protestants working in all of China. Listening to the diatribe, the young Hudson immediately said, "When I am a man I mean to be a missionary and go to China!" Biographer J. C. Pollock says that in spite of the fact that his father had prayed for his son to go to China, he thought the idea merely amusing that a boy as sickly as Hudson would ever go abroad.

God used that Yorkshire stubbornness to do what others with greater education, culture, refinements, and social standing never accomplished. Converted at the age of seventeen, Taylor immediately began his preparation for missionary service. Finally going to China, he labored for six years in Shanghai and Ningpo with mixed success.

For one thing, Taylor just didn't fit the mold. He was appalled at the way most missionaries lived, sequestered in an international compound where life wasn't much different than it would have been in Britain or America, with servants and afternoon tea.

Recognizing that the culture was a barrier, Taylor cut off his hair and wove a braid into the remaining locks, then dyed his scalp—something very painful since the container of lye he was using exploded, leaving facial burns—and began dressing in Chinese fashion.[19]

Still feeling unaccepted, Taylor returned to Britain and established his own mission—the China Inland Mission—and returned in 1866 with his first group of missionaries, who were committed to reaching China no matter what the cost. And Taylor paid plenty when it came to cost. He wrote, "If I had 1,000 pounds, China should have it. If I had 1,000 lives, China should have them. No! Not China but Christ!" Then he asked, "Can we do too much for Him?"[20]

When trouble came, Taylor always sought refuge in the Lord he loved. Trusting Him implicitly for their needs—whether it was finances or missionaries to help reap the harvest—he depended on the Lord. "God's work done

God's way will never lack God's supply," he used to tell his comrades.

In June 1900, an imperial decree from Peking ordered the death of all foreigners, a grim chapter of Chinese history that resulted in the deaths of 153 missionaries and fifty-three children, the majority of whom were connected with Taylor's mission. He never fully recovered from this great loss, yet he planted the cross of Jesus Christ firmly in Chinese soil. It not only survived the Boxer Rebellion but also the assault of Communism a half-century later.

It is amazing what God can do with a sickly boy who knows that his sufficiency must come from God the Father. It happened with James Hudson Taylor.

RESOURCE READING
John 4

INSIGHT
God wants all there is of you; and when you give Him everything that you are and have or hope to be, God has enough to accomplish what He wants done.

APPLICATION
Do you see in the life of this humble man the hand of God, which enabled him to press on and accomplish some truly great feats for the Lord?

Do you ever feel hesitant to step out and attempt anything for God because of your inadequacies? If so, never forget how God used Taylor.

FAITH

Jim Irwin

"You will seek me and find me when you seek me with all your heart."
Jeremiah 29:13

In 1971, long before personal computers, Colonel James Irwin went to the moon as part of the Apollo 15 flight. He's a man who has dined with kings and queens and been celebrated by world leaders for almost two decades, yet he is one of the most humble, gracious men I've ever interviewed on Guidelines.

What a man! What an experience! The flight medallions presented to the crew of the Apollo 15 astronauts read, "Man's flight through life is sustained by the power of his knowledge!" Jim often quoted that, changing one letter to a capital, so that it reads, "Man's flight through life is sustained by the power of His (referring to God's) knowledge."

"Man's flight through life is sustained by the power of His knowledge."

Is that true of your life, friend? Or have you considered God as someone out there whom you cannot really know? Jim Irwin believes that God is not just out there but that He can be within your life personally, changing your habits, your destiny, and your future. But how can you know this as a fact?

In our generation the scientific method has come into its own, and, of course, this has made not only the advancement of science possible but has put men on the moon and now explores the further reaches of space. But what is the scientific method? In simplest terms, the scientific method means that a great deal of research is conducted in the area of investigation. Then, after careful analysis of the revealed facts, conclusions are reached. First facts, then conclusions.

The scientific method works quite well in a laboratory, but can you find God through the same way? Well, if you mean, "Can you measure God and find out exactly how big He is or how far away His heaven is?" the answer is no, because that would be bringing God down to our size—a measured, limited, finite being. God is bigger than that, and Jim Irwin, a man who has experienced the power of the scientific method firsthand, has no doubt about science's limitations.

If you take time to examine the evidence of God's existence and read His revealed Word, the Bible, you will find that it is far more logical—yes, even far more scientific—to believe in God than to explain either the vastness of our universe or the emptiness that exists in human hearts without Him. It's much like the conclusion of the great biologist Albert Winchester, who said, "A deeper and firmer belief in God can be the only result of a better insight into truth."

I am absolutely amazed, however, at the vast numbers of people, some college students, some scientists, some professors and teachers, who have never, ever considered the evidence for God's existence and yet have shut the door to Him in their lives and thinking. Denying Him, they live as created individuals refusing to acknowledge a Creator, people without purpose and meaning in life. Don't be one of them. You undoubtedly believe in the scientific method, yet you may have come to a firm conclusion that there is no God, never having read the Bible or having considered the vast amount of evidence that points to His existence and purpose in our world.

You or I will probably never stand on the moon as did Jim Irwin, yet we can experience the same God who changed Jim's life and gave him a new direction and purpose. I hope you will go to the record, and as you do so, I have no doubt you will come to the same conclusion that Jim Irwin came to: There is one God and one mediator between God and humanity, the Man, Christ Jesus, and you can know Him personally.

Can God be known? Indeed He can, but in the final analysis, you must take His existence by faith and trust the evidence both in our world and in the Bible, the Word of God. Until a person finds God, that person's thoughts begin at no beginning and work to no end.

Think about it.

RESOURCE READING
John 1:1-14

INSIGHT

Jim Irwin said that every person he had talked with who had been in space had been profoundly influenced by the experience.

APPLICATION

While you probably will never walk on the moon as did Colonel Irwin, you can still face the evidence and encounter the same results. In John 1, the Son is presented as the Word—eternal and without beginning or end.

On a personal level, how has your relationship with God changed your life? Are you willing to publicly acknowledge God's power, just as Jim Irwin does?

FAITH
Galileo

*"He determines the number of the stars and calls them each by name.
Great is our Lord and mighty in power. . . ."*
Psalm 147:4, 5

He was a man born ahead of his time, and had he stayed with the organ and the lute, which he played very well, he probably would not have faced the Inquisition that sentenced him to an indefinite prison term in 1632. But the inquisitive mind of Galileo Galilei got him in trouble with the Church beginning in 1609, when he built his first telescope. Then a year later he discovered four bright satellites revolving around planet Jupiter.

"True science, is not at war with the God of creation."

These discoveries added fuel to the fire and brought him into direct conflict with the Church fathers, some of whom would have liked to send Galileo to his death as a heretic; however, with a display of mercy, the Church allowed Galileo to live under house arrest until he died, broken and disheartened, in 1642. But in those last few years of his life, under house arrest, he wrote *Dialogues,* which formed the basis of Sir Isaac Newton's three laws of motion, formulated some forty-nine years after the Inquisition.

Lately, I've been thinking of Galileo in light of the Hubble telescope that is in space, and I've been wondering just what Galileo would say if he could see the massive new telescope that now hovers as a giant eye in the sky some 370 miles above the surface of the earth. The Hubble space telescope is a window to space unlike anything that Galileo ever dreamed of in the wildest stretch of his vivid imagination. While Galileo's telescope provided only a few powers of magnification, the Hubble telescope is some 500 million times the power of the naked eye.

Would Galileo be surprised? Undoubtedly he would be surprised at the price tag, but I rather doubt that Galileo would be greatly surprised to understand what's happening, because he formulated the principle, a man born out of due season.

The great new Hubble space telescope is really five pieces of equipment in one, the largest of which is a telescope with a mirror eight feet in diameter, the most perfect ever made. A news magazine says, "No bump or ripple on the reflecting surface deviates more than one-millionth of an inch from perfection. If the mirror were the diameter of Earth, its highest peaks would be no taller than 3 inches." Wow!

While Galileo could tinker with his telescopes, perfecting the grinding of the lens, if anything further goes wrong with the Hubble telescope, scientists will have to go into space to repair the unit, something that would take more than a year to accomplish.

Fifty years after Galileo's death in Florence, the city erected a monument at the church where he was buried. This was slightly too late, but it points out the conflict that existed between science and the Church, which held to an Aristotelian system of the heavenly bodies and refused to listen to the evidence Galileo discovered.

True science, however, is not at war with the God of creation any more than God is at war with those who determine to find out more about what He has done. Werner Von Braun, the man who launched the U.S. space program, said, "The greater our knowledge of the universe, the greater my faith!"

Galileo didn't confuse the dictum of the Church with

what he saw when he looked through his telescope. He knew that men can be wrong, and though he was forced to publicly deny and abandon his position, history and further research proved him to be right. This, of course, works on both sides of the issue, which is why the actual findings of science harmonize with the actual statements of Scripture–something that resolves many a conflict.

RESOURCE READING
Psalm 147

INSIGHT
There are not two Gods: one of creation and one of science. There is one God who has revealed His Word in the Bible, His works in nature.

APPLICATION
Should science and the church be enemies? Why or why not?

There are many top-notch scientists today who are Christians. Do you know of some? Make a list.

FAITH
Martin Neimoeller

"Blessed are you when people insult you, persecute you and falsely say all kinds of evil against you because of me. Rejoice and be glad, because great is your reward in heaven, for in the same way they persecuted the prophets who were before you."
Matthew 5:11, 12

The ominous clouds of war were hanging over Europe in 1937. Claiming that he could turn the economy around and put people to work, Adolf Hitler began to strengthen his grip on Germany. Those who dared to oppose him were silenced as the detention camps, eventually to be known as concentration camps, were opened.

"Don't ever forget that the Lord is a fortress that endures forever for the righteous."

A former submarine captain turned pastor was one of the few who spoke openly against what Hitler was doing, and Hitler hated him with a passion. Martin Niemoller had to be silenced.

Eventually the knock came at the door and he was taken by the S.S. troops and put in prison. On February 7, 1938, Martin was to face his accusers in court.

A strange thing happened on that morning as Martin was led through an underground tunnel from the prison to the courtroom. Suddenly he heard the words of Proverbs 18:10, "The name of the LORD is a strong tower; the righteous run to it and are safe."

What so disturbed Martin was that there was no one

who could have spoken those words. He was both shocked and surprised. Was this the audible voice of God speaking courage to his troubled heart? No matter whose voice it was, God used that incident to bring both comfort and encouragement to a man who was beginning an ordeal that he neither deserved nor should have faced.

A Christian guard had learned that the acoustics in the tunnel would allow someone to whisper into the wall and to be heard by the prisoner a considerable distance away, and a man who was a brother in Christ wanted to encourage Martin. He never forgot those words: "The name of the LORD is a strong tower; the righteous run to it and are safe."

Neimoeller was acquitted of the charges that had been made against him, yet he was imprisoned for more than seven years. "On what charges do we send a man to prison who has been acquitted?" the prosecutor asked Hitler, and the Fuehrer replied, "He is my personal prisoner!"[21]

Martin Neimoeller was neither the first nor the last individual to be falsely accused and imprisoned. As the gates of the concentration camp swung shut on Martin, he was in the company of some of the world's saints–from Paul the Apostle to John Bunyan, who was imprisoned in the old Bedford jail in England.

Jesus put it: "Blessed are you when people insult you, persecute you and falsely say all kinds of evil against you because of me. Rejoice and be glad, because great is your reward in heaven, for in the same way they persecuted the prophets who were before you" (Matthew 5:11, 12).

Most of us would just as soon do without the blessing of wrongful imprisonment, yet at the same time, no person who stands boldly for truth and integrity, who stands for the right, is immune from the sarcasm and jibes of those who love darkness rather than light.

Have you ever heard comments like, "What's the matter with you? Too good to go along with us?" Notice the labels of "radical right" that are often hung on those who protest. Watch how the secular media often pictures

Christians as being weird or out of touch with society in an attempt to discredit their influence. Their enemies cannot silence them by putting them in prison, but they do their best to discredit them through misinformation and deceit.

"The name of the LORD is a strong tower; the righteous run to it and are safe" said the psalmist. Have you experienced that great truth, friend?

The person who commits himself to anything worthwhile will always experience the hostility of those who stand for nothing. Don't ever forget that the Lord is a fortress that endures forever for the righteous.

RESOURCE READING
Psalm 43

INSIGHT
The reward of courage is not that you always get your way, but that you know you have done the right thing.

APPLICATION
Do you know of others who have done right at tremendous cost?

Do you think Neimoeller ever regretted his decision even though it cost him his freedom?

FAITHFUL TO YOUR CALLING
Jeremiah

"Before I formed you in the womb I knew you,
before you were born I set you apart. . . ."
Jeremiah 1:5

If ever a man was called by God to fail, that man was the prophet Jeremiah. The son of a priest, Hilkiah, who lived in the little village of Anathoth, two and a half miles northeast of Jerusalem, Jeremiah lived a pretty normal life, that is until he heard the voice of God calling him to a mission that forever wrote his name in the annals of history.

"Jeremiah was convinced that if Israel would only grasp at the straw of God's mercy, they would be saved from destruction."

In all probability Jeremiah was about twenty when God said, "Before I formed you in the womb I knew you, before you were born I set you apart; I appointed you as a prophet to the nations" (Jeremiah 1:5). Was Jeremiah excited? "Ah, Sovereign Lord," he replied, "I am only a child." But Jeremiah's concern was put to rest with the great promise, "I am with you and will rescue you" (Jeremiah 1:7), and then God touched his mouth with a coal from the altar of heaven and sent him to call God's people to repentance.

The life of Jeremiah is a study of vivid contrasts—dark days penetrated by the brilliant light of God's personal intervention. As the world views success, Jeremiah didn't have it together. First, God called him to a tough task: to convince his own nation that they were headed for destruction by resisting the growing powers of Babylon to the east. For at least twenty years before the nation finally collapsed, Jeremiah thundered forth diatribes of gloom and doom. He was one of the most hated men of his day, so much so that his enemies accused him of being a traitor. Repeatedly beaten and thrown in prison, Jeremiah was a man of few friends.

Presiding over the death of a nation is never an easy task, but with Jeremiah it was especially difficult because God further denied him the comfort of a wife and family (Jeremiah 16:1). Even when Jeremiah wept for his nation, God said, "Do not pray for the well-being of this people. Although they fast, I will not listen to their cry; though they offer burnt offerings and grain offerings, I will not accept them" (Jeremiah 14:11). So unpopular was this man with the government, that King Jehoiakim took his penknife and cut up the scroll containing the prophesies of Jeremiah and threw it in the fire.

Yet a study of this man reveals a sensitive, deeply caring, emotional person, who dearly loved his country and, far more, loved his God, a man who was consumed with the mercy of God, absolutely convinced that if Israel would only grasp at the straw of God's mercy, they would be saved from destruction.

Nonetheless, without wavering, Jeremiah held to his position that destruction was absolutely certain unless God's people did an about-face and repented of their sinful wrongdoing. Though he was faithful, with unswerving loyalty to the calling of the Almighty, Jeremiah wept for his fellow citizens bent on destruction, who ignored the voice of Him who said, "My people have committed two sins: They have forsaken me, the spring of living water, and have dug their own cisterns, broken cisterns that cannot hold water" (Jeremiah 2:13).

If Jeremiah were alive today, undoubtedly he would make world leaders, intent on fulfilling their own agenda, just as uncomfortable as he did the leaders of his day, because his integrity was like an abrasive file that cut

163

against the grain of sinfulness. "The heart is deceitful above all things and beyond cure. Who can understand it?" he cried (Jeremiah 17:9).

God give us more Jeremiahs today who stand like granite against the trends of the day and hold with unflinching tenacity to the call of the Almighty.

RESOURCE READING
Jeremiah 1

INSIGHT
The relationship Jeremiah had with the Lord gave him the strength to do what God wanted him to do. He knew that God was with him in spite of the fact that his message was unpopular.

APPLICATION
Do you ever feel alone when you are forced to speak out for what is right?

The mentality that says "to get along" (meaning to avoid conflict) you must "go along" runs contrary to everything Jeremiah believed. How do you find the strength to stand for that which is right? Have you learned that when you do right, there are almost always others who will follow you?

FAITHFUL TO YOUR CALLING
Jeremiah

"The harvest is past, the summer has ended, and we are not saved."
Jeremiah 8:20

Before his death in 1984, Francis Schaeffer developed what some have called a "theology of disagreement." Schaeffer never abandoned his position that the true mark of a Christian is the ability to love unconditionally, yet he was also convinced that one cannot really love without hating the opposite of what one loves.

Schaeffer was not the first to articulate a "theology of disagreement." He was largely indebted to a man who lived some 2700 years before and who made a "theology of disagreement" a science. His name was Jeremiah; and when you really get to know this man, you discover that he was not a cantankerous sort of fellow whose teeth were on edge, always wanting to pick a fight to get his name in the headlines. He was a sensitive, caring individual intent on doing the will of God no matter what it cost him, and it cost him plenty.

"His word is in my heart like a fire, a fire shut up in my bones."

Why was Jeremiah almost always on the unpopular side of issues? Because that's where God was, and no matter what the cost, Jeremiah came down on God's side. He said, "His word is in my heart like a fire, a fire shut up in my bones." He said, "I am weary of holding it in; indeed, I cannot" (Jeremiah 20:9). He didn't hold it in, either. He spoke fluently, boldly, and without consideration of who would be displeased at what he said.

Jeremiah was called by God to be a spokesman, calling God's people back to Himself. And when they refused to budge, Jeremiah told them the price they had to pay. He became a hated, despised individual, persecuted and belittled. He was thrown into prison, put in stocks, even thrown in a slime pit or a tar pit and left to die. But a foreigner, an Ethiopian, rescued him by putting rotten rags under his armpits and using ropes to pull him from the clutches of death (see Jeremiah 38).

It is no wonder that his name has become a byword for someone who is pessimistic and discouraged. Was his the only voice that was denouncing the corruption of his day? Not at all. Contemporary with Jeremiah were voices such as Ezekiel and Daniel, both young men. Ezekiel, a fellow priest, was preaching in Babylon. Daniel was in the palace of Nebuchadnezzar. Habakkuk and Zephaniah were working alongside Jeremiah in Jerusalem. Nahum was announcing the fall of Nineveh, and Obadiah was predicting the ruin of neighboring Edom.

How does all of this fit into your life today in the late twentieth century? Are there qualities in the life of this man that we ought to emulate? Have we become so intimidated by what is happening around us that we fear the consequences of speaking out against the corruption of our day or the wrongdoing of society? Have we become so fearful of the hostility of those who accuse us of being intolerant that we hide for fear of drawing their wrath?

There is one thing you must never forget. The God who told Jeremiah not to fear because He was with him makes that same promise to His child who has the courage to denounce wrong when truth is on the scaffolds.

For far too long we who are committed to integrity and values not popular today have been intimidated by those who say exactly what Jeremiah heard long ago. Read the book that bears his name, found in your Bible. You'll be amazed how old is the battle for righteousness—one which never goes away.

RESOURCE READING
Jeremiah 38:1-13

INSIGHT
For Christians today there will always be a certain tension between the cross and the world, for they are in the world but not of the world.

APPLICATION
If Jeremiah were alive today, what issues do you think he would speak against?

When you see something that is wrong—no matter what it is—try to use your influence to help correct the situation. Write a letter, talk to the appropriate person, register your dissent. Do it in a positive way and see how you can make a difference.

FAITHFUL TO YOUR CALLING
Hosea

"I will heal their waywardness and love them freely,
for my anger has turned away from them."
Hosea 14:4

When his first child was born, he gave him a Hebrew name, Jezreel, which meant, "God will scatter!" The second child was a girl, and the father named her Lo-ruhamah, which meant, "No mercy!" In the meanwhile tongues began to wag, pointing out the fact that Gomer was often seen in the company of other men. Yet Hosea fell back on the assurance that no matter how poor a wife she was (at least in the eyes of other people), God had commanded him to marry her.

"You must return to your God; maintain love and justice, and wait for your God always."

As strange as it may seem to us, God had commanded Hosea to marry Gomer, a woman with a jaded past, because God wanted the marriage of this man to be a picture of how Israel as a nation had turned her back on Jehovah God.

Some well-meaning individuals undoubtedly must have reminded Hosea that he couldn't expect much more out of Gomer. "After all, look at her background," they said. "Prostitute" was the term that others used. And who could deny that she did have a past? Others turned their heads and cried, "What a shame! He could have married much better than he did!"

When the third child was born, there was no question

in his mind. What he had suspected and hoped was untrue was now altogether evident. He knew he had not fathered the child. So the infant bore the name, "Lo-ammi," meaning "Not my people!" Soon thereafter, Gomer disappeared.

I've often visualized what must have taken place, as Hosea put the children to bed night after night and tried to answer the same question, "Daddy, where is Mommy? Why doesn't she come home?" And the father, with pained expression and dark circles under his eyes, would reply, "We must pray for Mommy and ask God to bring her back to us."

God did bring Gomer back, but not before it became obvious that she had sold herself cheaply to a variety of men. In his own words, here is how Hosea described it, "The Lord said to me, 'Go, show your love to your wife again, though she is loved by another and is an adulteress. Love her as the LORD loves the Israelites, though they turn to other gods. . .' "(Hosea 3:1).

We are many years removed from the scene I've just described, yet the problem of broken homes is as current as this morning's newspaper or a phone call from a close friend. Hosea's problem is our problem. And, in a very real sense, what God illustrated so graphically is our problem as well—that the nation that forsakes the Almighty reaps grave consequences.

In the book that bears his name, Hosea talks about the issues that destroy nations: dishonesty, adultery, blood-shed, violence, and corrupt religious leaders. And he faithfully records the words of God: "My people are destroyed from lack of knowledge. Because you have rejected knowledge, I also reject you . . . ; because you have ignored the law of your God, I also will ignore your children" (Hosea 4:6, 7). Strong words!

"They sow the wind and reap the whirlwind," Hosea cried (Hosea 8:7), yet the theme of his messages is not entirely doom and dismay. He offers a solution: "You must return to your God; maintain love and justice, and wait for your God always."

And how does God respond to Hosea's proposal? He says, "I will heal their waywardness and love them freely, for my anger has turned away from them" (Hosea 14:4).

There's good news, friend. No matter how far you have strayed from the right path, you can come back and find healing and forgiveness. It happened to Gomer long ago, and it can happen to you, too.

RESOURCE READING
Hosea 1

INSIGHT
The entire book of Hosea is a picture of God's great love for Israel, a truth that is reflected in Christ's love for the Church.

APPLICATION
What lesson do you see in the fact that Hosea was a loving, caring, forgiving husband when he had every right to reject Gomer because of her unfaithfulness?

When infidelity takes place, is divorce the answer? Or can there be forgiveness, restoration, and healing? Do you know of a situation that could have resulted in a broken home, but because of forgiveness and healing, a home was kept intact?

FOCUS
Paul

*"I am a Jew, born in Tarsus of Cilicia, but brought up in this city.
Under Gamaliel I was thoroughly trained in the law of our fathers
and was just as zealous for God as any of you are today."*
Acts 22:3

For a moment pretend that you have received a letter
from a friend who gives the following description of a person she recently met. She writes that he was "a man of
middling size, and his hair was scanty, and his legs were a
little crooked, and his knees were
far apart; he had large eyes, and
his eyebrows met, and his nose
was somewhat long."[22] Now, honestly, would you be much
impressed? Probably not, yet the
description I just gave you is the
only one in history with any cred-
ibility that tells us what the Apostle Paul looked like.

> *"Concentration,
> forgetfulness, and
> anticipation—
> the threefold secret
> of a great life."*

No wonder his critics said, "His letters are weighty and
forceful, but in person he is unimpressive and his speaking
amounts to nothing" (2 Corinthians 10:10). He was the
greatest convert Christ's gospel ever produced. He was the
theologian-missionary of the New Testament, and he traveled thousands of miles, often by foot, preaching that Christ
died for our sins, He was buried, and He rose again the
third day.

Paul's credentials were good—plenty good. He was of the
tribe of Benjamin, a Roman citizen by birth in the university

and cultural center of central Asia Minor, Tarsus. He had studied with Gamaliel and was zealous in his commitment to Judaism (see Philippians 3:5). His first encounter with believers in Jesus Christ was in Jerusalem, as he held the coats of those who stoned Stephen.

Shortly after that came the defining moment of his life. He was on his way to the city of Damascus, intending to arrest and harass believers, when Jesus Christ revealed Himself to him. His life was forever changed. No longer was he Saul of Tarsus, but Paul, the Apostle of Jesus Christ.

Three great missionary journeys took him throughout the Roman Empire, and almost everywhere Paul preached, he established a church. Then, as he moved on to another place, he wrote letters back, thus giving us the thirteen books in the New Testament that give us so many insights into the heart of this great man.

One of the warmest and most personal letters of Paul is his letter to believers in Philippi (the Book of Philippians). In this, Paul, I believe, revealed the source of his faith and the secret of his life. Here's what he said: "One thing I do: Forgetting what is behind and straining toward what is ahead, I press on toward the goal to win the prize for which God has called me heavenward in Christ Jesus" (Philippians 3:13, 14). In three words, he revealed the secret of his life: concentration, forgetfulness, and anticipation.

Concentration: This one thing–not a dozen, not even two; only one thing. No person can really succeed apart from being completely focused. In the realm of the spiritual, concentration is important as well. Jesus said, "No one can serve two masters. Either he will hate the one and love the other, or he will be devoted to the one and despise the other" (Matthew 6:24).

Then Paul mentions, "forgetting what is behind"–a wise forgetfulness of the past. Forget your failures; they only hurt you. Forget your victories; they are history. Forget your losses; they will cripple you.

His third secret was anticipation, looking ahead. Paul

put it graphically as he wrote that he was "straining toward what is ahead." He was using the imagery of his day, comparing life to a race and the world to a vast arena where athletes vied for the prize. There was no thought of turning back for Paul, of settling for less than his best effort. He was committed. He had burned the bridges behind him. There was but one way to go—God's way.

When you make the decision Paul made, there is only one way to go and that is up. Concentration, forgetfulness, and anticipation—the threefold secret of a great life. Make it your secret as well, today.

RESOURCE READING
Matthew 6:25-34

INSIGHT
Paul's life was completely focused. He knew what God wanted him to do, and he had made that his goal entirely. No person can really accomplish much apart from that same focus, whether it is in the realm of education, science, industry, or serving God.

APPLICATION
Make a list of the projects you are involved in right now and ask yourself whether or not you are spread too thinly.

What is the "main thing" in your life? On a scale of 1-10, how focused are you on your immediate goals?

FORTITUDE
Elijah

"Then the woman said to Elijah, 'Now I know that you are a man of God and that the word of the LORD from your mouth is the truth.' "
1 Kings 17:24

Spurgeon called him "The Iron Prophet." Ahab, the king of Israel, called him "the troubler of Israel" (1 Kings 18:17). His contemporaries called him things even a great deal less complimentary. His name, Elijah, meant "Yahweh is God," or "Jehovah is God," and certainly his life demonstrated that he believed that with no wavering.

"Despite my faults and failures, God will honor the desire of my heart to seek and serve my heavenly Father."

Like a hero who appears out of nowhere to rescue a damsel in a burning building, Elijah appears in Scripture with the suddenness of a thunderstorm on a spring day. But unlike a rainstorm that brings relief to a parched land, Elijah's sudden appearance in the courtyard of the palace brought panic and terror, as he announced that, as the Lord God lived, there would be no dew or rain except at his command.

Then he disappeared and could not be found! But the prophesies of this strange man were a hundred percent accurate. The few brief chapters covering the story of this great man are found in the first and second books of Kings, and they are punctuated with the miraculous, including the remarkable story of Elijah's being swept into heaven by a chariot of fire at the end of his life's work, a fitting exodus for a man who was no stranger to the supernatural.

There is a common misconception today that the Old Testament record is filled with marvelous events we would term supernatural, but the fact is that the supernatural events of the Old Testament were remarkable but uncommon occurrences, often separated by many, many years, when God was demonstrating the weakness of pagan religions and calling His people, Israel, to repentance and faith. One Bible expositor speaking of Elijah says, "One measure of his stature is found in the fact that he was the man raised up by God at the time that Baal worship threatened the very existence of the worship of Yahweh [God] in Israel. His place in the New Testament also underscores his importance."[23]

Elijah was to the prophets what Moses was to the giving of the law. Henry Halley offers this tribute to the man, saying, "Elijah's rare, sudden and brief appearances, his undaunted courage and fiery zeal, the brilliance of his triumphs, the pathos of his despondency, the glory of his departure, and the calm beauty of his reappearance on the Mount of Transfiguration, make him one of the grandest and most romantic characters Israel ever produced."[24]

From these grand words we might assume that Elijah was no less than the iron man Spurgeon alluded to, yet the fact is, what made this man so great is that he was human as we are, filled with the same emotions of fear and love, hatred and compassion, and yet had a heart after God that separated him not only from his contemporaries but from the generations of history as well.

Here's the perspective of James, the half brother of Jesus: "Elijah was a man just like us. . . ." Stop! Just like us? Exactly. Read the story of his life in 1 Kings 17 through 2 Kings 2 and see the highs and lows of a man who experienced the gamut of human emotions. Read how he pled with God to just let him die and fade from the scene. But James continues, "He prayed earnestly that it would not rain and it did not rain on the land for three and a half years. Again he prayed, and the heavens gave rain, and the earth produced its crops."

Elijah is the champion of the common man. He tells me that God will hear my heart cry; despite my faults and failures, He will honor the desire of my heart to seek and to serve my heavenly Father. Thank God for Elijah, friend, and take heart. The God of Elijah is not dead nor does He sleep. The God of Elijah is the everlasting Father who will meet you today. Don't forget it, not even for a moment.

RESOURCE READING
1 Kings 17

INSIGHT
The strength of Elijah's life is that he was completely human—just as we are today. His life tells us that the emotional, the spiritual, and the physical cannot be separated.

APPLICATION
How do you account for the fact that Elijah was on top of things spiritually on Mount Carmel but turned and ran when Jezebel decided to go after him?

Do you see something of Elijah in your heart?

GETTING IN SHAPE
Kenneth Cooper

"Do you not know that your body is a temple of the Holy Spirit, who is in you, whom you have received from God? You are not your own; you were bought at a price. Therefore honor God with your body."
1 Corinthians 6:19, 20

Dr. Kenneth Cooper is a man who practices what he preaches—literally! Cooper's name is synonymous with physical fitness. He has been advisor to presidents, astronauts, movie stars, and common people the world over. In Brazil, his fitness programs have been so popular that they call jogging "Coopering." He coined the term *aerobics,* which is now included in dictionaries. He himself has run more than 27,000 miles, twice the distance from the North to the South Pole.

"Our body truly is a temple of God and we owe it to Him and to ourselves to keep it in good shape."

Cooper's commitment to physical fitness goes far beyond the "this makes me look good" mentality that motivates most people to get into shape—a rather selfish motivation. His drive for fitness also includes a spiritual dimension. "Our body truly is a temple of God," says Cooper, "and we owe it to Him and to ourselves to keep it in good shape."

Though he is now in his seventies, Cooper's physical fitness ranks him as a man of forty-nine years of age, based on the scale he has developed at his clinic. How did Cooper do the transition from the pudgy, overweight man he was in med school, surviving on junk food and caffeine, to the lean, wiry man who strides through empty streets in the early hours of the morning?

He recalls that on a water skiing trip, his heart began to beat like a trip hammer to a rate of over 250 beats a minute. He thought he might even die; and at that moment, he said he knew God was trying to tell him something. God didn't have to speak twice. He began to change. He began to develop a program that came to be known as aerobic exercise. It worked for him, and he began to market it. He lost thirty-five pounds and ran a marathon. His love for physical fitness turned into a passion that he marketed very successfully.

But speaking engagements and travel began to take their toll on his spiritual life. Though he was raised in a church, his spiritual life was challenged by doubts and uncertainty. He felt that he just wasn't connected with God, so he began to change his pattern of feeding the inward man. He became involved in his church, but more importantly, he began spending thirty minutes every morning in God's Word, the Bible. He began praying and integrating spiritual lessons into his lectures. His life changed for the better, and subsequently he has been able to help thousands of people spiritually as well as physically.

Cooper believes that there is no greater motive for staying in shape than spiritual commitment. Bringing today's commentary home where you live, may I ask, "How physically fit are you?" The busyness of our lives today combined with the stress of living and working indoors can be lethal. So what can you do? First—realize that your body is the temple of the Holy Spirit. Take time to reread and study 1 Corinthians 6, where Paul makes a big point of the fact that God indwells your body, a temple of the Holy Spirit. Then get into some kind of a "temple fitness" program. Start eating right, which means cut out the fat and start moving. Walk up stairs instead of taking the elevator. Ride a bike instead of driving. Learn moderation, and prioritize your schedule.

Strike the phrase "I don't have time!" from your vocabulary, because you have time for what you really consider to be important. Dr. Kenneth Cooper practices what he preaches, and so can you. It may well keep you from a heart attack or even something worse, but in the meanwhile, you'll feel better and be a lot more pleasant to be around. That's a fact.

RESOURCE READING
Romans 12:1-3

INSIGHT
It is just as harmful to your body to allow it to become run down or abuse it through overeating as it is to abuse drugs or alcohol.

APPLICATION
How many periods of exercise of at least twenty minutes do you get each week?

Try walking up stairs instead of taking the elevator.

If you feel you don't have time for keeping your body in shape, what does that tell you about your priorities?

HARMONY
Arturo Toscanini

"Nothing in all creation is hidden from God's sight.
Everything is uncovered and laid bare before the eyes of Him
to whom we must give account."
Hebrews 4:13

When the NBC Symphony was about to be formed, David Sarnoff, chairman of NBC's board of directors, gave this instruction, "Do not hire away any players from existing orchestras because that would only weaken other orchestras."

"God knows our every heart cry and our every thought."

Under the direction of Arthur Rodzinski, a fine orchestra was assembled with one exception—the first clarinetist.

George Marek, vice president of RCA, tells how when Toscanini was about to arrive, everything was in order—except for one thing. The clarinetist was weak. Sarnoff was asked how they should handle the problem. Should Toscanini be left to find out for himself? Or should they warn him ahead of time. "Let's tell him," said Sarnoff. His colleagues said, "You tell him."

And that was how Sarnoff happened to be heading the delegation that went down to the ship with the grim news that the weakest link in the great NBC Symphony was a clarinetist who tried but didn't seem to have it. Before they could say anything, though, the great Toscanini greeted the delegation in his stateroom with the comment, "That's a fine orchestra you got together—very fine, all except the first clarinetist."

180

Sarnoff was taken aback. "Maestro, how did you find out?"

"I have been listening on a little shortwave radio I had in Milan," said Toscanini, "and I could tell."

The upshot of the story was that Toscanini began to work with the clarinetist, who in time became one of the world's greatest and stayed with the orchestra for seventeen years. How amazing that with no more fidelity than a little shortwave radio picking up a signal beamed across the Atlantic, the great Toscanini could pick out the sound of the first clarinetist. He not only could identify it above the other instruments, but he could tell exactly what the clarinetist needed to do to correct his imperfections.

If Toscanini can do that, we shouldn't be surprised that God can hear our feeble cries and can just as easily tell us what we need to do to correct our flaws. Toscanini was an incredible maestro, but he was only human. God, on the other hand, knows our every heart cry and our every thought. Hebrews 4:13 says, "Nothing in all creation is hidden from God's sight. Everything is uncovered and laid bare before the eyes of Him to whom we must give account." Toscanini, like God, was intent not on destroying the one who ruined the harmony—he wanted only to change the dissonance to the harmony of life.

It was not by chance that God made it possible for harmony to come into our lives. Music is not by happenstance. Before the foundation of the earth was ever laid, God provided for our dissonance to be made harmonious when He provided for humanity's redemption through Jesus Christ. The dissonance of life is the result of sin in that man rejected the fellowship that God first provided. When Christ gave Himself for us, He bridged the gulf of separation and made it possible for us to have harmonious fellowship with God.

The making of music is often slow and difficult; there are no shortcuts to harmony. The person who finds God's help is the person who bluntly and completely admits that sin has created dissonance and is willing to ask God to bring harmony to life. There is hope for the dissatisfied clarinetists in life who realize that only the divine Maestro of life can ever help them become the people they ought to be.

One last thought: Toscanini's imperfect clarinetist learned from the Master and stayed with the NBC Symphony for seventeen years. But the person who looks to Christ as Savior becomes a member of another group, the church made up of Christian believers, and membership in this group lasts forever. No, not a local church, but a part of that innumerable group of men and women who have found harmony in life as they have found God.

RESOURCE READING
Hebrews 4

INSIGHT
If Arturo Toscanini could detect the weakness of an instrumentalist by listening to very poor fidelity on a shortwave radio, never think that God does not know our flaws. And He is far more willing to help than any human could ever be.

APPLICATION
Does God hear prayer because we are good? Or does He answer prayer because we are His children?

Strive to develop patience with those who do not measure up to your standard of excellence. Ask God to help you in this area. Remember the difference that Toscanini made, helping a mediocre musician to become an excellent one.

HUMILITY
Mrs. Oswald Chambers

"He will be great and will be called the Son of the Most High. The Lord God will give him the throne of his father David, and he will reign over the house of Jacob forever; his kingdom will never end."
Luke 1:32, 33

The aphorism "Behind every successful man is a woman" was never any more true than it was of Oswald Chambers. Walk into just about any Christian bookstore, anywhere in the world, and you will find something authored by Chambers. His book, *My Utmost for His Highest*, has become the world's best-selling devotional book, translated into many languages. Yet had it not been for Gertrude Chambers, the little known and unrecognized driving force behind Chambers's writings, very few people today would even recognize the name Oswald Chambers.

"She believed that in Oswald's writings, people would see Christ."

Her name never appeared on any of the fifty books that bear the name Oswald Chambers. In the foreword to *My Utmost for His Highest*, she wrote, telling how the selections had come from various speaking engagements, yet she signed only with the initials "B.C."

Who was this remarkable woman who insisted on remaining entirely hidden behind the work of her husband? Her maiden name was Gertrude Hobbs, and her family called her Gertie or Truda; but when she became Mrs. Oswald Chambers, for whatever reason, her husband affectionately began calling her Biddy—a term of endearment not bearing the connotation the term has acquired in our day.

Before his death in 1917, a few of Chambers's sermons had been published. Some of them had been printed as booklets, but not a single book had gone to press. Oswald died as the result of complications following an appendectomy in Egypt, where he had been ministering to British troops in conjunction with the Y.M.C.A. His untimely death at the age of forty-three was mourned by thousands of people. So well loved was he by the men he ministered to that in spite of the fact he was not part of the military, he was given a full military burial in the old British cemetery in Cairo. At his funeral, battle-hardened soldiers wept over the passing of this gangly Scotsman.

A cable was dispatched from Cairo to family and friends at home, bearing the simple message "OSWALD IN HIS PRESENCE." That was all. Oswald and Biddy had been married for just seven years. And at the age of thirty-four, she had become a widow and the single mother of a little girl.

The real story behind the man's fame began at his death. Before she met Oswald, Biddy had become a stenographer. She could take shorthand faster than people could talk, and from the time she first began listening to her husband's messages, Biddy took shorthand notes—hundreds of them—never thinking that one day they would be transcribed to become the texts of his books and that she would become the editor-in-chief as well as publisher of many of them.

If you have been blessed by the writings of Oswald Chambers as I have been over the years, you would agree that the Christian world owes a tremendous debt of gratitude to a humble, gracious, and generally unknown woman whose gargantuan efforts have blessed so many. The story that I have shared with you today is told fully in a powerful new biography entitled *Oswald Chambers: Abandoned to God.*

It's published by Discovery House Publishers and authored by David McCasland, who has done us a great service by his careful research and honest evaluation.

Today, we think it somewhat strange that a woman–almost anonymously–would so devote herself to editing and publishing her husband's works. Yet Biddy wanted it that way. She believed that in Oswald's writings, people would see Christ. As David McCasland comments, it was "their utmost for God's highest."

May God give us more women with the heart of Biddy Chambers!

Resource reading
Proverbs 31

Insight
It is amazing what can be accomplished when we are willing to let God have the credit and are not concerned about our getting the glory. Apart from the selfless efforts of Biddy Chambers, the world today would have forgotten her husband, Oswald.

Application
D. L. Moody once said that there is no limit to what can be accomplished if a person doesn't want personal credit and gives the glory to God. Do you agree?

Do you think that using only her initials, "B.C.," was a mark of humility or a feeling of inferiority? Why do you feel as you do?

Do you think that if she were alive today, she would do it differently?

INTEGRITY

Joseph Jacobson

"Like a bad tooth or a lame foot is reliance on the unfaithful in times of trouble."
Proverb 25:19

If you had been falsely accused of a sex crime and had been thrown in prison with no real hope for release and you could have three wishes, what would you ask for? I suspect you would ask for: 1) your freedom, 2) your identity as a person, as opposed to being a number in a penal system, and 3) revenge on the person who framed you and sent you to prison unjustly.

"Situations that are not of our choosing, nor of our liking, either make or break us."

It happened to a man whose story is stranger than fiction. His name: Joe Jacobson. Well, that's not exactly how his name was listed on the role of Pharaoh's prison in Egypt long ago. His name was actually Joseph, and he was the son of Jacob.

The rest is exactly the truth. Here's the record: ". . . Now Joseph was well-built and handsome, and after a while his master's wife took notice of Joseph and said, 'Come to bed with me!' But he refused . . ." (Genesis 39:6-8). When he continued to refuse her advances, in anger she accused him of rape, and Joseph was framed and sent to prison.

There is no questioning the fact that Joseph would have preferred life outside the prison to what faced him. No person gives up his freedom easily and no doubt he would have preferred his identity and would have liked to be able to go back to his homeland where he had been kidnapped by his own brothers and forced into slavery. But there is no indication that Joseph lived for revenge.

There are lots of people, like Joseph, who are forced into situations that are not of their choosing. Some go to prison. Some face business reversals that make them slaves to schedules and harsh lenders who demand more than a fair share of repayment. Some are trapped by circumstances and by illnesses that put them in a prison of suffering or loneliness. Situations that are not of our choosing, nor of our liking, either make or break us. How we cope with them depends on how we view them.

Joseph could have become vindictive and angry. He could have said, "God, is this what I get for trying to do the right thing?" If he ever thought of it, he never voiced it. But there is a postscript to the story that makes all the difference. It says simply, "the Lord was with him; he showed him kindness and granted him favor in the eyes of the prison warden" (Genesis 39:21). Your anger with circumstances, and even with God, often keeps you from understanding and certainly acknowledging that God is with you. Better to know that God is with you and dwell in a prison than to wonder if He is with you and live in a palace.

Joseph learned some hard lessons while waiting for God to vindicate him and to give him his freedom—lessons that can make a great deal of difference in your life today. For one, he learned that you can't count on friends to help get you where you want to go. When the cupbearer found his freedom, assisted by Joseph, he promptly forgot his old friend; but Joseph learned he could count on God.

In time, Joseph was released and given the position of prime minister in the whole of Egypt, something that would have never happened had he not been in the place that cost him his freedom. Later, in assessing the wrong done to him by his brothers, Joseph told them, "You intended to harm me, but God intended it for good to accomplish what is now being done, the saving of many lives" (Genesis 50:20).

A final question: Can we, like Joseph, have the assurance that God is with us? You can if you are His child, for to those who belong to Him, Jesus said, "Never will I leave you; never will I forsake you" (Hebrews 13:5). And with that assurance, you can face what Joseph faced, and you can win. For one plus God always forms a team far stronger than any prison. Of that, you can be sure!

RESOURCE READING
Genesis 39

INSIGHT
Short-term gains have long-range consequences. Sacrificing the permanent on the altar of the immediate destroys character and affects a person's future.

APPLICATION
Could Joseph have justified what he was tempted to do?

Have you found that it is always easier to do wrong than to do right?

When you are tempted to do something that violates your conscience, how do you handle it? Do you see some insights into the way Joseph ran from temptation? See 1 Corinthians 10:13.

KNOWING GOD
Eric Liddell

"If you love those who love you, what reward will you get?
Are not even the tax collectors doing that?"
Matthew 5:46

When a major production company in Britain decided to do a film about an athlete of the 1920s, media experts predicted they would lose millions. But as it turned out, the picture became an Academy Award winner, and *Chariots of Fire* roused something of hero worship that the experts did not know was still there.

As good as the picture is, it falls short of actually demonstrating how great a man Eric Liddell really was—not in the sense of being a great athlete, but above and beyond that, of being a man great in character and integrity.

"What was his secret? He unreservedly committed his life to Jesus Christ as his Savior and Lord."

Chariots of Fire focuses on the contests that took Liddell to the 1924 Olympics in Paris, where his convictions kept him from running the 100-meter race, his specialty, because it was held on a Sunday. Instead, Liddell chose to run in the 400-meter race and was further handicapped because he drew an outside lane where there were no other runners to help him set his pace. Liddell, of course, raced to victory and later returned to his native city of Edinburgh as a great hero.

The story of Eric Liddell's life, however, had just begun at that point. Turning his back on a life as an international hero and one of Scotland's favorite sons, Liddell chose to follow in the steps of his father and became a missionary to China. In 1925 Liddell went to China to begin missionary work at the Anglo-Chinese Christian College. Although Liddell ran some, the Chinese could not quite understand the strange Anglo-Saxon who ran through the crowded streets. Since it was not culturally very acceptable to the Chinese, Liddell stopped running. He did, however, accept an invitation to Japan in 1928–three years later–to run in a 400-meter, international event. Running in his own unique style, Liddell outclassed his opponents and swept the field, to the delight of the Japanese crowd.

What the crowd did not know was that Liddell's ship back to China was due to leave fifteen minutes after the event. Liddell mystified officials and spectators alike by continuing to run under the grandstand and out of the stadium to a waiting taxi, which rushed him to the docks. The ship had already cast off from the jetty. In a final sprint, Liddell ran down the pier and leaped to the deck of the ship fifteen feet away.

Ironically, Liddell spent his last days with the Japanese, but as their prisoner. When the Japanese invasion of China seemed imminent, Liddell sent his family home but remained behind to work as a missionary. He was soon arrested and placed in a Japanese prisoner-of-war camp. A man who knew Liddell, who was also in that concentration camp, wrote the following: "For Eric Liddell death came just a few months before liberation. He was buried in the little cemetery in the part of the camp where others who had died during internment had been laid to rest. I remember being part of the honor guard made up of children from the Chefoo and Weihsein Schools. None of us will ever forget this man who was totally committed to putting God first, a man whose humble life combined muscular Christianity with radiant godliness.

"What was his secret? He unreservedly committed his life to Jesus Christ as his Savior and Lord. That friendship meant everything to him. By the flickering light of a peanut-oil lamp early each morning, he studied the Bible and talked with God for an hour every day. As a Christian Eric Liddell's desire was to know God more deeply; and as a missionary, to make Him known more fully."

That is the real Eric Liddell story.

RESOURCE READING
Hebrews 12

INSIGHT
God honors the person who honors Him.

APPLICATION
If Eric Liddell were alive today, do you think he would compete on Sunday?

Thousands of professional athletes do compete or play on Sundays. How do some of them seek to honor the Lord with their lives?

How do you feel when you hear a sports celebrity share his or her testimony publicly?

KNOWLEDGE OF THE WORD
H. A. Ironside

"My people are destroyed from lack of knowledge. . . . Because you have ignored the law of your God, I will also ignore your children."
Hosea 4:6

When Henry Allan Ironside was just two years old, his father died of typhoid fever and left the family destitute. His mother was forced to take in sewing to provide for the two little boys who were left without a daddy. Money was always tight, but biographers tell about one particular occasion when there was nothing to eat. Henry's mother, nonetheless, set the table and poured water. The two little boys and their mother sat down, and in spite of the fact there was no food on the table, they bowed their heads to give thanks to God for at least the water. But no sooner had they finished their prayer when a resounding knock at the door brought them to attention.

"A little knowledge of God is worth far more than a great deal of knowledge about Him."

A man who owed Mrs. Ironside some money was standing there with a bushel of potatoes. He asked if she would accept the potatoes instead of the money. God used this to meet their immediate needs. Though money was scarce, Mrs. Ironside gave to her two sons what money cannot buy—a spiritual heritage that included a thirst for God's Word.

At the age of nine or ten, Henry heard someone tell how he had made it a practice to read the Bible through every year. He decided to try it. The more he read, the more fascinated he became with the narratives of Scripture. At the age of fourteen, he "caught up with himself," as he described it. He had completed reading the entire Bible not once, but fourteen times, a feat that few adults have ever accomplished.

And what became of the teenager with a thirst for a knowledge of God's Word? Had you lived a century ago, you probably would know the answer, for Henry Ironside became known as H. A. Ironside, one of his day's most prominent preachers. His name was affixed to over a hundred books, mostly commentaries on the Book he had so grown to love. Thousands of men and women were mesmerized by the grasp of Scripture this man had and listened spellbound as he related the Scriptures in simple, ordinary language.

Question: Have you ever read the Bible through from cover to cover? "Well, that would take a long, long time," you may be thinking. Not so long. If you are an average reader, and took just fifteen minutes a day to read, you would read four to five chapters a day; and in eight months, you would have read the Bible from Genesis to Revelation.

"I look upon it as a lost day when I have not had a good time over the Word of God"; so commented George Mueller who was a busy, busy man yet found time to read the Bible through more than a hundred times.

According to the Bible Societies, whose primary task is to distribute the Bible to as many people as possible, there has never been a time when the Bible is more readily accessible to men and women. Yet an ignorance of this grand Book is often only multiplied by the number of translations a person has. Have you made a trip to a Christian bookstore recently? You may be amazed at the number of translations that are geared to specific groups socially—couples, singles, teens, and so forth—as publishers market this grand old Book.

Why bother reading this Book? Among the many reasons, consider this: No other book in the world will introduce you to God. If you want to know Him, read the Book. As J. I. Packer said, "A little knowledge of God is worth far more than a great deal of knowledge about Him." Remember, just fifteen minutes a day will put you through this book in less than a year. It's well worth the time, as H. A. Ironside's life clearly shows.

RESOURCE READING
Exodus 19

INSIGHT
Taking advantage of wasted time can result in doing far more profitable things, including making the knowledge of Scripture a reality.

APPLICATION
Have you ever read the Bible through in a year? Why not consider it?

Why do we consider someone like Ironside unusual or even strange?

LEADERSHIP
Golda Meir

"Deborah, a prophetess, the wife of Lappidoth, was leading Israel at that time. She held court under the Palm of Deborah between Ramah and Bethel in the hill country of Ephraim, and the Israelites came to her to have their disputes decided."
Judges 4:4, 5

Few would dispute the statement that Golda Meir has taken her place as one of the outstanding women of our century if not of all time. In her biography entitled *My Life*, Golda Meir told about her birth in terror-shrouded Russia, her stormy adolescence in Milwaukee, and her years sharing in the birth of a nation who proudly flies the six-pointed Star of David on its flag. In spite of the fact that her lifestyle and habits often differ from mine,

"How can you criticize a woman who asks only to bear her share of the load?"

I profoundly admire this woman whom David Ben Gurion humorously called "the best man in my cabinet."

In her book, Golda tells about herself and what she thinks of the contemporary feminist movement. Says Mrs. Meir, who was both a mother and grandmother several times, "I am not a great admirer of the kind of feminism that gives rise to bra burning, hatred of men, or a campaign against motherhood. . . . The fact is that I have lived and worked with men all my life, but being a woman has never hindered me in any way at all. It has never caused me unease or given me an inferiority complex or made me think that men are better than women—or that it is a disaster to give birth to children. Not at all. Nor have men ever given me preferential treatment. But what is true, I think, is that women, who want and need a life outside as well as inside the home have a much, much harder time than men because they carry a heavy double burden. . . . And the life of a working mother who lives without the constant presence and support of the father of her children is three times harder than that of any man I have ever met."

I am confident that any mother who works and has no husband to support her in the task of raising a family would agree. Thrust into public life almost from her marriage to Morris Goldson, Golda often felt pulled between her responsibility to her country, Israel, and to her children. When she traveled, she often felt guilty and wrote them regularly, "but," says Golda, "I was also never free of the feeling that I was injuring them in some way."

Golda Meir is often referred to as a modern Deborah, one of the judges who ruled Israel before the days of the kings. In fact, the precedence of a woman in Israeli government, though it happened more than three thousand years ago, was an encouragement to religious sectors of life to accept a woman prime minister.

Golda Meir's brand of equality for women lies pretty much in the scope of Judeo-Christian teaching, though it identifies more closely with a New Testament concept of a woman's role than with the ancient rabbis who used to pray daily, "I thank thee God that I am not a heathen nor a woman."

Speaking of those gallant women who helped carve a land flowing with milk and honey out of barren and desolate desert, Golda says, "Their struggle wasn't for equal 'civic' rights, which they had in abundance, but for equal burdens. They wanted to be given whatever work their male comrades were given—paving roads, hoeing fields, building houses or standing guard duty—not to be treated as though they were different and automatically relegated to the kitchen."

When Peter, one of the twelve, often identified as the Big Fisherman, wrote about women's roles, he told husbands to honor their wives as the "weaker vessel" (physically, since men possess greater upper body strength than do women) but that a husband should do this in love and kindness–not condescendingly. The relationship that both pleases God and produces happiness in a marriage is the one where two share the burdens of life as well as the joys and happiness. For only in this way are burdens lightened as two bear them together. Happiness is multiplied because two mutually share it. One thing is sure: Golda Meir's brand of women's equality leaves few men in the critics' corner. How can you criticize a woman who asks only to bear her share of the load?

RESOURCE READING
Judges 4

INSIGHT
Though women are often called "the weaker sex," the fact is that women often are tougher emotionally and stronger spiritually than are men.

APPLICATION
Read Ephesians 5 and notice the balance that Paul stresses in the relationship between men and women.

What other women do you know about who profoundly influenced society or history?

Do you agree with this statement: "The Bible teaches the diversity of the sexes and through diversity there is harmony." If that's true (which I believe it is), then why so much disharmony between men and women today?

LONELINESS
Auntie Wang

"Never will I leave you;
never will I forsake you."
Hebrews 13:5

It is said that behind every great man is a great woman. Unquestionably, that was true of Wang Ming Dao. The woman, Deborah Wang, a frail but vibrant saint, endured what no woman should ever have to face. Her husband, Wang Ming Dao, was one of the unofficial architects of the house church movement in China. When her husband was sentenced to prison for what the Chinese government termed "anti-revolutionary" activities, his wife followed. For twenty years, this saintly woman was in a separate prison, facing the bitter cold of northern Chinese winters with thin clothes and insufficient food, but she never complained.

" I am sure of one fact: While she was alone, she was not lonely."

In 1989 I met the Wangs for the first time. I'll never forget the afternoon I sat in the humble little apartment in Shanghai and listened to them recount their experiences. While I deeply admired and venerated Wang Ming Dao, I was drawn to the strength of this saintly woman whose smile came from her heart. As she talked about the years of imprisonment, I asked, "Did you ever lose hope?" (After all, twenty years of separation from the one you loved so deeply, with very little news and few letters, is a long time.) Her eyes spoke far more than her answer as she said, "No, never!"

After the Wangs were released from prison, their home became a refuge for those who needed encouragement and counsel. God only knows how many cups of tea Auntie Wang (as her friends called her) served to weary men and women who traipsed up the stairs to their flat for encouragement and help.

What a woman! Two weeks after her husband passed away at the age of ninety-one, I again visited Auntie Wang. The ashes of her late husband were in an urn on the table near the chair Brother Wang had used as a pulpit to share the Word. My son-in-law and I sought to comfort her with some of my favorite passages of Scripture. But it was Auntie Wang who really comforted us. She was in her mid-eighties. Successful surgery a few months before had removed one of the cataracts from her eyes, and few details escaped her. When a small piece of paper fell from my lap, it was she who quickly leaned over to pick it up.

"Auntie Wang," I said, "I will pray that you will not be lonely."

Pausing for just a moment, she spoke with a clear and resolute tone of voice, "I will not be lonely; I was not lonely before." It was what she didn't say that spoke the loudest. On a previous visit, she told me that she had seen her husband only three times during the twenty years of imprisonment. That one word, "before," said so much. I knew what she was thinking.

Those words rang in my ears when a close friend told how Auntie Wang had developed pneumonia and was taken to a Shanghai hospital. With no rooms available, she was given a temporary bed in a hallway, and there in the early hours of the morning on April 18, 1992, she met Him who had been her stay and companion for so many years. As the leaves of the trees were budding, following the cold of a Shanghai winter, Deborah Wang made her entrance into the presence of the Lord, where a faithful and devoted husband awaited her.

The saddest part to me was that she couldn't be surrounded by friends and flowers when the angel sweetly took her hand and escorted her across the threshold of death. But I am sure of one fact: While she was alone, she was not lonely. She had the promise of her Lord, who said, "And surely I am with you, always . . ." (Matthew 28:20). Deborah Wang experienced that, both in life and in death.

RESOURCE READING
2 Timothy 3

INSIGHT

Jesus Christ has promised never to leave or forsake His own (Matthew 28:20, Hebrews 13:5). Though others may abandon you, the presence of Christ will always be there; and in our darkest hours, we can find His unmeasured strength and presence.

APPLICATION

In your Bible underline the passages referred to in the insight passage. Better yet, memorize them.

Why is it that we, at times, don't feel the presence of the Lord? Is this a feeling to be experienced or a fact that is to be accepted and appropriated?

LONELINESS
Ann Scheiber

*"Jesus. . .watched the crowd putting their money into the temple
treasury. Many rich people threw in large amounts. But a poor
widow came and put in two very small copper coins,
worth only a fraction of a penny."*
Mark 12:41, 42

Ann Scheiber was a lonely little woman who pretty much
stayed to herself. She lived in a tiny little apartment with
paint peeling off the walls and badly in need of repairs. A
product of the Depression, Ann
was of the old school, who lived
on a small pension and a government stipend. She never spent
money on clothes. Without close
friends, she seemed to be a real
loner. In her years of government
service, she was never promoted
and in all her lifetime received only a token pay increase.

*"Do your giving
while you're
living."*

Neighbors, however, knew that every day without fail,
she made a trip to the local library. Though they didn't know
it–the librarian did, however–she always read a financial
journal, *The Wall Street Journal,* from cover to cover. Only one
person really knew how brilliant she was–her stock broker
who saw her nominal investment of $5,000 grow into a for-
tune of over $22 million.

At her death she left her entire estate to a local Jewish
university she neither attended nor had ever visited. She
became their benefactor because she wanted others of the

same ethnic background to be possibly spared the discrimination that she had felt in her lifetime.

When she died, people asked, "How did she do it?" And the answer was that she invested in blue chip companies and major corporations, never living on her interest and profits. She plowed her dividend back into the purchase of more stock. But those who ask only how she was so successful making money have missed the whole point of her sad life.

Her stock broker knew her better than any other person and he observed, "She was obviously very intelligent and very unhappy. It would have been so much happier for her if she had done it [given the money while she was living] so she could see the benefits accrue to others."

There is another sad thing about this lonely little lady. Her own existence could have been so much more comfortable had she used even a small amount of her earnings for herself.

Expanding her portfolio was the driving force of her life, though she gained nothing from it save the satisfaction of knowing she was doing what millions would like to have done. She died, having lived over a century, and in the process her life was as barren and empty as her apartment.

Money, of course, does not buy friends, and perhaps her generosity will allow some who otherwise might never have had that opportunity to receive training in the medical college she endowed. But by sitting on her investments she also deprived those who were eventually helped of the opportunity of expressing gratitude and thanks.

Nothing is stranger than life! There is one thing commendable that needs to be said about Ann Scheiber. At least she had a will instructing that her estate be put to work for the good of humanity, something more than one person has failed in doing. She was a hero, for she changed others' lives with her selfless saving.

I'm thinking of another little lady who helped her nephew through seminary, and then as he served as a missionary she sent him token gifts. Over the years, she collected stock from the Kodak company where she worked, and when she died–without a will–her considerable estate went to the state, and relatives, including those whom she really wanted to help, received nothing. Unfortunately, the law never recognizes the force of good intentions.

As someone well put it, "Do your giving while you're living so you're knowing where it's going." Not bad advice. Yes, not bad. Don't put off changing the world.

RESOURCE READING
Mark 12:41-44

INSIGHT
Relationships with people are of far greater value than stocks and bonds.

APPLICATION
If Anne Scheiber had been able to overcome her sense of isolation and loneliness, how would her life have been different?

Do you know someone who is lonely? Is there anything you can do to help that person?

OBEDIENCE
Amy Carmichael

"Charm is deceptive, and beauty is fleeting;
but a woman who fears the LORD is to be praised."
Proverbs 31:30

Amy Carmichael was a woman who didn't fit the mold, a fact that resulted in a lot of problems for people who were more committed to order and tradition than to the teaching of God's Word. If you have never been introduced to Amy Carmichael, I highly recommend Elisabeth Elliot's book, *A Chance to Die.* A former missionary herself, Elliot is quick to reveal her prejudice—she has Carmichael on a pedestal and, I think, rightly so. Yet Elliot is candid in accurately portraying the humanity as well as the charity in the life of this woman, who was one of the greatest of all missionaries in modern history.

"It is not at all that we think that ours is the only way of living, but we are sure that it is the way meant for us. . . ."

Born on December 16, 1867, on the north coast of Ireland, Amy Carmichael was never destined to mediocrity. From her strict upbringing, Amy quickly learned that more was expected of her than others. While other children were given peppermint candies to pass away time in the long church services, the Carmichael children were expected to sit in quiet obedience.

In the early years of her missionary experience, Amy seemed to flounder. She first served in Japan, then China, then Ceylon, then back to England, where no small amount of pressure was put on her to stay home. Finally God sent her to India, and there she spent the rest of her life.

Among the many things that Amy Carmichael will be remembered for is her work among the children, especially the girls who were forced into temple prostitution. She became part of the work that had been established at Dohnavur, and that name eventually became synonymous with what she did.

If the greatness and complexity of this woman could be captured in three words (which I think is not probable), I would chose these: 1) obedience, 2) loyalty, and 3) tenderness. From the beginning she had a fierce and unswerving obedience to the Word of God and what she felt was God's will for her life, something traditional missionaries neither understood nor appreciated. In the early years of her work, there was a "Get-Amy-Carmichael-out-of-India" movement among missionaries and other Indian Christians. "She was a thorn in their sides," writes Elizabeth Elliot, because she donned Indian saris and insisted on doing the work of a servant.

Out of obedience to the will of God came loyalty to those with whom she worked. She refused to speak against her critics and would not allow her çoworkers to do so either. She insisted on absolute, unflagging loyalty to her brothers and sisters in Christ, no matter how they appeared to be enemies of the work.

In her book, *Roots*, she wrote, "It is not at all that we think that ours is the only way of living, but we are sure that it is the way meant for us. . . ." She did not believe that you could pray with someone or for someone and speak harshly of the same one. She wrote, "But how can you pray—really pray, I mean—with one against whom you have a grudge or whom you have been discussing critically with another? Try it. You will find it cannot be done." In the dining room of the missionary home of Dohnavur hung a sign that read, "May the absent one always be safe at our table!"

Finally, tenderness marked this great woman's life, but not the kind of tenderness often associated with weakness.

Hers was more that of an iron fist in a velvet glove. She would wade through a hostile crowd of shouting, angry people to rescue a little girl from temple prostitution, yet weep openly with the child over the pain and hurt she had sustained.

At the age of 84, on January 18, 1951, Amy Carmichael slipped into the presence of the Lord after a long illness. Under a tamarind tree, in a grave marked only by the Indian word for mother, AMMAI, lie the remains of a woman who was as much a saint as any woman who ever lived.

As I've read and pondered the life of Amy Carmichael, I asked myself, "Was this woman like a meteor that streaks across the darkened sky, something that will never be repeated, having burned itself out? Or are there others made out of this sterner stuff who are willing to give themselves without reservation to the cause of God and suffering humanity?"

I refuse to believe that the God who so challenged an Irish lass to go to India is not still calling women to serve Him. Perhaps you are one of them.

RESOURCE READING
Jeremiah 1

INSIGHT
God is still calling those who are brave enough, tough enough, and love Him enough to hear His call and say, "Yes, Lord, I'll follow You wherever You lead me."

APPLICATION
Have you ever asked yourself why it is often women alone who take on the tough task? Why are most missionaries (though certainly not all) women? Are women more sensitive to God's voice, or are men stubborn?

Have you ever prayed, "Lord, whatever You want me to do is what I want. Just show me, and make it very clear"? Never be afraid to take that position. The safest place in the world is in the center of God's will.

OPTIMISM
Bill Eaton

"Unless the Lord builds the house, its builders labor in vain."
Psalm 127:1

Most people called it "an absolute disaster!" But Bill Eaton called it an "adventure!" It all started following several weeks of drenching rain, when California took on the appearance of an Asian monsoon. The rains finally softened the earth beneath Bill and Lee Eaton's family home, and a massive hole began to swallow up their four-bedroom house, which had been home for twenty-three years. That home was full of memories, too. Here their family grew up. Christmases and birthdays, a wedding and scores of good memories were all associated with the pale green house.

"It's not a disaster; it's an adventure."

To make matters worse, a wrecking crew got the wrong address and punched several massive holes in the roof before they discovered they were tearing down the wrong house.

Yet Bill says, "It's not a disaster; it's an adventure!" Talk about optimism! And how does Lee feel? She's with Bill. "It looks ominous to me right now," she said, adding, "but it's not an impossible situation."

How do people stay so positive when insurance won't cover the loss and they are not exactly rich? Bill and Lee Eaton are not the average sort of people. They have an optimism born of faith. I know because for a number of years this gracious gentleman, who is an accountant by profession, has helped scores of people with their problems, including our staff at Guidelines, often without taking anything in return.

Naturally, Bill and Lee weren't exactly joyful when a city building inspector condemned their house as unsafe. They had to pick up what they could and gingerly move out, careful not to make too much noise or create too much stress for the rickety house. Even as they packed, they could feel the house moving under their feet.

What would be a disaster to some is a challenge, an opportunity to Bill and Lee Eaton! As I heard about the Eaton's positive optimism, I remembered that the Chinese character for crisis is a combination of two other characters that mean "danger" and "opportunity"!

There is an optimism born of faith when you understand that there is more to life than just what you see. Long ago, Paul spoke of this, saying, "For our light and momentary troubles are achieving for us an eternal glory that far outweighs them all. So we fix our eyes not on what is seen, but on what is unseen. For what is seen is temporary, but what is unseen is eternal" (2 Corinthians 4:17, 18).

Years ago, I stood outside a burning home. Flames were coming out of the doors and windows as a young couple stood watching, obviously overwrought with grief, having lost everything they had. The mother was sobbing, and the dad was wringing his hands. I arrived, hoping to help, just as the father, a young man in his late twenties, was saying, "My God, everything we have is lost!" A little girl, about four or five reached up and took the hand of her daddy and said, "Everything's not lost, Daddy; you got Mommy and me!"

Frankly, everybody doesn't handle trouble like Bill and Lee Eaton, but then Bill and Lee have something going for them some folks don't have either—a positive faith in God that affects their value system. They realize some things are more important than just a house. You see their home survived the destruction of the house. They know that the psalmist was right when he wrote, "Unless the Lord builds the house, its builders labor in vain" (Psalm 127:1).

With faith in God we see that which is invisible and it takes us beyond our losses. That's the stuff that will help Bill and Lee Eaton rebuild the house that is their home.

RESOURCE READING
Psalm 27

INSIGHT
An optimism born of faith isn't wishful thinking but is based on the fact that God is a good God and no matter what happens, He can turn evil into good in our lives.

APPLICATION
If your home had burned down, do you think you would look upon it as an opportunity or a disaster?

To what degree does your faith in God influence and affect your outlook on life?

Overcoming
Nehemiah

"The God of heaven will give us success."
Nehemiah 2:20

Anyone who has ever undertaken a building project knows that what looks great on paper never takes the same shape in the real world. I don't know if Nehemiah had ever heard of "Murphy's law"–whatever can go wrong will go wrong. There must have been a Persian equivalent, because a man who lived 2600 years ago experienced the full force of that reality.

"When challenged and confronted with danger, he prayed, and he kept on doing what he knew was right."

Possibly, the name Nehemiah doesn't ring a bell with you, in the event you read only the New Testament; but an Old Testament book, sandwiched between Ezra and Esther, contains the story of this great man's life and what he accomplished, which is well worth discovering.

Nehemiah was a man with a mission. He had papers from King Artaxerxes of Persia that would allow him to build the wall surrounding Jerusalem. Sounds like a nice project, right? Put in a garden and get someone to plant flowers! Everybody would be happy, right? Dead wrong!

Nehemiah knew it wouldn't be easy. When he arrived in Jerusalem, he told no one of his intentions. Why? He knew that opposition would immediately mount. Finally, he brought together the leadership and gave it to them straight. He described the disgrace and dangers that resulted from having no wall around the city, and they responded (like babes without knowledge), "Let us rise and build!"

More than one person has aspired to build a castle, but having faced the reality of the real world, settled for a shack. It's called "compromise"–giving up on your dream to settle for second best.

No sooner had Nehemiah begun the project when he was faced with severe antagonism. Local political adversaries tried to stop them. As the work progressed, the opposition tried scorn and ridicule. "What they are building–if even a fox climbed up on it, he would break down their wall of stones!" (Nehemiah 4:3) Their enemies mocked in derision.

But stop building they did not!

When the wall was nearly half built, the enemies mobilized and began to attack them. Undaunted, Nehemiah instructed that half the people should stand guard while half worked on the wall.

Finally, the wall was built and everybody lived happily ever after! Right? Wrong again! As the wall was going up, trouble broke out among those who were building, as some of the folks took advantage of their brethren by charging them high prices. The rich got richer and the poor got poorer, but in all of this Nehemiah didn't quit or give in to weariness.

When Tobiah and Sanballet, the chief antagonists of the project, knew that their resistance was failing, they tried to trick Nehemiah into a peace conference. "Come," they invited, "let us meet together in one of the villages on the plain of Ono." Again, doesn't peace make sense? But Nehemiah realized this was a trick, and they sought to kill him. "I am carrying on a great project and cannot go down," he replied (Nehemiah 6:2, 3). Four times came the invitation, and four times came the reply.

If Nehemiah were alive today and we should ask him, "What lessons did you learn from all of this?" surely he would reply: "I learned that God will honor His Word, and that it is no sin to grow tired or weary; the sin comes when you yield and compromise your conviction. I learned that the greatest enemies, however, are not those outside the walls. They are the ones within, which we later experienced when we ourselves yielded to what we knew was wrong."

Throughout his life, Nehemiah was a man of prayer. When challenged and confronted with danger, he prayed, and he kept on doing what he knew was right. Yes, God give us more Nehemiahs today.

RESOURCE READING
Nehemiah 2, 3

INSIGHT

The God who strengthened Nehemiah will also strengthen the hand of the person who will trust Him, whether it be in business, the classroom, the church, or the home.

APPLICATION

Do you see parallels between the enemies of Israel today and those who faced Nehemiah long ago?

What strength do you see in this man's life?

Why did he survey the walls under the darkness of the night before he called a meeting?

Overcoming

Fred Whiteman

*"Why then be downcast? Why be discouraged and sad? Hope in God!
I shall yet praise him again. Yes, I shall again praise him for his help."*
Psalm 42:5, TLB

When I asked Fred Whiteman how old he was, he replied,
"I'm forty-seven on the outside and thirty-one on the inside.
I've had more trouble than most senior citizens, and I still
look at life through the eye of a child." What kind of an
answer was that? Chronologically, Fred had seen forty-seven
birthdays. Within his chest cavity
beat the heart of a man thirty-one
years old—the result of having had a
heart transplant. Had Fred really
seen more trouble that most senior
citizens?

> *"God will meet you
> at the point of
> your deepest need."*

Within a six-month period of
time, Fred lost his best friend, who
died with cancer of the liver, his mother died, and his wife
died, having gone to work perfectly healthy one morning
and then dying later that day in what most would term a
"freakish accident." In addition to that, Fred's heart failed
him; and even then, following a successful heart transplant,
Fred himself faced surgery for cancer, as well as being sued
by the bank where his wife worked. And all of this happened to one man in a period of months. Yes, I think you
could say very fairly that Fred has known more trouble
than most people experience in a lifetime. When Fred gets
to heaven, he may well have some advice for Job himself.

Now, had all of this left Fred bitter and cynical? Not at all, but you do get the feeling talking to Fred that you are talking with a man who has nothing to fear from life because he has faced its bitter challenge and has found the strength that comes from the God who helped him meet the challenge. Anyone who faces the fire as he has either comes through as gold refined by the fire or is burned up by the heat.

How does Fred explain what he has been through? Fred falls back on the fact that we are made by a loving God "for His glory," and he quotes Bob Harrington, who said, "When we can't figure it out, we have to faith it out." Unlike some who face times of difficulty and have nothing to fall back on, Fred is a committed believer in Jesus Christ and has spent most of his life serving the Lord.

The words of a popular song go, "When all hope is gone, go into your room and turn on a sad song." Instead, Fred did what the psalmist recommended, who cried out, "When my heart is overwhelmed, lead me to the rock that is higher than I" (Psalm 61:2, KJV). "I never had a moment," says Fred, "when there was no hope!"

Why should one man have so many difficulties? Fred doesn't fully understand, but neither is he spending time trying to solve that question. I suppose anyone who faces what he has gone through becomes somewhat philosophical about the valley through which he has traveled. He quickly says that difficulty does several things for a person: (1) It gives you a knowledge of yourself that also makes you aware of your intense need for God. It makes you fully understand your humanity and the fact that we live one heartbeat away from eternity. (2) Difficulty produces character in your life and refines the integrity of the heart. It strips you of the desire to play games and pretend to be what you are not. (3) And it allows God to use you as a witness to other people, showing them that at the point of our deep need, God can and does meet His children.

When Fred was asked to talk with three different psychiatrists, one of whom had asked why he just didn't commit suicide, Fred began to explain his relationship with Jesus Christ. All three psychiatrists, professionals who deal with grief and difficulty every day, were left in tears.

Fred doesn't understand why some face difficulty and grow with it, as he has, and why some face similar circumstances and wither. But he does know that God will meet you at the point of your deepest need. He's been there and learned that firsthand.

RESOURCE READING
Job 1

INSIGHT
Difficulties only show you how big your God is.

APPLICATION
If you faced a fraction of the problems that Fred has faced, would you be bitter? Or would you strive to maintain the same attitude that he has?

Make a note of the three things difficulty does for you and apply this to your life.

OVERCOMING

Isaac Watts

"Lord, thou hast been our dwelling place in all generations. Before the mountains were brought forth, or ever thou hast formed the earth and the world, even from everlasting to everlasting, thou art God."
Psalm 90:1,2, KJV

He had a nose with a crook, about two sizes larger than the rest of his face. Though he had a beautiful, artistic soul, Isaac Watts's personage wasn't much to look at. One observer noted that "his head seemed too large for his five foot tall body; his small, piercing eyes and hooked nose did not enhance his appearance any either."

"Where the Psalmist describes religion by the fear of God, I have often joined faith and love to it."

He never married, though as the result of reading his poetry, one woman did fall in love with him. A romantic courtship by correspondence followed, but when she met him, her love quickly dissipated to a friendship that didn't include matrimony.

At the age of four he learned Latin from his father. Eventually he read Greek, Hebrew, and French. He was brilliant, approaching the level of genius, but because he refused allegiance to the Church of England, he was denied entrance to the University of Cambridge and Oxford. He attended an academy sponsored by independent Christians.

Nonetheless, he left his mark on the world as have few men. He wrote more than six hundred hymns, including some still sung today. He authored scores of publications, including fifty-two books on subjects as diverse as logic, grammar, pedagogy, ethics, astronomy, geography, and theology.

As a little boy, Isaac, one of nine children, had a gift for verse and often spoke in rhymes. So annoyed was his father that, on one occasion, the young Isaac was told to stop this or else he would be punished. Sure enough, when he continued, his father began to spank him and Isaac cried out, "O father, do some pity take, And I will no more verses make."

At the age of seven he wrote his first hymn. Though he felt resentment and rejection, Isaac was a person of deep compassion, sensitivity, and feeling. Those emotions found body and soul in the hymns that came from his pen. Yet the focus of his energy was never, "Look at me! See how I hurt." "Sure I must fight if I would reign," he wrote. "Increase my courage, Lord; I'll bear the toil, endure the pain, Supported by thy word."

A study of some of the hymns that came from his pen shows that most of what he wrote embodied the great themes of Scripture: the faithfulness of God, His majesty, His wisdom, and the strength of God's Word—themes that have been sadly neglected in our day.

His hymn "O God, Our Help in Ages Past" was based on Psalm 90, the words of Moses, who wrote, "Lord, thou hast been our dwelling place in all generations. Before the mountains were brought forth, or ever thou hast formed the earth and the world, even from everlasting to everlasting, thou art God" (Psalm 90:1, 2, KJV).

His beautiful hymn, often sung at Christmastime, "Joy to the World," is patterned after Psalm 98, where the psalmist wrote, "Make a joyful noise unto the Lord, all the earth. . ." (Psalm 98:4, KJV). Watts believed that the Psalms should be interpreted in the full light of the New Testament. ". . .Where the Psalmist describes religion by the fear of God," he wrote, "I have often joined faith and love to it."

It would be well worth your time to take a hymnal and look up the hymns of Isaac Watts. Reflected in his soul, you will see the image of God. At his death on November 25, 1748, a monument was erected to Watts among the great and mighty in Westminster Abbey. However, his greatest tribute is the fact that after almost two hundred and fifty years (nearly ten generations), we still sing his hymns and songs of praise.

RESOURCE READING
Psalm 100

INSIGHT
Your appearance has nothing to do with your worth. Isaac Watts knew his nose was large. This, however, probably added to the sensitivity that was reflected in his ministry. Thus, a handicap became an asset.

APPLICATION
Strive to look beyond physical appearance to the soul within. Looking beyond the physical, we see the real person. Strive to do this with people you know who are different, whether they come from a different culture or background, or look or dress differently from you.

Does physical appearance increase or decrease emotional sensitivity?

OVERCOMING
John Mark

" 'Come, follow me,' Jesus said, 'and I will make you fishers of men.'
At once they left their nets and followed him."
Mark 1:17-18

If the life of any person ever demonstrated that success is never final and failure is never fatal, it was a man who lived in Jerusalem in the first century. His name was John Mark, often referred to as just Mark. We are introduced to him when a prayer meeting was held in his mother's home in Jerusalem. And on that occasion he met a man who was to leave a deep impression on his life, Peter, who had just miraculously been released from prison. All of this you can read about in the New Testament Book of Acts, chapter 12.

"Success is never final and failure need never be fatal!"

About the same time persecution arose under Nero, Paul took Mark along with his cousin Barnabas and started his first missionary journey. But things didn't go well. Perhaps part of it was the food. Perhaps the weariness of travel contributed to it. But for sure, it was homesickness. John Mark quit and came home.

Paul didn't like it. He didn't want a quitter in the ranks. When it came time for the next journey, Paul wouldn't allow Mark to join him and Barnabas; so the two cousins dropped out, and Barnabas took Mark and went to Cyprus.

If they had logged air miles in those days, Mark would have been a gold card frequent flyer, but travel was by ship and by foot. After the Cyprus experience, Mark returned and spent time with Peter, whose style deeply impressed this young man so much that Mark eventually wrote the manuscript we know as the second Gospel in our Bibles today–the Gospel of Mark.

Beginning to see how failure doesn't have to be fatal? In your New Testament you will find four books often referred to as Gospels–Matthew, Mark, Luke, and John. But in reality there is but one gospel recorded by four different men with different viewpoints.

The shortest is the one Mark wrote, consisting of but sixteen chapters. Sometimes called, "the businessman's Gospel," it is fast moving, almost staccatolike, a series of encounters with Jesus Christ joined together by a Greek word, *euthus,* which means "straightway," "immediately," or "right away."

Mark reflects the world view of his travels and seems to write from a Roman viewpoint. He pictures Christ as a servant whose birth is unimportant. Whereas Matthew and Luke devote quite a bit of narrative to the birth of Jesus Christ, tracing His lineage and telling of the events surrounding His birth, Mark skips the event entirely and immediately begins to describe the deeds of Jesus Christ. Some fourteen times he refers to Him as "the son of man."

The foreword to the Gospel of Mark in one study Bible says, "Matthew and Luke present what might be described as a series of colored slides, while Mark's Gospel is like a motion picture of the life of Jesus." Actually what Mark wrote is not a biography but selected events in the life of Jesus Christ, so that all might know the servant became the Savior of the world.

Was the rift between Paul and this young man ever healed? When Paul was languishing in prison shortly before his execution in A.D. 67, he wrote to Timothy and asked him to come and to bring John Mark with him.

Looking beyond what Mark wrote, you see the heart of a man deeply dedicated and committed to the cause of

Jesus Christ. He emphasizes the importance of commitment and decisive action, possibly acknowledging his own failure in his early years.

Sixteen action-filled chapters give you a new appreciation for the Servant-Savior Mark wrote about. Read it for yourself.

RESOURCE READING
Mark 1:1-20

INSIGHT

Success is never final and failure need never be fatal! A mistake or a failure is often a learning experience taking us in the right direction.

APPLICATION

Someone said that the person who eventually gets to the top climbs the ladder of success "wrong by wrong." Do you agree? In other words, people who never make mistakes, never learn and never reach their goals.

"Quititis"–the attitude of "I think I'll just quit"–never allows you to learn from failures. Your outlook on life makes the difference. In our spiritual lives, God forgives failures (1 John 1:9) and then gives us His grace and strength to succeed and overcome the weakness or flaw that resulted in wrongdoing.

OVERCOMING

D. L. Moody

"I sought the Lord, and he answered me;
he delivered me from all my fears."
Psalm 34:4

Although this book can't contain the exploits of all my heroes, certainly it would be incomplete if I did not include a man who had a great heart for God, who radically challenged two continents for God, and laid the foundation of a multifaceted Christian ministry that has encompassed the world and continues to grow even stronger with the passing of time.

"Out of the depths
I cried unto my Lord,
and He heard me
and delivered me
from all my fears."

Dwight Lyman Moody was a hero in his day. He's still at the top of my list. But I've chosen to include a little-known incident in the life of this great man which demonstrates that heroes are not superhuman individuals, but normal people who struggle with the very emotions and feelings we have. They simply are not overcome by them.

A century ago, Moody was as well known as Billy Graham is today. All over the world English-speaking people had been affected by this forceful, energetic evangelist.

In the fall of 1892, Moody boarded a ship from Southampton headed toward New York. Three days into the journey, disaster struck. In his memoirs, Moody told how he was lying on his bunk, reflecting on his good fortune, and how he had never been involved in an "accident of a serious nature."

At the very moment he was thinking about it, Moody was startled by a loud noise and the vessel began to shudder as though it had been "driven on a rock."

It was serious, very serious. The large shaft that drove the propeller had broken and smashed through the side of the ship. Water began pouring in and soon it became apparent that the ship would sink.[25]

D. L. Moody was no stranger to dangerous situations. In the American Civil War, he had been shot at, but the bullets missed him. He was in Chicago during the great cholera epidemic and went with doctors to visit the sick and dying, but the sickness spared him. Moody said, "I remember a case of smallpox where the sufferer's condition was beyond description, yet I went to the bedside of that poor sufferer again and again. . . . In all this I had no fear of death. But on the sinking ship it was different. It was the darkest hour of my life."[26]

Moody had never before known the cold, gnawing reality of fear. By his own testimony, "I had thought myself superior to the fear of death," but that illusion quickly vanished. "I could not endure it," he said. Moody went to his cabin and on his knees poured out his heart to God in prayer. What happened? Moody said, "God heard my cry, and enabled me to say, from the depths of my soul, 'Thy will be done!' "

Moody had gotten through to God and his fear left him. He went to bed and fell asleep almost immediately. He said, "I . . . never slept any more soundly in all my life. I can no more doubt that God gave answer to my prayer for relief than I can doubt my own existence."[27]

At three in the morning, Moody's son awakened him with the good news that a steamer had heard their distress signals, and seven days later, they were towed into safe harbor.

"The darkest hour of my life" was the way Moody described it. Keep in mind this was a man who had preached to hundreds of thousands. In his day he spoke to more people than any man alive. He was a man who had never before experienced real fear. Moody said it was not because he feared dying, but he feared leaving behind his family and the friends whom he loved.

Two thoughts: First, no one is immune from the dark hours of the soul when fear gnaws at your innermost being. Even heroes who are spiritual giants are susceptible to the weaknesses of the flesh. I take great heart in James saying that "Elijah was a man just like us" (James 5:17). The second thought is that in the dark hours of our lives, we must yield to the will of our Father, for in doing so, we are reminded that we are His children and He has promised to keep us.

Moody said, "Out of the depths I cried unto my Lord, and He heard me and delivered me from all my fears," echoing the words of David in Psalm 34. Scores of men and women can testify to the fact that at the darkest hour of their life, God broke through, giving them peace and courage to say, as did Moody, "Thy will be done!"

Are you in the midst of the darkest hour of your life? As you say, "Thy will be done!" you will sense His presence and find His deliverance.

RESOURCE READING
James 4

INSIGHT
Courage is fear that has prayed. Heroes are not exempt from fear, but they pray and stand their ground instead of turning and running.

APPLICATION
Describe at least one time when you were fearful. What happened? How did you overcome your fear?

Does this chapter help dispel the thought that heroes are without the same emotions and feelings everyone experiences?

OVERCOMING
Williamette Rudolf

*"Whatever I have, wherever I am, I can make it through anything
in the One who makes me who I am."*
Philippians 4:13, The Message

In 1960 a slender, gangling young girl was described as the
fastest woman alive. At the age of twenty, Williamette
Rudolf collected three gold medals in the Olympics and
became the idol of thousands of men and women everywhere. But to many, what really was important was not so
much what she did, but what she
overcame in doing what she did.

You see, Willie could not walk
without braces until she was thirteen years of age. When she was
just a child, she fell victim to the
crippling disease known as polio.
At age thirteen, Willie started run-
ning to regain the strength of her legs and she did not stop
until she had become the fastest woman alive and the
proud owner of three gold medals.

*"We are as weak
as we believe ourselves
to be and as strong
as our faith."*

The physical handicap was not the only hurdle that
faced this young woman. There were two other barriers,
perhaps even more formidable than the physical. Willie was
the twentieth of twenty-two children born to a black couple,
so this admirable young woman had to hurdle the psycho-
logical barriers of poverty and racial antagonism as well. Yet
what this young woman did brings faith and courage to
untold thousands who live with their own handicaps and

have to battle them in their own way.

At times the emotional handicaps are even more forbidding than the physical ones, for they are the ones that cause you to lose faith and to stop trying. Sometimes the people with the greatest physical attributes are the ones who face the greatest handicaps psychologically. Take, for instance, Saul, the King of ancient Israel, who stood head and shoulders above the rest of the people. In spite of his strength and appearance, Saul was timid to the point of being cowardly.

At times your physical strength or personal beauty actually works against you. I am thinking of one of the most beautiful girls I ever knew, who committed suicide at the age of twenty-five—having gone through four unsuccessful marriages. She confided to a friend that she often wished she were not so beautiful so that people would seek her out for what she really was rather than what she looked like.

What is the handicap you live with? Even the Apostle Paul said that he lived with a thorn in the flesh—perhaps a myopic condition that caused his eyes to matter and run. Yet Paul said that through his weakness God's strength could be more evident. When Paul asked God to remove his handicap, God replied, "My grace is sufficient for you, for my power is made perfect in weakness."

"Therefore," Paul said, "I will boast all the more gladly about my weaknesses, so that Christ's power may rest on me" (2 Corinthians 12:9). That is an intriguing thought—that in spite of human weakness, no matter what it may be, God's strength and beauty will be evident.

That means there can be beauty in life when a face is quite plain. It means there can be strength in spite of physical weakness. There can be courage and integrity in spite of any physical affliction. The strength that really counts—and the one that changes the external—is the strength of character and integrity that begins within.

When you face a handicap or a difficult situation—

regardless of what it may be–there are two choices open to you. You can use the handicap as a crutch to fall back on, excusing your failures and shortcomings, or you can take it as a challenge, asking God to help you overcome your weakness. We are as weak as we believe ourselves to be and as strong as our faith.

Paul's secret can be yours. He said, "I can do all things through Christ who gives me strength" (Philippians 4:13). It is His strength and help that make the difference.

RESOURCE READING
Philippians 4

INSIGHT
You can use a handicap as a crutch to fall back on, an excuse for your failure, or you can take it as a challenge, asking God to help you overcome your weakness.

APPLICATION
How would you define an "excuse" as opposed to a "reason" for something?

What, in your opinion, causes someone like Williamette Rudolf to rise to the challenge while others give up and quit?

PERSEVERANCE

Adonirom Judson

"The disciples were called Christians first at Antioch."
Acts 11:26

They called him "Jesus Christ's man in Burma"! The title was no compliment, but a term of derision scornfully hurled at a young missionary by the name of Adoniram Judson, who had gone to Burma with the intention of evangelizing the beautiful little country where people bowed to the image of Buddha. He was all of twenty-five years of age, his wife but twenty-one, when the ship, *The Georgian,* dropped anchor in Rangoon Harbor on July 13, 1813.

"Judson. . . wanted only a cross and a crown."

Was he greeted warmly upon arrival? Not exactly! Told by government officials that he was not wanted there, a friendly customs agent told him that the best thing he could do would be to get back on the ship and go home. "I know what I'm talking about," he said, "when I say to you . . . there's nothing for you here but heartache."

Time proved his words to be prophetic, but even the King of Burma, as well as the combined military forces of the country, couldn't stop this determined young man from planting the cross on Burmese soil. It was not without a price. Death eventually claimed not only two of his children, but his dear wife whom he deeply loved. Still, Judson wouldn't quit.

Right now you may be thinking to yourself, "Didn't

you say that this fellow—what's his name—yeah, Judson, went to Burma in 1813? That was a long time ago. Why bother to even mention someone who lived so long ago?"

There's a good reason. You see, the kind of stuff Adoniram Judson was made of is the kind of stuff we badly need today. We've lost sight of goals, of character, of commitment, and fierce determination. Taking the path of least resistance, we often settle at the level of mediocrity and accomplish nothing. Judson, unlike some today who settle for a pension and a paycheck, wanted only a cross and a crown.

When the British invaded Burma, although Judson was an American and not a subject of the English crown, he was thrown into prison. In the eyes of the Burmese king, he was a foreigner and was, therefore, suspect. For two long years the task of translating the Bible into Burmese was set aside as Judson languished in prison, being subjected to ongoing torture, harassment, and sickness. He despaired of life itself. Fearful that his precious manuscript of the translation of the Bible into Burmese would be destroyed while he was in prison, his wife sewed the translation into a pillow and took it to the filthy prison where Judson was interred. He slept on it, prayed over its pages, and wondered whether he would ever live to finish the task before him.

When the British forces advanced toward the capital city, Judson, anemic and weakened by continual bouts of dysentery, was forced to interpret for the Burmese government and help negotiate a truce. Finally, Judson was free, but his translation was gone. Instead of cursing his fate, Judson thanked God that he could start the task all over again.

He was ready to start over when a faithful servant appeared one morning, dangling a dirty bag with a string loosely holding its contents. Judson looked inside, and his heart leaped with joy. Was it? Yes, it was! The precious manuscript he had used as a pillow was found outside on the trash heap by a faithful friend. It had been thrown out by the executioner, who found it too hard to use as a pillow.

"Jesus Christ's man in Burma," a term of derision that was in reality a title of honor and praise. What a man!

Can it be said of you, whether you are in business, teaching, or farming, that you are "Jesus Christ's man"? A term of derision—or a title of honor?

RESOURCE READING
Isaiah 6

INSIGHT
Today Christianity is firmly established in Burma largely because of the efforts of a man who wouldn't quit.

APPLICATION
Are you facing a difficult challenge or task? Tempted to quit? Why haven't you?

Try taking life just one day at a time, one task at a time, asking God's help in facing this day. Ask Him to give you His grace and help in getting through today.

PERSEVERANCE

Anacleto Lacanilao

"Andrew, Simon Peter's brother, was one of the two who heard what John had said and who had followed Jesus. The first thing Andrew did was to find his brother Simon and tell him, 'We have found the Messiah' (that is, the Christ). And he brought him to Jesus."
John 1:40-42

Charles Spurgeon once said, "By perseverance, the snail reached the ark!" I don't know whether an unknown missionary laboring in the Philippines a generation ago ever heard that, but I know he believed it. Laboring in a Catholic country where, a generation ago, Protestant missionaries were not always appreciated, he began to tell Anacleto Lacanilao that he needed to be born again and have a personal relationship with Jesus Christ. Lacanilao, who was the father of eight children, didn't buy this new concept and shrugged off the witness of his friend, who wasn't rebuffed but just kept coming back. Seven, eight, nine times the missionary came to the Lacanilao home and urged him to invite Jesus Christ into his life.

"If your witness has been rejected, remember the man who led Anacleto Lacanilao to the Lord."

On the eleventh visit, Lacanilao told the unwelcome visitor, "If you come back one more time, I'm going to kill you!" It was not idle talk when he made that threat. And what happened? The man came back the twelfth time! Suppose someone told you, "If you talk to me one more time about Jesus Christ, I am going to kill you," what would you do? A lot of folks would assume that it might not be too healthy, but not the man who witnessed to Anacleto Lacanilao, because he came back the twelfth time and that was when Dad Lacanilao became a believer in Jesus Christ. He later said, "When he came back the twelfth time, I figured there must be something to this experience he was talking about, and I had better listen to him!"

Today, he and his wife are both in heaven, but their eight children are all serving the Lord, some as outstanding Christian leaders in the Philippines and the United States. One of the sons is Mike Lacanilao, former president of FEBIAS College of the Bible and head of Back to the Bible Ministries in the Philippines. Another served as head of Youth For Christ; but all of the eight children followed in the footsteps of Mom and Dad Lacanilao. It all happened because a faithful witness, whose name is unknown to me, didn't stop when he faced opposition.

When I heard that true story, I couldn't help but think how quickly most of us give up when a colleague or a friend whom we have been talking to about Jesus Christ begins to give us a cold shoulder. Quickly we think, "Religion is a personal matter—he has his and I have mine!" Nothing causes enemies quicker than talking about religion or politics, right? At least, that's what we often tend to think.

At some point we have to decide, "Is what I believe real? Did Jesus Christ really rise from the dead as Scripture says? Is there any other way that people can get to heaven?" If there is any other way, then Luke was wrong when he wrote, "Neither is there salvation in any other: for there is none other name under heaven given among men, whereby we must be saved" (Acts 4:12). If Jesus came to provide a way to heaven and there is no other way you can get there, better be concerned about your neighbor or friend, your husband or wife, or the person you work with.

You have an influence that I do not have, that your pastor doesn't have, that Billy Graham or Mother Teresa doesn't have. You rub shoulders with men and women daily, and you, as a believer, are the only one who represents Jesus Christ to them. If you have talked to someone, and your witness has been rejected, remember the man who led Anacleto Lacanilao to the Lord. You can count the pieces of fruit on a tree, but you can't count the trees in a piece of fruit, right? What a difference would have resulted if an unknown missionary had given up when he was rebuffed. Think about it and be encouraged!

RESOURCE READING
John 1:43-50

INSIGHT
You touch the lives of people who will never be influenced by Billy Graham or probably a minister. You are the gospel to these people.

APPLICATION
Make a list of five friends who need Jesus Christ. Now put that list in your billfold or purse and begin to pray for them every day.

If you are uncertain how to lead someone to Christ, talk to your pastor or youth minister and tell him or her you want some training so you can bring your friends to the Lord.

PERSEVERANCE
Peter Bird

"I can do everything through him who gives me strength."
Philippians 4:13

He rowed alone across the Pacific Ocean 8,990 miles but fell short of his goal thirty-three miles away. Peter Bird attempted to become the first man to single-handedly row from San Francisco in the United States across the Pacific. He almost succeeded, but approaching the east coast of Australia's Great Barrier Reef, Bird encountered stormy weather and choppy seas. He was looking for a passage through the coral. Actually he was within one nautical mile of the reef when he had to radio for help, fearing that he could not make it.

"Hang in there.
God will send
the help you need
to make it."

The Royal Australian Navy rescued the photographer turned sailor, and as they towed his thirty-three-foot-long craft, it broke up in the heavy surf. Though most would never dare to attempt what Peter Bird did, you have to have a profound admiration for one who would pit his life against such odds. To succeed in crossing almost nine thousand miles of ocean and yet to fall short of the goal by a mere thirty-three miles is rather sad. He was so close to the finish. Of course, he would have preferred doing it on his own. But he came a long, long way, nonetheless.

In the first chapter of the Book of Judges in the Bible, the chronicler of old tells of another situation in which men almost succeeded but failed at the last. God had promised the land of Israel to Joshua and the children of Israel. He had told them to go up and to conquer the land, that He would go with them and that He would surely give them a complete victory. But this is what happened according to the writer: "The Lord was with the men of Judah. They took possession of the hill country, but they were unable to drive out the people from the plains . . ."; and "Manasseh (one of the tribes or groups of people) did not drive out the people of Beth Shan . . ."; "When Israel became strong, they pressed the Canaanites into forced labor but never drove them out completely."

It is one thing to have your craft broken up on the Great Barrier Reef and quite another thing to give up when victory is in your grasp. When the antagonism was too sharp, the writer of the Book of Hebrews encouraged struggling believers to get their eyes on the Lord—not circumstances, not the Great Barrier Reefs of life—but to look to Jesus as the author and finisher and the One who completes our faith (Hebrews 12:2).

In the tenth chapter, five times the writer of Hebrews uses the phrase "let us." He says, "Let us draw near to God with a sincere heart"; "Let us hold unswervingly to the hope we profess"; "Let us consider how to spur one another on toward love and good deeds"; and "Let us not give up meeting together, but let us encourage one another." Notice those two phrases that stand as sentinels against the tides: "Let us not give up . . ." and "let us encourage one another."

Perhaps you have come a long, long way in your Christian walk, but you are discouraged and you feel like giving up. Hang in there. God will send the help you need to make it.

Peter Bird did reach Australia, but he had to have the assistance of the Australian navy; that didn't mean he wasn't still a hero. To reach your destination on heaven's shore may require that you let someone else give you a hand also. It's all part of refusing to be destroyed on the Great Barrier Reefs of life. As Scripture says, "Let us not give up. . . . Let us encourage one another."

RESOURCE READING
Philippians 4:10-20

INSIGHT
God never leaves us at the mercy of circumstances. He knows the limits of our strength and endurance and will be there at our time of need.

APPLICATION
What does the phrase "Man's extremity is God's opportunity" mean?

Would you consider doing what Peter Bird did? Why? Or why not?

Are you working on a project now that is near completion? How much more effort will it take to finish? Considering giving up?

PRAGMATIC
Thomas

"Thomas said to him, 'Lord, we don't know where you are going,
so how can we know the way?' Jesus answered,
'I am the way and the truth and the life.' "
John 14:5,6

Tradition characterizes him as being strong-willed, stubborn, and doubting. His name: Thomas, one of the twelve who walked with Jesus. Mentioned a dozen different places in the New Testament, Thomas is usually thought of as a "show me" sort of person, short on faith and long on doubt. But is this a caricature—an impression passed from person to person without any real foundation? Or was Thomas a perpetual pessimist, the kind of person who describes a partially filled glass of water as "half empty" instead of "half full"?

"Christ met Thomas (and He meets us as well) at the point of his need."

Of one thing you can be certain: There are individuals who constantly are negative. You've no doubt met the kind of person who always feels bad when he feels good because he's afraid that he will feel worse. But is it fair to think of Thomas in such terms?

This may surprise you, but I believe that to so describe Thomas isn't really fair to the man. Certainly, he was practical, pragmatic, cautious; but there is a great deal of evidence that suggests Thomas was not so much of an "unbeliever" as a "nonbeliever." What's the difference? The individual who is nonbelieving only wants evidence. He wants the truth. He wants an object for his faith. He or she is merely looking for rational evidence to support his or her faith. This person wants the facts, then responds to them in a positive manner.

The unbeliever, however, is often biased and prejudiced. The attitude of unbelief is that which refuses to accept any evidence no matter how well substantiated and certain.

It is the former attitude to which God always responds.

After the resurrection, Thomas was missing when Christ appeared to the disciples. When the others said, "We have seen the Lord," Thomas didn't attack them for what they had seen. He simply spoke for himself saying, "'Unless I see the nail marks in his hands and put my finger where the nails were, and put my hands into his side, I will not believe it'" (John 20:25).

A week later Jesus appeared to the disciples. The doors were locked and the curtains veiled the windows, and suddenly Jesus appeared in their midst. Then Jesus spoke directly to Thomas and said, "Put your finger here; see my hands. Reach out your hand and put it into my side. Stop doubting and believe" (John 20:27). What happened? A nonbeliever became a believer.

There is nothing in the text to suggest that Thomas put his hand in the nail prints of our Lord, but the text says, having been confronted with the risen Christ, he immediately cried out, "My Lord and my God!" His confession was personal—"My Lord and my God!" That was it. The matter was settled.

Frankly, two things impress me about this whole issue. The first is that Christ met Thomas (and He meets us as well) at the point of his need. When an individual is honest and sincere—he or she truly wants to know—Christ will always reveal Himself to that person. Early in His ministry Christ challenged, "If anyone chooses to do God's will, he will find out whether my teaching comes from

God or whether I speak on my own" (John 7:17). That promise is still valid today.

The second observation is that Christ met Thomas at the level of his faith. He didn't reject him because of his personality or his cautious reserve. Commit as much of yourself as you can based upon what you do understand. And in time, you will find that more and more becomes apparent. That's the way faith works.

RESOURCE READING
1 John 1:1-10

INSIGHT
For those who sincerely want answers, Jesus Christ is always willing to reveal Himself and meet them at the level of their needs.

APPLICATION
"Doubting Thomas" is the label history has tagged this disciple with. Do you think this is valid?

Do you see a personality type who simply wanted evidence for his belief?

Have you learned that what you do understand bothers you more than what you don't understand? Focus on living up to the light you have, and ask God to show you answers to the questions you do have.

PRAYER

George Mueller

"This is the assurance we have in approaching God:
that if we ask anything according to his will, he hears us."
1 John 5:14

George Mueller was educated in the universities of Germany during the period of time when rationalism was the dominant philosophy of the day. Rationalism is a humanistic philosophy that leaves God pretty much out of life, and Mueller certainly did that very thing for his first twenty years. As a young man, Mueller's life consisted of wine, women, and song. He ended up in jail, to the disgrace of his father and family, who wanted their son to become a clergyman. Mueller wanted anything but that!

"May God help us to discover the power of the bended knee."

At the age of twenty, while studying at the university, he was invited to the home of a friend who was a Christian. That evening Mueller was intrigued to see his friend kneel and pray–something Mueller had never seen before. At his home following the meal, the host read a chapter from the Bible–the same one that a professor of Mueller's had earlier ridiculed–and the reading of Scripture was followed by a hymn. Mueller felt so awkward that he apologized for even being there, but that night changed his life.

When he wrote his autobiography, Mueller could not remember if it was that night that he went home and knelt down for the first time to pray as he had seen his friend, George Wagner, do. But it is certain that Mueller was shortly thereafter converted to Jesus Christ. After his conversion, he quickly learned the secret of prayer.

In the university, Mueller had excelled as a scholar; and with the same fervent dedication, he now turned to the Scriptures and began to apply them to his life. Rejecting a rationalistic approach to life, Mueller believed that faith is believing the promises of God and then standing on them completely. At the same time, Mueller began to be concerned for the orphans that wandered the streets of Bristol in England, where he had taken a church. This was the beginning of the orphanages that Mueller established, which were operated on the principle of faith in God.

During his lifetime, George Mueller never asked for money for his work, yet in response to his faith, God sent in the equivalent of well more than one million U.S. dollars. There were times when there was no food, yet Mueller would not allow his staff to send out an SOS for money—unlike some organizations today. Instead, he would go into his room and bend his knees in prayer. Often, he would instruct, "Set the table for dinner," although there was nothing to cook, and then he would go to prayer . . . and God provided.

The power of the bended knee—in a world of ICBM's and bombs measured in megatons, a world where so much that happens, even in the Christian world, is a result of good promotions and clever psychology. We need to rediscover the power of the bended knee—the power of prayer.

When Mueller was in his eighties, he was asked to speak to a group of seminary students. One of them raised his hand as the old man finished his address. He said, "Mr. Mueller, there is a question which some of us would like to ask."

"Yes," answered Mueller as he strained to hear.

"What is your secret?" the youth queried.

The eighty-year-old man pushed his chair back and began to bend his old limbs to the floor as he knelt in prayer. "This is the secret," replied Mueller.

One of his biographers wrote that when Mueller died, it was discovered that there were two ridges, or grooves, worn into the wooden floor by his bed. Mueller had literally worn two depressions into the wooden floor by his knees as he knelt beside his bed in prayer. The God of George Mueller is yet alive and well today, and He still answers prayer. May God help us to discover the power of the bended knee.

RESOURCE READING
1 John 3

INSIGHT
What God did for George Mueller, He will do for you as well, for God is no respecter of persons.

APPLICATION
Do you think that the manner in which God answered prayer—without vocal financial appeals and four-color promotional pieces—was something special for just Mueller? Or do you think that God will meet those involved in His Word the same way today?

Hudson Taylor, a friend of Mueller's, used to say, "God's work done God's way will never lack God's supply." Do you agree?

How many ministries do you know that make no financial appeals?

Prayer

Chris Milbrath

"Is anyone of you sick? He should call the elders of the church to pray over him and anoint him with oil in the name of the Lord. And the prayer offered in faith will make the sick person well; the Lord will raise him up."
James 5:14, 15

When Chris Milbrath was working with Co-Mission in Ukraine, the last thing he ever thought would happen to him was a trip to the hospital for surgery. After all, Chris is twenty-five years of age and a handsome, healthy, strong specimen of young manhood. He's six feet, five inches tall with a shock of blond hair and is endowed with the kind of good looks that turns the heads of young women.

"God's work— as well as His workers— is energized by prayer."

But then unexpectedly, a stomachache didn't go away. It had to be more than indigestion. Eventually a doctor told him, "You've got a ruptured appendix, and unless you have surgery immediately, you're going to die." A second opinion would have been comforting, but the hospital where Chris was hadn't paid their phone bill, and the phone had been shut off.

Surgery took place the next day. It didn't go well. Infection threatened his life. A roommate who understood a little English said that he prayed and praised the Lord in his delirious stupor.

Then, halfway around the world, an older woman, a

friend and supporter, suddenly woke in the middle of the night. She felt an irresistible burden to get out of bed and pray for her young friend. She didn't know why. She just knew that she should pray. Later as they compared notes and made adjustment for the difference in time zones, Chris and the friend were amazed that this strange prayer burden came at the very time his life was hanging by a thread.

What happened? Within twenty-four hours, word got through to a medical missions group in Moscow that things hadn't gone well and that the hospital didn't have the resources or equipment to save his life. A small jet just happened to be available and was sent to airlift him to Geneva, where one of the best surgeons in Switzerland just happened to be available for additional surgery, which undoubtedly saved the life of this young man.

As Chris shared his experience with me, preparatory to going back to again serve in the same city where he went through this trauma, I couldn't help wondering, "What might have happened if that woman had turned over and said, 'I'll pray for Chris tomorrow' "?

"Okay," you say, "God could have woke up someone else." Of course, and besides God isn't restricted in His purposes by people who don't answer a wake-up call in the middle of the night. What He wants done, He's going to do.

But just a minute. When something like this happens, several powerful things come together. First, there is no questioning the fact that there is a link between prayer and the circumstances that led to Chris's recovery. The Bible makes it very clear that there is a link between prayer and sick people's recovering (see Mark 16:18 and James 5:13). Then there is joy on both ends, knowing that someone played a part in the redemptive work God wanted accomplished. Do you remember how Jesus said, "Ask and you will receive, and your joy will be complete" (John 16:24)?

A final thought. There are those occasions when God does prompt someone to pray specifically for a person in time of need—but don't wait until you are jolted from a deep sleep with an urgency to pray before you intercede for those who are serving the Lord.

God's work–as well as His workers–is energized by prayer. The measure of our accomplishment is really the reflection of the prayer base supporting those of us who are involved in His work. Make prayer for others a vital part of your support. Your prayers make a difference. Chris Milbrath knows for sure.

RESOURCE READING
James 5:13-19

INSIGHT

No human explanation can account for the fact that God, on occasion, sets aside the natural laws that govern the world and does the miraculous as the result of fervent prayer.

APPLICATION

While Chris's experience is out of the ordinary, answered prayer should be a normative experience for God's children. Jot down verses of Scripture you are familiar with that say God answers prayer. If you cannot remember any, take a Bible concordance and look up verses on prayer and mark them in your Bible.

PRAYER

Armin Gesswein

"Again, I tell you that if two of you on earth agree about anything you ask for, it will be done for you by my Father in heaven."
Matthew 18:19

It happens frequently. The door of my office is closed, and I'm quietly working or engaged in conversation with someone, when suddenly the door opens, and a lean, dignified, rather tall man with angular features—now in his nineties—comes marching in, having done an "end run" around the receptionist and my secretary much as a defensive tackle would in breaking through the line of scrimmage in a football game. In his hand is a magazine article or something encouraging he thinks will help me. He stays for only a few brief moments. Then he's gone, often reminding me of Elijah, who appeared unannounced in the court of King Ahab.

"Learn to plead the promises of God."

"Who is that?" people ask.

"That," I explain, "is Armin Gesswein, and he has executive privilege. He's been a dad in the Lord to me for a long time, and he's a very special person. This saint—a real man of God if ever there was one—for more than seventy years has born a name synonymous with prayer, having conducted prayer rallies for Billy Graham's crusades and establishing an organization known as Revival Prayer Fellowship that brings pastors and Christian leaders together in prayer.

How did Armin learn the importance of prayer?

Armin was a young Lutheran pastor, age twenty-four, striving to plant a church on Long Island, New York, and things were not going terribly well. In his church fellowship was a retired blacksmith, about fifty years his senior. Armin had noticed that when this man prayed, things happened. He said, "The prayer and the answer were not far apart—in fact, they were moving along together." Armin explains, "His 'prayer muscles' were extremely strong because of much exercise." Wanting to learn his spiritual secrets, Armin asked if he might join the old blacksmith in prayer.

Going to the blacksmith's home, they crossed the driveway and went to the old barn, where they climbed up into the hayloft. Armin prayed. Then Ambrose Whaley, the old blacksmith, prayed. Finally Armin turned to him and said, "You have some kind of a secret in praying. Would you mind sharing it with me?"

"Young man," said the blacksmith, "learn to plead the promises of God." The old man had knelt between two bales of hay, and on each bale of hay was an open Bible. His two large hands, gnarled and toughened by years of hard labor, were open, covering the pages of each Bible.

Armin learned his lesson well. "I learned more about prayer in that haymow," says Armin, "than in all my years of schooling for the ministry." Now in his tenth decade, Armin Gesswein is still actively speaking, encouraging, and exhorting. The only heritage Jesus left the Church, he believes, is a prayer meeting.

With him, prayer is not an appendage tacked onto a planning session or a business meeting. It is the main thing, the frontal assault. He's convinced that one of the reasons both churches and individuals are powerless and over-whelmed with spiritual impotence is that they have not learned the secret of praying, pleading the promises of God.

Understanding the relationship between the promises of God's Word and what we ask our heavenly Father to do has helped me immensely in my personal life. God honors

His word. Jesus said candidly, "The Scripture cannot be broken" (John 10:35). He also said that the equivalent of crossing a "t" or dotting an "i" would not pass from the law until every bit was fulfilled (see Matthew 5:18).

Learn a lesson from a man who constantly says, "Let's pray!"–and he doesn't mean some other time. He means "now!" And don't just pray, but pray and stand upon the authority of God's Word. Some spiritual secrets are too good to keep to yourself.

RESOURCE READING
Matthew 17

INSIGHT
God answers prayer–not because of my goodness or my merit–but because of His promises, which cannot be broken.

APPLICATION
Have you thought much about the relationship between the promises of God's Word and answered prayer? Begin marking prayer promises in your Bible.

Keep a prayer journal with dates, requests, and then a column where you can record how God has answered your prayers.

PRAYER

Mother Sala

"As a mother comforts her child, so will I comfort you;
and you will be comforted over Jerusalem."
Isaiah 66:13

Benjamin Moore, the great painter of the last century, said that a kiss from his mother made him a painter. In my youth, it was the prayers of my mother that kept me from straying, and in my adult life her encouragement and love sustained me in times of personal doubt and difficulty. She may not be a hero in the eyes of the world, but she was my first real hero and that image never dimmed.

"She was a mother who knew how to pray and prayed, reflecting the image of Christ in her personal life."

When I was a teenager and I would go out in the evening, to reach my bedroom I had to go down the hall, past the partly closed door of the study where Mother prayed. Night after night, I would find her down on her knees praying. I never had to ask, "Praying for the missionaries, Mother?" No, I knew who she was praying for—my brother and me—yet she never used prayer as a cudgel to keep us from straying. Reflecting on the influence of my parents, I have to say that what most influenced my life was not the often loud, stentorian sermons of my dad, but the gentle, loving care and counsel of my mother.

People marry in life, I have noticed, to complete themselves, which explains why opposites attract; but when there are too many dissimilarities, opposites repel. No two people could have been much different when it comes to temperament and personalities than my two parents. Frankly, though I loved and respected him, especially for his determination to succeed (which he did), Dad was not an easy person to live with. He was proud of himself (and his family) and often arrogant. On one occasion when Dad was being especially difficult, I said, "Mother, I don't know how in the world you can live with Dad when he is as difficult as he sometimes is."

"Harold," she said, "I learned a long time ago that when you love someone, you learn to put up with him." She was gifted in knowing when to speak her mind and when to remain quiet and to steer through the minefields.

Dr. Sam Sutherland, past president of Biola University, once told me that what he most admired about his wife was that she knew when to speak and when to keep quiet. Mother was like that. But her gentleness and patience did have limits. The only time that I recall ever seeing her angry–really angry–was the time when my parents owned and operated a Denver area motel and a patron lied to her, telling Mother that his companion was his wife. When she learned that she had been deceived, she picked up the phone and said, "Mister, I've learned that this woman isn't your wife so you have five minutes to vacate your room, and if you don't, I'll call your real wife (she already had looked up the phone number) and let her know where you are." I don't think I ever saw anyone leave so quickly.

I was in Korea when Dad called with the sad news that Mother was hospitalized with a heart attack and was not expected to live. But Mother had said for Dad to tell me, "Not yet. It's not yet," and wanted me to stay there and minister. A few days later the call came. "She says to come home."

I spent three days at her side as we talked, laughed, and cried. On the morning of the fourth day, she said, "Harold, I want you to pray that the Lord will take me home today. I've lived a long, full life, and it's time to go." The one who had prayed for me for eighty years, was now asking me to pray for her release. That was tough.

About 10 P.M. that night, I encouraged my dad to go home and get some rest. "Mother," I said, "I'm going to stay with you tonight. I owe you a few, you know."

In the quiet of the night, with tears in my eyes, I quoted Psalm 91, her favorite psalm and her grandmother's before her. We prayed together, her bony hand in mine; and then in just moments her gaze focused on something I couldn't see. Her eyes were intense, and I distinctly remember that the pupils of her eyes narrowed.

Some forty years before, my sister, at the age of twenty-six, was dying with Lupus. She suddenly sat straight up in bed as she reached out, saying, "Jesus, Jesus!" Mother asked, "Honey, what did you see?" but got no answer; those were my sister's last words. This time, she was the one who saw what I couldn't see, though I looked again, fully expecting to see something.

In moments, the line on the heart monitor went flat, and I knew she was gone. I gently combed her hair, then knelt by the side of that hospital bed and thanked God that He had given me a praying mother.

After Mother was no longer with us, what I think I missed most was the knowledge that she was praying for me. Yes, to me she was my first and most enduring hero, a mother who knew how to pray and prayed, reflecting the image of Christ in her personal life.

RESOURCE READING
Proverbs 31

INSIGHT
People may spurn your counsel and ignore your suggestions, but they cannot escape your prayers.

APPLICATION
Who has been a great influence in your life? Why?

How would you respond to the person who says, "My mom sure isn't like that"?

Have you ever really told your mother how much you love and appreciate her?

PRAYER

Peter Cao

"You intended to harm me, but God intended it for good to accomplish what is now being done, the saving of many lives."
Genesis 50:20

If you question the fact that truth is stranger than fiction, let me tell you about Peter Cao and the uncanny set of circumstances that brought his family back together again after they were torn apart by the conflict in Vietnam. You see, when Vietnam fell, Peter knew his future was in jeopardy. He was pastor of a church and he also ran an orphanage filled with children whose Amerasian heritage was considered a stigma by the Vietnamese, whose racial purity had been defiled by the American soldiers.

". . .against almost unbelievable odds. But that's the way it almost always is when God steps in and answers prayer."

To save his "family," Peter put five of his ten Amerasian children on military flights to the U.S. His third youngest daughter Lehang recalls, "When parents would decide at the last minute to remove orphans from an airlift, our father would fill the empty slots with the youngest of us."

Eventually, Peter's five children were separated from each other, their hopes dashed of ever seeing each other again. One morning, Lehang awakened at the temporary shelter where she had been placed to hear a child crying. You think that all crying children sound the same, do you? Not so! This had to be a Vietnamese child. But that voice also had a familiar ring to it. Could it be? Was it possible that it was her little brother? Lehang says, "His face and eyes were so swollen from crying, I could not recognize him immediately. But when I looked closer and saw this boy's unusually large feet, I realized he was my two-year-old brother, Buu!"

But Lehang couldn't speak English. And try as she did, she just couldn't make anyone understand that this child was her brother. Lehang tried to tell an interpreter, but the records had been mixed up, and the nickname she used for her brother was different from the official name on the documents. The next day Lehang was forced to leave and fly to another state. It was like having a life ring within your grasp, only to have it swept away by the tide. Lehang was broken-hearted. Would she ever see her little brother again?

When the plane arrived at its destination, the children were placed on five different buses en route to a processing center. On board each bus was a Vietnamese interpreter. As Lehang boarded the bus, she looked at the interpreter and looked again. She couldn't believe what she saw. Before her eyes was her elder sister, who had come on an earlier flight and was now serving as an interpreter. Soon the children were reunited.

But what of their parents? The children prayed fervently that God would allow them to be reunited—at the same time the parents were praying the same prayer. Thousands of miles of ocean and piles of government red tape separated them. Would God ever allow them to be one family again?

Meanwhile Peter, his wife, and five of the oldest children decided to risk everything by embarking on an old fishing boat. Before them were twenty-four grueling days at sea with nothing to eat but dry noodles and fish. For three days they went without food, and water was rationed out in a bottle cap.

Eventually, God answered prayer and the little fishing boat reached Guam. After nine months of separation, the family was reunited against almost unbelievable odds. But that's the way it almost always is when God steps in and answers prayer.

Jesus said, "If you have faith as small as a mustard seed, you can say to this mountain, 'Move from here to there' and it will move. Nothing will be impossible for you" (Matthew 17:20, 21). The Peter Cao family agrees.

RESOURCE READING
Matthew 18:1-9

INSIGHT
In answering prayer, God can override circumstances in such a way that we will know that only He could have done it.

APPLICATION
How would you respond to someone who said that the circumstances bringing the Peter Cao family together "just happened"?

Have you seen answers to prayer in your personal life which convinced you God did indeed answer your prayer? Try using a notebook and jot down specific answers to prayer that you have received.

PROVIDENCE
Constantine von Tischendorf

*"I tell you the truth, until heaven and earth disappear, not the
smallest letter, not the least stroke of a pen, will by any means
disappear from the Law until everything is accomplished."*
Matthew 5:18

In 1844, Constantine von Tischendorf, one of the finest
scholars of the past century, visited the monastery of St.
Catherine in Israel at Sinai. When he was in the library, he
noticed 129 leaves of a very old manuscript in a paper bas-
ket. The old pieces of parchment had been put there for the monks
to use in lighting fires. Tischen-dorf's interest was captured by
some ancient writing on the leaves of the manuscript, and what he discovered proved to be one of the greatest discoveries of biblical
manuscripts.

"No other book has ever or will ever make the difference in our world that God's own Word has."

Tischendorf arranged to secure forty-three of the leaves
that recorded part of the Old Testament written in Greek
about the year A.D. 400.

Nine years later, Tischendorf returned to the
monastery, intent on copying the remaining leaves of the
ancient document; however, to his horror, the remaining
leaves had been lost by the monks, who did not fully realize their tremendous importance.

In 1859 Tischendorf again returned, this time as envoy of
the Russian czar. But it made no difference. The priceless

manuscript was lost and no amount of investigation would reveal its hiding place. Tischendorf was to return broken-hearted. For the second time, he had failed to find the missing documents. On the night before he was to depart, his sorrow turned to the highest elation when the man who had been his host showed him a codex, thinking that this might be the missing link to the lost manuscript. It was! The codex contained the missing eighty-six leaves Tischendorf left behind in 1844. In addition, there were another 112 leaves of the Old Testament, plus the entire New Testament, along with two other ancient Church writings that had been lost for centuries.

Tischendorf's great discovery came to be known as Codex Sinaiticus, since it was found at the monastery at Sinai. It contains the Old and New Testaments, written in Greek about A.D. 400. The priceless manuscripts were taken to the Imperial Library in St. Petersburg, and then in 1933 were sold by the Russian government to the British Museum for the sum of $280,000.

How important was Tischendorf's discovery? Scholars are in general agreement that his discovery was the most important manuscript discovery of the last century. Codex Sinaiticus takes its place along with the Septuagint. Time and again ancient manuscripts have confirmed the fact that the book called the Bible is unlike every other book in the world in that it has been accurately passed down from generation to generation. When scholars compare ancient texts with our standard version, they are quick to admit that there are no major changes in your Bible from the manuscripts of the second to fourth centuries.

Did this just happen, or is it possible that God gave supernatural guidance in preserving the sixty-six books we know as the Bible? I would believe that this "just happened" about as quickly as I would believe that an explosion in a print shop made a book.

Over the centuries, people have recognized that the Bible is different—a divinely inspired Book—and consequently they have handled it differently than most books. Today we owe a big debt of gratitude to the scribes and Masoretes, who painstakingly copied the manuscripts of Scripture over the centuries. So careful with the text were they, that if a king or monarch should walk into the room while they were copying Scripture, they would not even rise until they had finished the sentence. Some were so cautious that if they made a mistake, they would start the manuscript all over again. As a result of their work and the providential guidance of God, we can open our Bibles and read with the assurance that we are reading the Words of God, supernaturally given.

The Bible is a textbook for living. It works as you follow its formula. Both the Old and New Testaments point to Jesus Christ, who said, "I am the way and the truth and the life. No one comes to the Father except through me" (John 14:6). The Bible tells us that in Jesus Christ a person finds eternal life and the answers to life's puzzle. Tischendorf was a hero for his persistence in seeking the Codex Sinaiticus, but the Bible itself rises above his heroic deeds. No other book has ever or will ever make the difference in our world that God's own Word has.

RESOURCE READING
Isaiah 40

INSIGHT
God has supernaturally preserved some of the ancient biblical manuscripts and allowed their discoveries at a time when scientific skepticism seems to be at its greatest.

APPLICATION
Ask yourself three questions each time you read the Bible: What does it say? What does it mean? How do I apply it to my life?

Keep a notebook and each day jot down the central insight or thought you have had as the result of reading the Word.

PURITY
Mary, Mother of Jesus

"Blessed are you among women. . . ."
Luke 1:42

"Why do you ignore the place of Mary, when it comes to the Christmas story?" a friend queried a couple of Christmases ago. I've been pondering on that question. Protestants sometimes accuse Catholics of glorifying Mary beyond the limits of what they feel is the scriptural framework, but is it possible in their attempt to glorify the Son, they have ignored the handmaiden of the Lord, who was the natural mother of Jesus?

". . .a woman of grace and beauty, with an essential, irreplaceable role in the Incarnation."

Who was Mary? How important was her life in the scope of redemption? What lessons can be learned by modern women today from her life?

You do understand that her position among women from the time of Eve to the present has been totally unique and without duplication. That alone demands that we take another look at her life and the qualities that were recognized by our heavenly Father, which resulted in her being the human instrument that enabled the Divine to be united with humanity.

May I ask you? What do you really remember about Mary? Think about it for a moment. Yes, you know that she was a virgin and that she was engaged (betrothed is the King James term, which means more than engagement does today) to a man whose name was Joseph. You remember the essential details of the Christmas story; but is there more, especially in relationship to women today?

I think there is. Matthew traces Mary's lineage to Abraham through David, establishing her pedigree. However, as Matthew lists the genealogy, he does something that is significant when he writes that Jacob was the father of Joseph, the husband of Mary, of whom was born Jesus, who is called Christ.

Normally, rules of grammar would have been to use a masculine pronoun when Matthew says, "Joseph the husband of Mary, of whom was born Christ," but he uses a feminine pronoun in reference to Mary to whom was born Christ. By doing this he tells us that there is no question in his mind that Mary was a virgin, not only at the time of conception, but that as Scripture says, Joseph did not have sexual relations with her until Jesus had been born.

There is little doubt that Mary was a young woman, perhaps as young as age twenty, or even younger, in that the custom of the day was for a bride to be considerably younger than her husband. Just how the wedding arrangements were worked out isn't quite clear. The betrothal had already taken place. It was official that Mary would eventually be married to the quiet carpenter in the city of Nazareth where they both lived.

The writers of Scripture never included detailed material that readers could weave into an intricate fabric. They gave the essentials: "God sent the angel Gabriel," writes Luke, a Syrian physician and the author of the third Gospel, "to Nazareth, a town in Galilee, to a virgin pledged to be married to a man named Joseph, a descendant of David. The virgin's name was Mary" (Luke 1:26, 27).

That's how it all starts. When it became obvious that Mary was with child, "Because Joseph her husband was a righteous man and did not want to expose her to public disgrace, he had in mind to divorce her quietly," so says Matthew 1:19. After all, who would believe her story that an angel by the name of Gabriel had appeared to her? Who had ever borne a child conceived without a human father before? Joseph knew how ludicrous this all appeared, and because he did care for her and was a good man himself, he wanted to spare her public disgrace and ridicule. It was at that point that an angel appeared to Joseph, convincing him that Mary had conceived a baby from the Holy Spirit.

Friend, take a new look at Mary's life. You will discover a woman of grace and beauty, with an essential, irreplaceable role in the Incarnation.

Resource reading
Luke 1:26-56

Insight
God's emphasis on sexual purity comes not only by statement but also by the example of Mary, the Mother of Jesus.

Application
Take time to read the resource reading and then make a list of the qualities you see in Mary's life that you would like to have in yours.

The grace of God brings forgiveness, restoration, and healing. It is never too late to begin living as God wants you to, so ask the Lord to help you make the qualities in Mary's life a reality in yours as well.

Purpose

Paul Kauffman

*"I hope in the Lord Jesus to send Timothy to you soon. . . . I have
no one else like him, who takes a genuine interest in your welfare.
For everyone looks out for his own interests, not those of Jesus Christ."*
Philippians 2:19-21

Long ago God gave to David "men of understanding of the
times," so that Israel would know what to do (1 Chronicles
12:32). Paul Kauffman, who spent most of his life in Asia,
was the same kind of man. His native home was China, but

*"Launch something
so great that it is
doomed to failure
unless God
supernaturally
steps in."*

when the dark specter of the Sino-
Japanese War was looming on the
horizon, Paul's widowed mother
brought him to safer territory. His
heart was always in Asia. Growing
up in China, Paul spoke Chinese
flawlessly, and if a Chinese heart
could indwell an American body,
Paul would have been the combination.

Establishing the first Chinese research center in Hong
Kong in the 1960s, Paul was a man ahead of his times. In
1968, when the bamboo curtain was strongly protecting
China from western influence, Paul and his organization,
Asian Outreach, launched a new translation of the Bible in
the simplified Chinese characters Chairman Mao had
insisted was necessary to teach the masses to read and
write. When major publishers scoffed at the idea of publishing a new Bible for China when the country was sealed
from the outside world, Kauffman set about to publish the

262

new Bible with his own organization.

There are three kinds of people in the world–those who make things happen, those who watch them happen, and those who never know that anything at all is happening. For more than fifty years Paul was on the cutting edge of making things happen, and when events inside China were reshaping the future of this massive population base, Paul interpreted them with accuracy and clarity. In the 1950s, he began disseminating information about China in a monthly newsletter; but then as the demand for information grew, the newsletter became a bimonthly publication known as the *Asian Report*.

Of all the men I have been privileged to know personally, Paul Kauffman ranked among the finest. He was a type A+ personality whose greatest legacy was his integrity and commitment to the cause of Jesus Christ. At a missions conference he once challenged people to launch something so great that it is doomed to failure unless God supernaturally steps in and undergirds the project. For a number of years I saw Paul quite frequently at the foot of the stairs leading to his office, just above our Guidelines' offices, and I will always cherish those conversations as he poured out his heart, often with tears, talking about his beloved China.

Though his books are among the finest ever written, his name was not a household word to most Americans. Yet he was known to millions in Asia as a man who knew what was happening and knew how to respond to the cataclysmic events of the past fifty years.

Silenced by a devastating stroke, the last two years of his life were frustrating for a man who lived to preach, teach, and write. My last conversation with Paul was strictly one-way. I told him of my impending trip into China and patted his hand knowingly. Though he could not speak, his eyes did. His seventy-seven years are now behind him, but of one thing I am sure: he left behind a legacy and an example that is far more valuable than diamonds or pearls.

When missionary Robert Morrison was on his way to

China, a destination that was never realized, the captain of the ship he was on sarcastically said, "So you expect to change China, do you, Mr. Morrison?" "No," he replied, "but I expect God to," and Paul Kauffman was one whom God used to do just that. May God raise up many more Paul Kauffmans.

RESOURCE READING
Philippians 2

INSIGHT
God uses ordinary men and women who are willing to make an extraordinary commitment to the Lord, seizing opportunities and making the most of them.

APPLICATION
Paul Kauffman refused to live with the word "No!" or the mentality that because things had not been done before, they could not be done. Would you call that faith?

Have you followed the growth of the church in China today? Watch newspaper accounts of believers who are still paying the price of persecution for their faith.

Have you considered a short-term missions awareness trip?

PURPOSE
Evangeline Booth

"Do not conform any longer to the pattern of this world, but be transformed by the renewing of your mind. Then you will be able to test and approve what God's will is—his good, pleasing and perfect will."
Romans 12:2

A thousand men proposed to her. She had offers from millionaires, farmers, businessmen, fishermen, and vagrants from the Bowery. Even after her seventieth birthday, propositions came in such quantities that her secretary did not bother to show her the letters. She was not an actress or a movie star, but she had a tremendous following of thirty-eight thousand men and women, who became ambassadors of good will in eighty-six countries. Her name was Evangeline Booth and she headed the Salvation Army. After retirement, she swam and did fancy diving as though she were still eighteen. She was a tremendous woman—administrator, musician, and friend to thousands. When she was interviewed by a reporter, she said that her secret was this: "I live for others. My deepest desire is to make every person I meet a little better because I have passed this way."

"I live for others. My deepest desire is to make every person I meet a little better because I have passed this way."

Another woman, a contemporary of Evangeline Booth, was Hetty Green, once the richest woman in America. She left an estate of $75 million at her death, yet she was one of the most penny-thrifty women who ever lived. In the winter, she padded her clothes with newspapers to keep warm. Though she owned two railroads and had stocks in every major company, she would sit up all night in a day coach rather than spend the money for a Pullman berth on a train. On a blistering summer day, a friend found her under a blazing tin roof in an attic–the sun made the temperature almost unbearable. What was she doing? She was sorting colored rags from the white ones because the junk man paid a penny more a pound for sorted rags. She died and left a fortune but no friends.

What distinguished Evangeline Booth from Hetty Green, and for that matter from thousands of others considered important?

First, her generosity. She gave of herself. Her secret, so she told people, was to touch the lives of others so they were "a little better" because she had crossed their path. She gave of herself without reservation, without thought of what she got in return.

The second quality that distinguished her was her genuineness. She was authentic and unpretentious. Her clothes or her looks were never what people remembered. She was remembered as a person who radiated warmth and care.

The third quality that motivated her was the fact that she had convictions and refused to take the path of least resistance. For a lad or a lassie to join the Salvation Army in Evangeline Booth's day meant they were willing to commit to a life of simplicity and pledged to engage the enemy in spiritual warfare. The term "army" reflected the lifestyle of those who signed on, and without convictions–strong convictions–no person could boldly lead others.

The fourth quality that distinguished this woman was her desire to please God rather than herself. She often quoted the words of Paul from the King James text, which read, "For do I now persuade men, or God? or do I seek to please men? for if I yet pleased men, I should not be the servant of Christ" (Galatians 1:10).

The fifth quality that separated her from not only the

women of her day but from the men as well is that she was her own person. Anyone who had the boldness to don a swimming suit in retirement and spring from the board just as she had done fifty years before, had to be secure, not caring a great deal what others might say. I, for one, have a deep respect and admiration for those who have outgrown the "cookie cutter" mentality and refuse to let the world force them into its mold.

May God give us more women who are as strong as Evangeline Booth and as committed to the cause of touching the lives of those around them. Yes, indeed.

RESOURCE READING
Luke 9

INSIGHT
What you do with your life is a choice.

APPLICATION
Take time to look up Romans 12:1, 2 in several different versions. Apply to your personal life what Paul says about not letting the world force you into its mold.

As radical as this one may be, sit down and write your obituary as it is now. Then write it as you want it to be and get to work making it what you would like it to be.

PURPOSE
Renny Scott

"The next day Jesus decided to leave for Galilee.
Finding Philip, he said to him, 'Follow me.' "
John 1:43

Just how much do we need? What kind of lifestyle does God want us to live? These are questions that as Christians we must consider seriously.

In all probability you won't arrive at the answers overnight. It may be a slow journey from the hills of suburbia to the inner city where people are hurting, or from where you are to a simple path of service. Rarely does a person wake up and say, "I've been living for an ego trip and I'm going to get rid of the big car, the fancy sailboat, and go live in the slums of Manila's Tondo working with the poor," but at some point you have to consider God's will and purpose for your life. I hasten to say that God deals with each of us on an individual basis, and what may be okay for some is not necessarily okay for others.

"It's time we began to look at the needs of our world in light of the trust of our possessions."

Take, for example, Renny Scott. Haven't heard of him? Probably not, but Scott is a fresh new voice saying it's time we began to look at the needs of our world in light of the trust of our possessions. Scott is an Episcopalian priest, and during his first stint in a parish, he began wrestling with the issue of materialism and how much is enough. He said, "I

268

just couldn't resolve the tension of living in a peaceful bedroom community while hell on earth was all around us in the form of hunger and poverty."

He went to Africa with a World Vision group, which was the beginning of involvement with the needs of other people. He sold everything and went to Africa–right? Wrong! But he did move into the inner city, where he lived and began thinking about those who were less fortunate than he. That was the second step. He took a church, a struggling one with a congregation of fifty that met in a school cafeteria. A year later he invited a Ugandan pastor to speak about the genocide taking place in Uganda under Idi Amin. The pastor used the story of Jesus with the loaves and fishes and challenged the people to do what they could.

Afterwards a deacon suggested they give the entire Sunday morning offering to help. Scott swallowed hard because that meant his salary was included. Eventually Scott and his wife, Margaret, came to grips with their lifestyle and did something that I have challenged many to do: put a cap on your lifestyle and say, "This much and no more"; and everything above that was given away no matter how much they received. The little church of fifty people grew into a body of people that averaged over 1800 in attendance and matched dollars for buildings with dollars for missions.

Today Renny Scott has taken on a new challenge: that of helping homeless people find housing that is affordable. Scott said, "I had to pause and ask myself what I would want to be doing if Christ returned today. And I found myself answering from Matthew 24 and 25. I needed to take my talents and invest them in the poor, the sick, and the naked." Hats off to Renny Scott, who discovered there is more to life than pastoring a large church with a good income.

Can anyone afford to be indifferent to the needs of others when the very example of Jesus dictated drawing a line somewhere and saying, "This much and no more"? When Nelson Rockefeller, one of the richest men in his day, was asked how much it takes to be satisfied, he replied, "Just a little bit more." The line between need and greed is a fine one, but it is there nonetheless.

RESOURCE READING
Psalm 1

INSIGHT
No child of God can be indifferent to the needs of others when the source of our blessing is the Father.

APPLICATION
Should you fear the result of being generous if you know Him who fills your barn? In other words, if you really believe God is the One who has given you what you have, and can give you more, should you fear giving to those in need?

In your life have you discovered the fine line between need and greed? At what point does "I want!" become "I need"?

Realizing Your Potential
Scott Hamilton

"My grace is sufficient for you,
for my power is made perfect in weakness."
2 Corinthians 12:9

"Hell," said Gian Carlo Menoti, "begins on the day when God grants us a clear vision of all that we might have achieved, of all the gifts which we have wasted, of all that we might have done which we did not do. . . ."

Scott Hamilton would agree. Scott is the Olympian gold medal winner who earned the admiration of the world for his 1984 performance at Sarajevo. It was his talent, as well as his wholesome "boy-next-door" image, that captured our hearts; but, for Scott, it represented another kind of triumph as well.

"Difficulties are either a challenge or a handicap."

When he was two years of age, Scott stopped growing, afflicted by a childhood disease that almost cost him his life. But Scott didn't die, and his adopted parents encouraged his rehabilitation by teaching him to skate. It was therapy for the little boy who was never quite as large as the rest of his classmates.

For Scott, his problem was not a handicap, but a challenge to be overcome, and overcome it he did. When individuals face challenges that can handicap them, they face an uphill fight, but Scott Hamilton for one did not give up.

Thomas Edison is another one who would have

understood Scott. From the age of twelve, Edison was afflicted with a severe hearing loss. Teachers urged his parents to take him out of classes. A "slow learner" was how educators classified him, but Edison turned his deafness into a creative tool that drowned out the distractions and allowed him to focus on what was of interest to him. Thomas Edison, the man labeled as a "slow learner" by teachers, gave our world more than a thousand inventions, including the incandescent globe and the phonograph. Like Scott Hamilton, he did not give up.

Helen Keller was another such person. She went through life not only sightless, but deaf as well. In her day, individuals who bore the label "deaf and dumb," as she did, were usually shunted to institutions where they lived as animals in an existence that was subhuman. Helen overcame her handicaps, though, and her indomitable spirit gave all humanity a legacy of courage. As the result of what she was able to conquer, thousands of individuals have refused to quit or crawl into the corner of despair. She, too, would have understood Scott Hamilton.

Brad Parks is another. Injured by an accident that put him permanently in a wheel chair, Brad could have looked for the "handicapped" spot for the rest of his life, feeling sorry that his athletic ability was gone and that he was permanently benched. Not Brad. He began to strengthen arm muscles by hitting tennis balls against the garage door, and, discovering that others could be motivated as well, formed the Wheel Chair Tennis Association. He's another in the same league with Scott Hamilton.

A well-meaning friend of mine tells about the time he offered condolences to a family who had a youngster diagnosed as being "retarded." "Don't be sorry for us," the child's mother replied. "All of us have been tremendously blessed by her presence in our home. We can't tell you," she said, "how much joy we have all found because of her presence in our lives."

What is normal? And what is a handicap? And who sets

the standard for normalcy, anyway? Is it being short or tall, thin or stout, a fast learner or a slow one? Is it your I.Q.? Or your ability to change a flat tire? Or your ability to see which way the stock market is headed? Hasn't God gifted each of us with abilities that can be explored to the depths? Aren't the real handicaps lethargy, indifference, the inability to shut off the TV set and pick up a book? The great handicaps do not belong to those who are born with challenges, but instead they limit the "normal people" who restrict their lives with mediocrity and boredom.

Yes, difficulties are either a challenge or a handicap for all of us. Would that we were all in Scott Hamilton's league.

RESOURCE READING
2 Corinthians 12:1-10

INSIGHT
Everyone in life faces challenges of one kind or another, but to hide behind the difficulty only keeps us from realizing the measure of God's grace that can make us what He wants us to be and do.

APPLICATION
When difficulties strike, do you consider them as opportunities or as challenges?

How do you turn difficulties into blessings? Who are some of the people you look up to, individuals who have turned handicaps into challenges?

SACRIFICE
Maximillan Kolbe

"Greater love has no one than this,
that he lay down his life for his friend."
John 15:13

It was three in the afternoon on one of the last days of July 1941, when the men of Block 14 were digging gravel outside the Auschwitz concentration camp. Suddenly the sirens began to shriek and German sentries shouldered their guns. There had been an escape. Silently the men of Block 14 prayed that the escapee had not been from their block.

That evening their worst fears were confirmed. The missing prisoner had been from Block 14. The entire camp was punished by receiving no evening meal, which usually consisted of a dried piece of bread and some cabbage soup or gruel.

"None of us has the right to live selfishly."

The next day the remaining six hundred men from Block 14 were forced to stand on the parade ground under the broiling sun. Men fell over from the heat and fatigue. Those who collapsed were left to die where they lay. "At the day's end," wrote newspaper woman Connie Lauerman, "the deputy commander, Fritsch, arrived in his crisply pressed uniform and shiny jackboots to announce the fate of the terrified men in dirty, blue-gray striped prison suits. The silence was absolute. 'The fugitive has not been found,' barked Fritsch. 'In reprisal for your comrade's escape, 10 of you will die by starvation. Next time it will be 20.' "

The men slated for starvation were selected. One of those men, Franciszek Gajowniczek, a Polish army sergeant, was sobbing, "My wife and my children." Suddenly a Polish Franciscan priest, Maximillan Kolbe, pushed his way to the front as S.S. guards sighted their rifles on his chest. "I want to talk to the commander," he said, looking Fritsch straight in the eye.

"Herr Kommandant," he began without faltering, "I wish to make a request, please."

"What do you want?" barked the commandant.

"I want to die in place of this prisoner," pointing to the sobbing Gajowniczek. "I have no wife and no children. Besides, I'm old and not good for anything."

Kolbe's request was totally out of the ordinary and completely unexpected. There was absolute silence, but soon it was broken with the words, "Request granted!"

Maximillan Kolbe died of starvation in place of a man who bore the sentence of death. Jesus Christ Himself said it: "Greater love has no man than this, that a man lay down his life for a friend" (John 15:13).

Maximillan Kolbe, now St. Maximillan to Catholics, will long be remembered for that heroic act of sacrifice. However, it seems to me that there are scores of men and women in the ranks of the saints who have never been canonized, those who care for the elderly, who wash the soiled linen and gently turn the frail bodies, the armies of nurses and doctors who tenderly minister to the needs of others who are repulsive and repugnant because of putrid illness. There are vast numbers of people who sacrifice themselves in a very real way for others. "God is not unjust," wrote the writer of the New Testament Book of Hebrews. "He will not forget your work and the love you have shown Him as you have helped His people and continue to help them" (Hebrews 6:10).

In all probability God will never, never ask you to make the decision that Maximillan Kolbe made, yet He does ask you to make a decision of your own, because real love demands your personal sacrifice for someone else. None of us has the right to live selfishly, for all of us have been the recipients, in some way, of the love that prompted Maximillan Kolbe to give his life. Remember, friend, it was Jesus Christ, Himself, who gave Himself freely and without compensation that we might live eternally. Yes, greater love has no man than this, that a man lay down his life for a friend.

RESOURCE READING
Daniel 6

INSIGHT
God never promised that life would be a Disneyland, but He did promise to be with us, to strengthen us, and to help us no matter where we may be.

APPLICATION
Do you think that Kolbe ever thought about becoming famous over what he did?

If you can locate a copy of Viktor Frankl's book on his concentration experience, read it and see how that horrible experience brought out both the best and the worst in people.

SACRIFICE OF LOVE
Sir Ernest Shackleton

"Greater love has no one than this,
that he lay down his life for his friends."
John 15:13

In the year 1908, the Irish explorer Sir Ernest Shackleton headed an expedition with the goal of reaching the South Pole in the Antarctic. The destination of the expedition was to cross the twenty-one hundred miles of antarctic wasteland and reach the pole, something that had never been done before.

The fact that they were traversing uncharted wasteland locked in by ice and snow didn't deter them. En route their ship was stopped by the ice pack, crushed, and destroyed. They loaded the supplies on the sleds and pursued their elusive goal.

"God honored the spirit of a man who was willing to give his last morsel of food to his brother."

Shackleton and his men came within ninety-seven miles of the pole and had to turn back. Those were the days when hardy men made a desperate run for it; if they succeeded, they were heroes. If they failed, they were statistics in the record book. Shackleton came closer to the pole than anyone had ever been before, but the time came when he and the men realized that to continue the expedition would not only endanger their lives but result in their deaths.

They were weary and exhausted and food was running

low. To continue would mean sacrificing some of the sled dogs, and with each loss, the burden of carrying equipment or even trekking would grow greater for every man. With heavy hearts, they turned and started back for the nearest outpost of civilization on South Georgia Island, some twelve hundred miles away.

Shackleton and his men had to trudge over two hundred miles of ice floes, dragging behind them a lifeboat weighing nearly a ton, taken from the ship that had brought them. When they finally reached open waters with the lifeboat, they faced an angry ocean with waves as high as ninety feet.

In his diary Shackleton told of the time when their food supplies were exhausted, save for one last ration of hardtack, a dried sort of biscuit, that was distributed to each man. Some of the men took ice or snow, melted it, and made tea while consuming their biscuit. Others, however, took the hardtack and stowed it in a food sack, thinking that they would save it for a last moment of hungry desperation.

The fire was built up, and weary, exhausted men climbed into their sleeping bags to face a restless sleep, tossing and turning. Shackleton said that he was almost asleep when out of the corner of his eyes, he noticed one of his most trusted men sitting up in his sleeping bag and looking about to see if anyone was watching.

Shackleton's heart sank within him as this man began to reach toward the food sack of the man next to him. This was one of his most dependable men. Never did he think that this man would steal from his neighbor. Shackleton didn't move and watched as the man took the food sack of the man next to him, opened it, and then took his own hardtack and put it in the other man's sack.

Jesus put it: "Greater love has no one than this, that he lay down his life for his friends" (John 15:13). When Shackleton and the rest of the party reached their final destination seven months after it had begun, they were so hardened and emaciated that friends did not even recognize them. How did they survive? One biographer wrote, "To a man, however, those who had completed the journey reported that they felt the presence of One unseen to guide them on their perilous trek. Somehow they knew they were not alone."

God answered the prayers of these hardy explorers, for a great deal more than Irish resolve was necessary for survival. God honored the spirit of a man who was willing to give his last morsel of food to his brother. Tough men, that Shackleton and his bunch. Truly tough, as only God can make us.

RESOURCE READING
John 15:1-13

INSIGHT

Difficulties are like hot water to a tea bag—they bring out what's inside, whether it is good or evil. Sometimes very difficult situations demonstrate how great individuals really are—generous, caring, and compassionate.

APPLICATION

Find out about the experiences of such individuals as Corrie ten Boom, who was in the Ravensbruck concentration camp during World War II.

When you find yourself tempted to take the last piece of something, ask yourself what you would like that person to do if he or she had gotten there first. Then do it yourself.

SPIRITUAL REVOLUTION

Rosario Rivera

"Then he said to them all: 'If anyone would come after me,
he must deny himself and take up his cross daily and follow me.' "
Luke 9:23

Rosario Rivera has been a revolutionary most of her life. Born out of wedlock in Lima, Peru, she grew up filled with anger over her poverty and hunger. Eventually, anger turned to hatred toward her mother, her teachers, and the system that had spawned her. At age thirteen she had given up school and was deeply involved in reading Marx and Lenin. By eighteen she was a militant revolutionary and a communist.

> *"Whenever a person receives Jesus Christ, a revolutionary change results."*

In Cuba she met the famed revolutionary, Che Guevara, and became his assistant. Upon his death she became all the more bitter and returned to her native Peru. She was there when another Latin revolutionary returned to Peru. His name: Luis Palau, but Palau was a revolutionary of a different kind. His commitment is to the Master, not Marxism.

Palau was speaking in the bull arena in December 1971 when Rosario decided that she had to kill him. She was enraged while listening to Palau's radio program in Spanish and decided that he had to die. With a gun on her person, she went to the arena. Telling about the incident later, Palau said, "During my message I spoke about the 'Five Hells of Human Existence'—murder, robbery, deceit, hypocritical home and hatred.

"Each sin I mentioned pricked Rosario's conscience—for she had committed them all—and only made her all the more determined to kill." Trying to maneuver into position to fire the fatal bullet, she came forward with three hundred people to receive Christ as personal Savior. A little old lady who was a counselor walked up to her and said, "Madam, can I help you receive Christ?"

Rosario did not know how to respond, so she hit the old lady in the face and ran away; but as she tried to sleep that night, God kept taking the words of Palau's message and pushing her toward the cross with them. "Cursed is the one who trusts in man. . . . Blessed is the man who trusts in the Lord. . . ."

After a sleepless night, she fell to her knees and received Jesus Christ as her personal Savior. Palau says, "The Lord absolutely revolutionized this Marxist guerrilla. Today she is an amazing testimony to the transforming power of the Word of God."

When her communist comrades came looking for her, she "machine-gunned" with the Gospel, as she puts it. Now years have passed, and Rosario still considers herself a revolutionary, but her weapons are totally different. She says, "If my heart burned for the revolution in the past, then it burns even more now, and if I did a lot for the poor before, then I do more now."

She has tackled poverty, corruption in government, injustice in the system, and the conditions of poor factory workers; but she's done so with the compassion of Jesus Christ. Scores of people, like Rosario, have switched allegiance and have begun to march to the beat of a different drummer, now serving Jesus Christ with far more fervency than they ever did as political revolutionaries.

How about you? With whose cause have you identified? Or are you simply living for self, one selfish day at a time? To know more about the transforming power of Jesus Christ, read the Gospel of John and decide for yourself. As

C. T. Studd wrote a century ago, "If Jesus Christ be God, then no sacrifice is too great for Him." Whenever a person receives Jesus Christ, a revolutionary change results–the kind that produces deep peace within instead of burning anger and hatred. Just ask Rosario Rivera.

RESOURCE READING
Acts 9

INSIGHT
Anyone who begins to look at life through the eyes of Jesus Christ will have his or her heart touched by the needs of people and respond to them.

APPLICATION
If Jesus were alive today, how do you think He would respond to some of the needs of the inner cities?

Are your friends a reflection of your values and attitudes? Or do you know someone whose ethnic background is different from yours?

Tough Love
Mary Slessor

" 'For I know the plans I have for you,' declares the Lord, 'plans to prosper you and not to harm you, plans to give you hope and a future.' "
Jeremiah 29:11

Scotland of the 1840s was as barren as the nursery rhyme cupboard of Old Mother Hubbard. The decade was known as the "Hungry Forties," as crops failed and migrant workers were driven to the overcrowded, desolate cities. In 1848, Mary Mitchell Slessor was born to an alcoholic shoemaker whose wife was a weaver as well as the eventual mother of seven children. When drink finally overcame her father, the scant wages of his wife drove the family to Dundee, where young Mary grew up. At the age of seven she was forced to work in the mill half-time. This meant schooling had to fit in with the work schedule. Home was a tiny, one-room flat with no water, no lighting, and no sanitation facilities.

"God plus one are always a majority— let me know Thou art with me."

It was a tough world for this redheaded, streetwise young woman. She finally dropped out of school to work in the mill, but the girl who knew how to use her knuckles with the local rowdies had a tender heart. When a missionary from the Calabar in Africa (now known as the Sudan) spoke in their local church, Mary's heart was inflamed. Everything, though, was against her becoming a missionary—everything and everybody but God. Nonetheless, God was able to use

283

all of these circumstances in a mighty way to her advantage.

Many years later, Mary Slessor, who became known as Mary, Queen of the Calabar, wrote in her diary, "God plus one are always a majority–let me know Thou art with me." Mary Slessor–the fighting Scot from the slums of Dundee– went to an Africa that was still reeling from the horrors of the slave trade. It was diseased by such pagan customs as killing all twins because the natives were convinced that one had been fathered by the devil. Since they were uncertain as to which twin was so fathered, they immediately killed both.

The Africa to which Mary went was competing for the white man's money, weapons, and booze. The impact of Mary Slessor, who sacrificed pleasure, health, and almost her very life, is so beautifully described in a book written by James Buchan entitled *The Expendable Mary Slessor*, which I highly recommend.

Buchan describes Mary's accomplishments: "She never opposed the African ways except where they degraded the Africans themselves. She had learned from St. Paul–'Paul, laddie,' she called him–that her Lord loved these people enough to give His life for them, but loving them never meant acquiescing to the base aspects of pagan culture. She threatened and begged in order to save lives; she adopted dozens of African babies that were left to die in the bush. She fought for the right of the African women to be free from death at the whim of a man. For nearly forty years–until her death in 1915–she lived as an African, often in a village hut. When she died, thousands of Africans wept for the Eka Kpukpro Owo–"Mother of all the peoples."

Buchan confirms a story I heard long ago. After many years in Africa, Mary returned to her native Scotland, a stooping, gray-haired woman, so wrinkled that her friends failed to recognize her. Recuperating at a friend's home, her hosts, the McCrindles, often heard her talking in her room. They thought the isolation and privation had actually affected her sanity; but upon listening to her conversation, they soon discovered that she was chatting with her heavenly Father–a habit Mary cultivated by keeping in constant touch with Him.

If it is true that "when the going gets tough, the tough get going," then certainly that was true of the Scot whom I consider to be among the great Christian leaders of the last century–Mary Slessor, Queen of the Calabar.

RESOURCE READING
Jeremiah 29:4-14

INSIGHT
God used the rough and tumble background of Mary Slessor to accomplish great things for Him, just as He can use your background, no matter what it is, to do something unique.

APPLICATION
If Mary had grown up in a more genteel home, do you think she could have been so successful in Africa?

If Mary had married and settled down, do you think she would have had the same freedom to serve the Lord?

TOUGH LOVE

Olga Robertson

"Don't forget about those in jail. Suffer with them as though you were there yourself. Share the sorrow of those being mistreated, for you know what they are going through."
Hebrews 13:3, TLB

How many men can one woman love? More than one woman has wrestled with that question, and today's commentary will not give you a definitive answer. I, for one, have come to conclude that one woman can love at least nine thousand men. Her name is Olga Robertson, and she's affectionately known as "Mommie Olga" to the nine thousand inmates of the new Bilibid Prison outside of the city of Manila in the Philippines.

"When you are really in love with Christ, you can love an infinite number of other people."

Unquestionably, Olga qualifies as one of the most interesting women you would ever meet anywhere. She is an unusual contradiction of what you would expect to find in a woman, which is part of the reason she has a heart big enough to love so many men–many of whom are rather unlovable. Olga carries an American passport, but actually she is Lebanese. She has reached the age where most women settle down and begin to think of leisure and grandchildren. However, "Mommie Olga" is a dynamic bundle of energy with projects going in all directions at once, from the supervision of a new chapel for prison guards to seeing that none is turned away when there is a spiritual need.

Most women would be frightened to move freely among tough convicts in one of the world's largest prisons, where gangs are a part of survival. She says she's a "scaredy-cat," but the fact that she has spent almost eighteen years as spiritual counselor and advisor at Bilibid belies the fact that she's afraid of anything. Olga's thin frame, her dancing dark eyes, and bouncing steps have endeared her to the hearts of men who see very little of women in a men's prison.

Olga is a very special kind of woman. She has a powerful weapon working for her, the kind that criminologists and law enforcement officials would do well to study. It is the power of an old-fashioned, dynamic love that changes lives for good—and for God.

I was with Olga recently and saw firsthand how God's love through her had transformed the lives of men who had been murderers, rapists, and hardened criminals. That is now all gone, and their lives have been drastically changed. As the men in the choir lined up to get their sample of after-shave lotion, given out personally by "Mommie Olga," I saw not criminals but men who laughed and joked and reflected a tenderness that is rare anywhere—especially in a prison. Their eyes glistened with tears as they sang and testified that Jesus Christ had changed their lives.

As I sat there and pondered the forceful impact of one lone woman presenting God, I could not help thinking that the human heart is an amazing thing. When you are in love with yourself, there is little room to love anyone else. Greed, selfishness, misery, and unhappiness are the symptoms; but when you are really in love with Christ, you can love an infinite number of other people—yes, even nine thousand men. I saw that gleam, that indefinable dynamic love of Christ in her eyes as she said, "God loves them, and so do I."

Hers is not a sentimental kind of love, but the kind that is durable and tough enough to take her to the side of the electric chair as men pay society's price for their crimes. That's the transforming power of God's love in a heart big enough to love as Christ loves in this loveless world.

RESOURCE READING
2 Timothy 4

INSIGHT
One person, doing what he or she can, makes a tremendous difference. A single light is more powerful than the combined darkness.

APPLICATION
If you find it somewhat difficult to love people who are different from you, read Romans 5:5 and ask God to fill your heart with Himself, who alone is love.

Take the concordance of your Bible and look up New Testament references to love.

TRUST
Ira Sankey

"Of the increase of his government and peace there will be no end."
Isaiah 9:7

More than a century ago, Ira Sankey led the singing for the great meetings of the American evangelist Dwight L. Moody, and on a certain occasion, Sankey was asked to sing. He did, singing a then-popular song called "The Shepherd Song." After the meeting was over, a man with a rough, weather-beaten face approached Sankey and asked, "Did you ever serve in the Union Army?"

"Yes," replied Sankey, curiously, "in the spring of 1860."

"Can you remember if you were doing picket duty on a bright, moonlit night in 1860?"

Again, Sankey replied, "Yes," this time very much surprised.

"It's time to lay down our weapons and let Him touch our lives with His peace."

"So did I," replied the stranger, "but I was in the Confederate Army." He continued, "When I saw you standing at your post I said to myself, 'That fellow will never get away from there alive.' I was standing in the shadow completely concealed while the full light of the moon was falling on you. At that instant, just as a moment ago, you raised your eyes to heaven and began to sing. Music, especially songs, has always had a wonderful power over me and I took my finger off the trigger. 'Let him sing his song to the end,' I said to myself. 'I can shoot him afterward.' But the song you sang then was the song you sang just now. I hear the words perfectly. 'We are thine, do Thou befriend us, Be the guardian of our ways.' Those words stirred up many memories in my heart and I began to think of my childhood and my God-fearing mother. She had many, many times sung that same song to me, but she died all too soon, otherwise my life would have been much different.

"But when you finished that song, it was impossible for me to take aim at you again. I thought the Lord who was able to save that man from certain death must surely be great and mighty and my arm of its own accord fell limp at my side."

Who would deny that truth is always stranger than fiction? Out of every war and every tragedy come stories that deeply touch the heart, such as the time that American and German soldiers in World War I were in their bunkers on Christmas Eve, and someone began singing, "O Little Town of Bethlehem," and men who had been shooting at each other only hours before, on both sides of the lines, blended their voices, some in German and others in English, singing, "O holy Child of Bethlehem! Descend to us, we pray; Cast out our sin and enter in, Be born in us today. We hear the Christmas angels The great glad tidings tell; O come to us, abide with us, Our Lord Emmanuel."

Strange isn't it, the effect that Christmas has on people, making friends of enemies and brothers of strangers? I, for one, am convinced that the only hope of peace in the world, the only glimmer of light that makes me think there is yet a chance for humanity, is through the babe born at Bethlehem who is now the King of Kings and Lord of Lords.

One of the titles Isaiah bestowed on him was "Prince of Peace" (Isaiah 9:6). Whether it is a sniper who is about to pick off a sentry or an angry wife who wants to blow her husband away with a divorce, anger and bitterness divide and destroy. You believe in Christmas, right? But do you believe in it enough to let the Prince of Peace bring peace to your troubled heart and life? He's the only one who can cause us to stack arms and surrender to the King of Love. It's time to lay down our weapons and let Him touch our lives with His peace—the real kind that changes our hearts and eradicates our sin. Yes, that's the abiding truth of Christmas.

RESOURCE READING
Luke 1:39-56

INSIGHT

The only solution to conflict—whether it is between nations or between family members—is to let the Prince of Peace control our lives.

APPLICATION

When you find yourself becoming angry with someone, take a deep breath, count to ten, and pray, "Lord, what is the right thing for me to do in this situation?" You will be amazed how that simple exercise can make a difference.

There are many, many references and titles given to Christ such as "Prince of Peace." How many more can you think of?

TRUST
Go Puan Seng

> *"Trust in the LORD with all your heart and lean not on
> your own understanding; in all your ways acknowledge him,
> and he will make your paths straight."*
> Proverbs 3:5-6

In his book *Refuge and Strength*, Go Puan Seng tells of the four
years during World War II when he and his family were only
one step from death as they eluded the Japanese soldiers in
the jungles of the Philippines. When United Press International reviewed the book, they
pointed out that the purpose of
Seng's book is not to re-open old
wounds, but to remind the world
that absolute and complete faith in
God and in the promises of His
Word is sufficient to take one
through the most serious crisis.

*"God will lead us
if we trust Him
with all our hearts."*

When World War II broke out, Seng was the publisher
of the influential Chinese newspaper based in Manila
called the *Fukien Times*. When the swords began to rattle,
Seng came out strongly against the Japanese for their
aggression in the Philippines. Seng strongly urged resistance. When Manila fell in December, 1941, Go Puan Seng
found himself a hunted man, with his name on the list of
most wanted men.

The days of his fiery editorials and rhetoric against the
invaders were over, and Jimmy Go, as he was known to his
friends, began to live one day at a time. In spite of the

constant danger to his life, God gave Seng a quiet confidence that He would guide and protect him.

Shortly after Seng took his family and escaped to the mountainous jungles some thirty miles from Manila, the former publisher found himself at the point of despair, and in desperation, he cried out to God. In the stillness of the jungle, God met him! And from that point on, Jimmy Go was never in total despair. At times the enemy was so close that their voices could be heard beating the bushes in pursuit of them. At other times God led them through the enemy lines, as they prayed fervently that God would spare their lives. And, in response to their prayers, the soldiers would wave them on, not realizing that one of the enemy's most wanted men was in the horse-drawn cart.

It was through the Word of God that specific guidance was given to the party in exile, guidance at times that seemed totally out of keeping with the circumstances. In his own words, Go tells of an instance when, "We were surrounded inside the Japanese General Yamashita's battle lines. That was in 1944 (about the end of December), when the retreating Japanese soldiers were pouring into our mountains from the west side. By all human instincts, we should go east, run deeper into the mountains to keep distance between us and the retreating Japanese soldiers. We prayed to God and God's answer was in the good book of Joshua. It said, 'Goeth down westward to the coast. . . .' When I told my group that we were going westward, many of them were against me. Some of them left me. Ten of them went east instead of westward. They never have returned. . . . We went westward. We did encounter Japanese soldiers retreating from the front lines, but they did not do us any harm."

The pressures of those four years, when they found refuge and strength in God, have produced two of life's choicest diamonds. The Sengs have never forgotten the God that brought them through the jungle. The honors that have been heaped upon their shoulders in the world of journalism have never caused them to lose sight of the fact that God will lead us if we trust Him with all our hearts, and lean not on our human understanding when God leads us contrary to human logic.

After we had lunch with the author and his wife, we walked through a busy department store, and as we were bidding the Sengs farewell, Jimmy said, "Brother, will you pray for me?" As I prayed, perhaps twenty or thirty people stopped to watch in curiosity as an American prayed quietly for a Chinese Filipino. When a man has found that God is our refuge and our strength, nothing else really matters but that He guides and leads us hour by hour.

RESOURCE READING
Proverbs 3

INSIGHT
The miraculous escape of the Seng family demonstrated that God will lead and guide His children, often in ways that seem to refute logic.

APPLICATION
Have you had a situation in your experience when you knew that God had guided you or protected you? Have you ever written it out? Do so and share it with a friend.

The Psalms say that the angel of the Lord camps around those who fear Him (Psalm 34:7). Have you ever experienced such protection?

TRUST

J. C. Penney

*"I am the resurrection and the life: he that believes in me,
though he were dead, yet shall he live: and whosoever lives
and believes in me shall never die."*
John 11: 25, 26

When the U. S. stock market crashed in 1929, J. C. Penney had made some unwise personal commitments. He became so worried that he could not sleep. Night after night, Penney tossed and turned and became obsessed with a fear of death. Out of this nervous condition, he developed a disease known as shingles. He was hospitalized and given sedation to relieve the intense pain. A combination of circumstances, physical and mental, led him to believe he would not live until morning. He wrote farewell letters to his wife and son. He sincerely believed that the monster of death was lurking for him in the hospital corridors.

> *"Simple faith in God goes beyond reason, yet it gives peace that is most reasonable."*

Somehow, Penney lived through the night. The next morning the fear-torn Penney heard a group of people singing in the hospital chapel. The words of the song drifted down the halls: "God Will Take Care of You." He listened to the words intently. They were followed by a reading of a Scripture passage and prayer.

Then, something happened. In Penney's own words: "I can't explain it. I can only call it a miracle. I felt as if I had been instantly lifted out of the darkness of a dungeon into warm, brilliant sunlight. I felt as if I had been transported from hell to paradise. I felt the power of God as I had never felt it before. . . . From that day to this, my life has been free from worry."

Penney's fear of death was suddenly cut down to size. It ceased to haunt him. Why? Neither Penney nor anyone else could explain it by reason; yet countless millions have discovered that when they committed their lives to Christ, they found the reality of a supernatural peace that cuts the fear of death down to proper size.

Knowing Christ links us to Him who has already fought the battle and won. Remember Christ's words, "Because I live you shall live also" (John 14:19). This is why the Apostle Paul could say, " 'Where, O death, is your victory? Where, O death, is your sting?' The sting of death is sin, and the power of sin is the law. But thanks be to God! He gives us the victory through our Lord Jesus Christ" (1 Corinthians 15:55-57).

Simple faith in God goes beyond reason, yet it gives peace that is most reasonable. What more beautiful expression of peace in the face of death is there than the Twenty-third Psalm: "The Lord is my shepherd; I shall not want. . . .Yea, though I walk through the valley of the shadow of death, I will fear no evil: for thou art with me."

John Bunyan expresses the attitude of those who have committed their lives to Christ: "Let dissolution come when it will, it can do the Christian no harm, for it be but a passage out of a prison into a palace; out of a vast sea of troubles into a haven of rest; out of a crowd of enemies, to an innumerable company of true, loving, and faithful friends; out of shame, reproach and contempt into exceeding great and eternal glory."

Christian faith is unique in its assertion that the grave is not the end but merely the beginning of an eternal tomorrow. How beautiful are the words of Christ: "I am the resurrection and the life: he that believes in me, though he were dead, yet shall he live: and whosoever lives and believes in me shall never die"(John 11: 25-26).

William Cullen Bryant penned these familiar lines:

"So live, that when thy summons comes to join
The innumerable caravan which moves
To that mysterious realm, where each shall take
His chamber in the silent halls of death,
Thou go not, like the quarry-slave at night,
Scourged to his dungeon, but, sustained and soothed
By an unfaltering trust, approach thy grave,
Like one that wraps the drapery of his couch
About him, and lies down to pleasant dreams."

RESOURCE READING
1 Corinthians 15:51-58

INSIGHT
Because our Lord promised to never leave us nor forsake us and told us He was going to prepare a place for us in heaven, death should never be feared.

APPLICATION
Look up Hebrews 2:15 and think about how that should take away the fear of death.

Have you lost a friend or member of your family who has gone to heaven? What do you know about heaven? For a start read Philippians 1:23 and 2 Corinthians 5:8.

TRUST
Hezekiah

"The LORD is good, a strong hold in the day of trouble;
and he knoweth them that trust in him."
Nahum 1:7, KJV

If ever a man had reason to feel that God had let him down, that man was Hezekiah. "Hezekiah who?" you may be saying. Hezekiah, the king of Judah who ascended the throne of David about 726 B.C. If you're a bit rusty on Old Testament history, I'll brief you.

"The same God who gave deliverance to Hezekiah is still giving deliverance."

Having replaced his father Ahaz, who had been a careless ruler, Hezekiah got his act together! He began a great reformation. He broke down the idols Ahaz had set up. He reopened the temple and restored the service of God. He even dipped into his own funds to provide for restoration and repairs.

In the sixth year of Hezekiah's reign, the Northern Kingdom (Israel) fell to Sennacherib, king of Assyria. True, Israel was often an enemy of Judah, but they were all related by blood through King David, who had established the kingdom. So when Assyria wiped out Israel, Hezekiah knew that his borders were more vulnerable.

Then Sennacherib moved against Judah. Here's the text: "After all that Hezekiah had so faithfully done, Sennacherib king of Assyria came and invaded Judah!" Did Hezekiah feel God had let him down? Did he feel that God owed him better treatment than he got? If so, he didn't say so. Why? Hezekiah had faced the enemy more than once and had learned that what counts isn't the strength of your enemy but the strength of your defense, and he had learned God can be that defense.

How Hezekiah faced a formidable enemy and won gives us insight for facing the enemies of life today, who in their own way are just as ferocious as any Assyrian warrior who ever lifted up a sword in battle. Before I tell you how he faced the enemy, I want to remind you that the Assyrian soldier was about as tough and mean a character as ever assembled on any battlefield. Go to some of the great museums of the world and you will see reliefs of Sennacherib's army with their coats of mail, their swords and weapons. It is said that Lenin, Hitler, and Stalin were all disciples of Assyrian military policy. It was a formidable adversary that confronted Hezekiah, one who had proved to be among the world's most terrible.

You will find the whole text in the Old Testament, in 2 Chronicles 32. In studying Hezekiah's response, you will notice two very important guidelines that will help you no matter who or what has come to invade your private world. First, Hezekiah did what he could do himself. He built walls supporting the walls that were already there. He made weapons; he encouraged the men in the army by reminding them that with Sennacherib was only the arm of flesh, but with them was the "Lord our God to help them and to fight their battles."

All of that was true, but Hezekiah didn't stop there. The second approach was this: "King Hezekiah and the prophet Isaiah. . .cried out in prayer to heaven about this" (2 Chronicles 32:20). The government and the religious community united their hearts in fervent prayer. They didn't talk about prayer. They prayed! And what happened?

God gave tremendous deliverance. In confronting the problems facing you, learn from Hezekiah. Do what you can yourself. Encourage others to join you, to stand together, and then seek God with all your heart. The same God who gave deliverance to Hezekiah is still giving deliverance. ". . .A strong hold in the day of trouble" as Nahum wrote, "and He knoweth them that trust in Him" (Nahum 1:7).

RESOURCE READING
2 Chronicles 32

INSIGHT
The greater the challenge, the greater the opportunity for God to do something so awesome and wonderful that you know it could never have just happened.

APPLICATION
Do you look on difficulties as problems or possibilities?

If the battle belongs to the Lord, why do we worry so much about it?

WISDOM
John the Baptist

"John. . .will be great in the sight of the Lord."
Luke 1:13, 15

One of the evidences for the supernatural character of the Bible is the manner in which the flaws of heroes are portrayed. The writers never gloss over their faults or omit their failures as we tend to do of ourselves. In unvarnished strokes the writers of Scripture describe people just as they are. Subsequently, a vast army of men and women march across the stage of redemption fully human, completely real. Such was the man who served as the forerunner of Jesus, a man described as "John the Baptist," a name given to him based on his desire to seal repentance with baptism so that all would know of the change of heart people had experienced.

"Those who walk the narrow pathway will always have plenty of elbow room."

Had John walked into a local church today, he probably would be asked to leave, or, at best, sit in the overflow area where more air circulated. John was unconventional, totally unconventional. Obviously his demeanor and dress were unconventional. Dressed in camel's hair, he had the appearance of an individual who was completely out of step with society, a social misfit. His hair was wild and his beard unkempt. Though I can't prove it, I've always thought that probably John's hair and beard were a sandy, burnished red. His skin was leathery and

301

tough. His eyes, bright and penetrating.

When someone asked Jesus about John's appearance, He replied, "What did you go out into the desert to see? A reed swayed by the wind? If not, what did you go out to see? A man dressed in fine clothes? No, those who wear fine clothes are in kings' palaces" (Matthew 11:7, 8). John's diet was unconventional as well. Locusts and wild honey were his staples, according to local reports. But then would you expect a man who lived in the desert to shop at the local supermarket and feast on bagels and smoked salmon?

John was also unconventional in his character. A man's man with a heart after God, John's character was without flaw. When the crowds came to hear him speak, instead of basking in the glory of notoriety, John made it clear that he was only the forerunner, the front man of the coming Messiah. Is it any wonder that Jesus said of him, "Among those born of women there has not risen anyone greater than John the Baptist" (Matthew 11:11). What a commendation! It was this man whom Jesus sought out when He began His ministry and asked to be baptized in water, thereby giving us an example that we ought to follow.

Yet with his rugged character and integrity, John was fully human. When he was thrown into prison as the result of making political enemies, he sent his disciples to Jesus asking, "Are you the one who was to come, or should we expect someone else?" (Matthew 11:3).

John was not only unconventional in his dress, his character, and his humility, he was unconventional in his message. He never pitched his message to the grandstand. He openly and even defiantly proclaimed the truth in spite of the fact that prison and death resulted. What a man who stood resolutely for what was right and godly!

John's life speaks clearly to the flaws of our culture today. His example tells us that those who really walk with God will be out of touch with the mindset and mentality of our age. This isn't to suggest that we adopt weird, strange dress and think that we are godly, but it does imply we should proclaim loudly and clearly that those who walk the narrow pathway will always have plenty of elbow room.

Long before John, God spoke to Samuel, "The LORD does not look at the things man looks at. Man looks at the outward appearance, but the LORD looks at the heart" (1 Samuel 16:7).

As God looks at your life, what is it that He sees? It is an issue well worth thinking about.

RESOURCE READING
John 1:5-36

INSIGHT
Every life makes a statement, negatively or positively, and it is when the heart is pure that your life message is powerful.

APPLICATION
Should your dress be more important than your life message? What made John's message powerful?

Does your dress become part of your life message?

WISDOM

A. W. Tozer

"Since we have these promises, dear friends, let us purify ourselves
from everything that contaminates body and spirit,
perfecting holiness out of reverence for God."
2 Corinthians 7:1

On his tombstone there is a simple epitaph that reads,
"A. W. Tozer–A Man of God." That's it. He was born on
April 21, 1897, and at the age of seventeen was converted
to faith in Jesus Christ. Shortly thereafter, he cleaned out a
corner in the basement of his
father's home and began to satu-
rate himself in the book that
became his master, the Bible.

"We must simplify
our approach to God.
We must strip down
to essentials. . . ."

Aiden Wilson Tozer, or A. W.
as he preferred, using only the initials of his name, never got a formal seminary education. He was
basically a self-taught student of the Book, yet his writings
touched a generation for God. The books that Tozer wrote
are not for shallow searchers looking for the "quick fix" or
an "instant solution" to a problem that leaves you feeling
good. He wrote deep stuff, the kind you can't really grasp
at one sitting. You don't read Tozer like a newspaper or a
Reader's Digest. Reading Tozer demands concentration, taking what he says in "bite sizes," allowing you as a reader to
digest what he says and understand God in a new way.

One of the unique things about Tozer is that he brings
you into direct confrontation with the Almighty, and when

you close one of his books, you know that you have confronted the claims of Scripture in a new way, one which demands a decision. Two of his books, *The Pursuit of God* and *The Knowledge of the Holy*, have become classics, a tremendous achievement for a man who never received formal theological education. Leonard Ravenhill once spoke of Tozer saying, "I fear that we shall never see another Tozer. Men like him are not college bred but Spirit taught." He was right.

In one of his books Tozer wrote, "God discovers Himself to babes, and hides Himself in thick darkness from the wise and the prudent. We must simplify our approach to Him. We must strip down to essentials and they will be found to be blessedly few."

While some describe themselves as being in the Reformed Tradition as Martin Luther or John Calvin, Tozer described himself as a mystic, a term that conjures up images of someone who walks about with his head in a cloud, not quite in touch with reality. Writing about Tozer, Warren Wiersbe says that Tozer's mysticism was different. He defines it saying, "A mystic is simply a person who: (1) sees a real spiritual world beyond the world of sense; (2) seeks to please God rather than the crowd; (3) cultivates a close fellowship with God, senses His presence everywhere; and (4) relates his experience to the practical things of life."

Tozer believed that a lot of people know a great deal about God—they know the language, the songs, and the culture—but they do not know God Himself. They have been taught about God, but not taught by God, and there is a difference.

Most of Tozer's books were an outgrowth of messages he preached, and they uniformly brought hearers into direct confrontation with God. He would ask, "Is God real to you?" "Is your heart hungering and thirsting after personal righteousness?" "Is yours a firsthand experience with Him, or a secondhand one through others?"

He never owned an automobile, and even after he became a successful author and public speaker, he was never affected by his money. To the contrary, he gave most of his money away to those who were hurting and in need. Some considered him strange, and his views on music and entertainment were out of step with his generation, but he walked in step with the Holy Spirit and gave us a legacy of holiness and truth. A. W. Tozer—a man of God as his tombstone truthfully asserts.

RESOURCE READING
2 Corinthians 7:1-10

INSIGHT
God often uses men and women who lack some of the requisites that usually make for success—education, a good family, money, and appearance. To realize our inadequacies and to depend totally on God allows Him to work through us, giving Him the credit for what He does.

APPLICATION
If you have never read anything by Tozer, get one of his books and read it slowly and thoughtfully.

Do you think that Tozer would have been more successful had he had a formal education?

WISDOM
Arnold Toynbee

"Blessed is the nation whose God is the Lord."
Psalm 33:12

Arnold Toynbee, a historian and critic of Western civilization, will long be remembered. Toynbee, who died at the age of eighty-six, was born on April 14, 1889 into a family of distinguished scholars and philanthropists. Although he was best known for his twelve-volume *A Study of History*, written over a thirty-four-year period, Toynbee was also vocal about a wide range of topics, from sex to religion to the spread of cities.

His extensive study of history notes a pattern in the rise and fall of civilizations, their birth, growth, and decay, and also demonstrates that moral and spiritual decay were common factors in the decline of a great world power. Toynbee has noted that nineteen of the past twenty-one great civilizations of the world were not destroyed from without but rather were destroyed by moral and spiritual decadence from within.

> *"History confirms what the Bible tells us about humanity's nature: the human heart is basically sinful."*

Toynbee also believed that humanity was the highest spiritual presence in the universe, and that the human race can be saved from spiritual destruction only by recognizing human beings' spiritual nature and by responding to the basic tenets of Christianity. Toynbee is not alone in his criticism of the contemporary world and its departure from Christian principles.

307

English journalist Malcolm Muggeridge, whose life we've already discussed, has noted, like Toynbee, the decline of civilization along with the rise of modern technology, and he believes that the farther away we move from the principles of Christianity, the more pagan we become. "Snuff out the light of the Gospel," he declares, "and only gross darkness will remain."

Christianity is not a way of life, though it vitally does affect the way people live; instead, it involves a personal experience with Jesus Christ as a living person. But no thoughtful mentor of history would deny that those who have followed the lonely Galilean have left behind institutions that have benefited all mankind. Consider that in the wake of Christianity, you will find the great colleges and universities of our day—many of which have been the very cradle of science and technology of the twentieth century. You will also find the hospitals in the big cities, as well as the far-flung remote mission stations of the world. Centuries ago the psalmist wrote, "Blessed is the nation whose God is the Lord" (Psalm 33:12).

History stands like an open book. Though people may disagree on interpretation, the facts of history stand; and none would deny what Toynbee so aptly observed, that civilizations follow a definite pattern. "History repeats itself," we say; and since this is true, there is a lesson to learn from history. History confirms what the Bible tells us about humanity's nature: the human heart is basically sinful. Christ said out of peoples' hearts proceed evil thoughts, murders, adultery, and sexual sins.

The marble tombstone of Arnold Toynbee may someday crumble like the civilizations of which he wrote, but one thing is certain. The principles observed by this great man, as well as the lessons of history he so aptly wrote about, will be just the same—be it ten years or a hundred years from now—because history *does* repeat itself.

RESOURCE READING
Revelation 1

INSIGHT

The lesson of history demonstrates that the sinful human heart can be changed by the personal presence of Jesus Christ, and that the change He brings forever affects the future of humanity on this earth.

APPLICATION

If we do not remember the past, are we doomed to repeat it?

Why is it that we see the same pattern of war and human failure repeated over and over? (See James 4:1 for a clue.)

WISDOM
Matthew Maury

*"What is man that you are mindful of him, the son of man that you
care for him? You made him ruler over the works of your hands;
you put everything under his feet: all flocks and herds, and the
beasts of the field, the birds of the air, and the fish of the sea,
all that swim the paths of the seas."*
Psalm 8:4, 6-8

Some of the greatest scientific discoveries of all time were
made by men who not only believed the Bible but followed its insights. Such was the
naval commander Matthew
Maury, whose research and charts
pioneered the field of oceanography and navigation.

*"Life ceases to be
a riddle when
you gain God's
perspective."*

It started almost a century
and a half ago, when Maury sustained a leg injury that left him
bedridden. Maury was a sailor who had been around the
world a couple of times. However, in 1839, while he was
recovering from the injury, his wife, who was a Christian,
read the Bible to him, especially the Book of Psalms.

One day Mrs. Maury was reading Psalm 8, the same
passage, incidentally, that astronauts quoted on the Apollo
8 mission. The psalm talks about God's creative power and
might. As she read the passage, the words seemed to ignite
her husband's imagination and thinking. These are the
words that spoke so loudly: "You [meaning God] have put
him [that's humanity] in charge of everything you made;

310

everything is put under his authority: all sheep and oxen, and all the beasts of the field, the birds of the heavens and the fish of the sea, and all that passes through the paths of the seas" (Psalm 8:6-8).

Maury began thinking, "How can the sea have paths or lanes?" Then he began thinking that if he ever got back to the sea, he would do research on the paths of the sea. Two years later Maury went back to the navy and was put in charge of their depot of charts and instruments. In this post, he launched an investigation of the ocean currents, which kept him busy for the next twenty years and won him the title "Pathfinder of the Seas."

He designated logbooks and gave them to sea captains from many nations. He asked them to keep a daily record of their location, wind speed, and weather conditions. He persuaded sailors to drop bottles in the sea with messages recording the date and location.

Eventually Commander Maury was responsible for charting the Gulf Stream and the Labrador Stream and laid the foundation for the U.S. Naval Observatory. Maury's work cut precious days from travel time as captains took advantage of the natural currents of the sea. His discoveries saved countless lives by helping navigators avoid dangerous storms at sea. And all of this resulted from the discoveries of a man who believed that the phrase "the paths of the seas" was not poetic license the psalmist took three thousand years ago, but was an accurate statement science had not quite caught up with yet.

Maury believed the Bible was true. Most importantly of all, the Bible is *spiritually* true. It will show you how to receive eternal life, how to know that you have become God's child and that your sins are forgiven. Life ceases to be a riddle when you gain God's perspective, and that is the secret of the Bible.

RESOURCE READING
Job 38

INSIGHT

The Bible is accurate in the statements that it makes regarding our world and its order. Often the statements of a scientific nature were totally out of sync with current thought when the authors penned them.

APPLICATION

Find out more about oceanography, the study of the sea and its currents.

The Old Testament references to oil helped geologists locate sites containing oil in the Negev of Israel today. Be alert to articles in the news where archaeology or biblical statements give direction in our day.

A Few
Final Thoughts

In the pages of this book, we have thought about people who have made a difference in our world, common ordinary people with an extraordinary purpose in life. I have written about men and women who have made a difference in the lives of others.

In all probability you read only a few pages before you began to notice a pattern. In the lives of many of the people I have described, there was a spiritual encounter with God through His Son, Jesus Christ. Though they may have described it in different terms, it was the same experience had by Nicodemus, a religious leader who came to Jesus by night. Jesus told him simply that he needed to be born again. "Except a man be born again," said Jesus, "he cannot see the kingdom of God" (John 3:3, KJV).

"Success is seeking and knowing and loving and obeying God."

This personal encounter with Jesus Christ—whether it was the unusual kind of encounter that Saul of Tarsus had on the road to Damascus or the slow, gradual understanding of who Jesus is and what He did, whereby someone embraces Him as Lord and Savior—is what gave so many of my heroes direction and purpose for their lives. And when they found Him, their goals changed with a redirected focus in life.

No, I have not included Jesus Christ as one of my heroes. Frankly, when you come to understand who He is, both Lord and Savior—God incarnate in the flesh who freely laid down His life that we might have life through His death—He ranks far above the plain of my heroes, and I would not detract from His person or glory by putting Him in the same category as the men and women I admire and venerate as heroes today.

Having stressed that real purpose in life comes through a personal relationship with Jesus Christ, by way of contrast, let's focus on the lives of a few other people who were rich and famous and by virtue of their attainment, beauty, or fame were considered to be heroes in their day.

First, let me tell you about George Eastman, whose goal in life was financial success. He reached it, too. In camera shops the world over, you will find the yellow boxes of film made by the Eastman-Kodak company. You see, George Eastman was a Scandinavian-born inventor who had an idea: "You click the shutter and we do the rest." That idea turned rags into riches for Eastman, but reaching his goal didn't satisfy him. Eastman lived in a thirty-room mansion where he had a magnificent pipe organ that was played during meals, but Eastman was far from happy.

One morning he conferred with his business associates, then went to his room and scribbled these words on a piece of paper: "My work is finished. Why wait?" He then took a German Luger semiautomatic and, putting it to his head, pulled the trigger, thus ending his life in suicide.

If fame or beauty is your goal in life, consider Marilyn Monroe. On August 5, 1962, newspapers told how this gifted and beautiful woman overdosed on Nebutol—a drug that stopped her heart. Her psychiatrist finally smashed down the door to find her lifeless body. My hometown newspaper editorialized, "Marilyn Monroe died Sunday proving that even $10,000 a week won't buy peace of mind."

She was beautiful, but her fame didn't satisfy.

If accomplishment in life is your goal, then consider the life of Ernest Hemingway, one of the heroes of my youth. When I was in college I thought, "If I could ever

314

write like Hemingway, wow, I'd have it made." Hemingway won the Nobel Prize for literature. He was famous for his pungent character descriptions in works like *A Farewell to Arms, The Old Man and the Sea,* and *For Whom the Bell Tolls.* Still in my possession is a yellowed newspaper, the front page of the *Los Angeles Times* dated July 3, 1961. The headline reads, "GUNSHOT BLAST KILLS HEMINGWAY." The story reads, "Ernest Hemingway, Nobel Prize-winning novelist who wrote of violence and death, shot himself fatally in the head Sunday with a 12-gauge shotgun at his home. . . ." Obviously, a person can be tremendously talented and yet unfulfilled and miserable.

In 1923, a group of men who were considered winners met at the Edgewater Beach Hotel in Chicago. Present were eight of the world's most successful financiers. Like whom? Charles Schwab, president of Bethlehem Steel, was there along with the president of the world's largest utility company, Samuel Insull. Richard Whitney, the president of the New York stock exchange, was there. Also attending that meeting was Albert Fall, then a member of the U.S. president's cabinet, along with Jesse Livermore, Ivan Kruger, and Leon Frazer, heads of the world's largest investment firm, the greatest monopoly in the world, and the Bank of International Settlement, respectively.

And what happened to these men who had clawed their way to the very top? Charles Schwab, the man who headed the largest steel company in the world, died bankrupt and lived on borrowed money for the last five years of his life. Samuel Insull, the man who headed the largest utility company in the world, ended his days as a fugitive, broke, and living in a foreign country. Richard Whitney, the man who was president of the New York stock exchange, was released from Sing Sing prison to die at home. Albert Fall, the man who was a member of the U.S. president's cabinet, was pardoned so that he also could die at home. The last three that I mentioned—Jesse Livermore, Ivan Kruger, and Leon Frazer—all died as suicides.

These individuals made it to the top. They had the world at their feet; but once they reached their goals, something went wrong. Plenty wrong. What price success? What cost in winning?

For a few moments, focus your attention on these individuals, people also considered to be winners: Viscount Castlereaugh, the British foreign secretary; Lee Ki Poong, vice president of Korea; Edwin Armstrong, who invented FM radio; Arthur Chevrolet, the designer of the automobile built by General Motors; Lester Hunt, governor of the state of Wyoming; and James Forrestal, the American secretary of state. And to this group I could add the names of Ernest Hemingway, Marilyn Monroe, and Kurt Cobain for a beginning. What do they have in common? Two things: they were successful and they were also suicidal.

Just a minute. I said they were successful. But were they really? Perhaps that depends on how you define this nebulous word. If reaching the top is success, they made it; but as Dr. Charles Malik, the Lebanese statesman and former president of the U.N. General Assembly defined success, they fell dismally short. "Success," said Malik, "is seeking and knowing and loving and obeying God; and if you seek, you will know; and if you know, you will love; and if you love, you will obey."

Success from God's point of view, from the vantage of looking back over life and valuing relationships, is vastly different. Jesus put it, "What good is it for a man to gain the whole world and lose his soul? Or what can a man give in exchange for his soul?" (Mark 8:36).

I think if Jesus were alive today, He might well say, "So what if a person gains the company presidency, or climbs the greasy ladder to the top but loses his family and his integrity, his self-respect, and finally his very soul in the process?"

In coming to the end of this book, may I challenge you to ask yourself, "For what am I living? What drives my life?

What purpose is before me? Is a relationship with God through His Son the missing ingredient of my life?"

A closing thought: It is never too late to change directions in life. Some people strive for survival, some for success, but some achieve significance, and with that level of accomplishment comes the peace of God that means your life was worth living. Don't simply occupy space on Planet Earth.

If a relationship with God has been missing in your life, right now pray a simple prayer something like this: "Father, I believe You sent Your Son into the world to make a difference in my life. I do believe that He lived, died, and rose again. I not only want Him to forgive me of my sins, but I want Him to be my Lord and Savior. Lord, Jesus, please take over my life and give me a purpose in living."

Then I hope you will write to me and let me know what happens. I'll be glad to answer your questions.

With God's help you can make your life count for something lasting and worthwhile, something that will endure the fire. You, too, can be a person who makes a difference in our world.

Write to me at this address:
    Dr. Harold Sala
    Box G
    Laguna Hills, CA 92654

In Asia write to:
    Dr. Harold Sala
    Box 4000
    Makati City, MM
    Philippines

You can access our home page and send me e-mail at: www.guidelines.org

REFERENCE NOTES

1. Billy Graham as quoted in "Portraits for Spiritual Growth," *In Touch,* published by Charles Stanley, April 1993, pp. 8, 9.

2. The idea for this chapter is from E. K. Cox's book, *Lives That Oft Remind Us* (Moody Colportage, 1940), pp. 26-33.

3. Kitty Muggeridge, "Mother Teresa," *Eternity,* December 1983, p. 101.

4. Lori Sharn, "Mother Teresa's Heart Never Left the Poor," *U.S.A. Today,* September 8, 1997, p. 17A.

5. Diego Ribadeneira and Indira Lakshmanan, *Seattle Post-Intelligencer,* "Mother Teresa," Sept. 6, 1997, p. 1.

6. Ruth Tucker, *From Jerusalem to Irian Jaya* (Grand Rapids: Zondervan, 1983), p. 277.

7. Taken from Jim Reapsone, "Final Analysis," *World Pulse,* April 23, 1993. For additional information about Borden's life, see *Borden of Yale,* by Mrs. Howard Taylor (Minneapolis: Bethany House, 1988).

8. Carl Henry, "Twilight of a Great Civilization," as quoted by Cal Thomas, *The Things That Matter Most* (New York: Harper Collins, 1994), p. 113.

9. Bruce Shelley, *Church History in Plain Language* (Chicago: Word, 1982), p. 119.

10. "Towering Witness to Salvation," *Time,* July 15, 1974, p. 90.

11. "A Prophet with Honor," *Christianity Today,* January 18, 1985, p. 70.

12. *Time,* op. cit.

13. "A World Divided," *Open Doors,* November-December, 1978, p. 10.

14. *Time,* p. 92.

15. Billy Graham, *Just As I Am* (San Francisco: HarperCollins Zondervan, 1997), p. 24.

16. Ibid.

17. Eliot Wirt Sherwood, *Billy* (Wheaton, Ill.: Crossway Books, Wheaton, 1997), p. 20.

18. J. C. Pollock, *Hudson Taylor and Maria* (New York: McGraw-Hill, 1962), pp. 15,16.

19. Ruth Tucker, *From Jerusalem to Irian Jaya* (Grand Rapids: Zondervan, 1983), p. 176.

20. James Hudson Taylor III, "Pioneers with Commitment," *East Asia Millions,* Summer, 1990, p. 355.

21. From James Bentley, *Martin Niemoller* (New York: Free Press, 1984), p. 139.

22. From "The Acts of Paul and Thecla," as quoted by *Christianity Today,* August 11, 1997, p. 39.

23. D. Guthrie and J. A. Motyer, eds., *The New Bible Commentary* (Leicester, England: Intervarsity Press, 1986), p. 342.

24. Henry Halley, *Bible Handbook,* published by Henry Halley, 1955, p. 184.

25. William R. Moody, *The Life of Dwight L. Moody* (New York: Fleming H. Revell, 1900), p. 402.

26. *Moody,* p. 403.

27. Ibid.